THE MAKING
of a
ROYAL NAVAL OFFICER

For the present and
future generations of the
Carne family

THE MAKING
of a
ROYAL NAVAL OFFICER

CAPTAIN W. P. CARNE CBE RN

FOREWORD BY ADMIRAL LORD WEST GCB DSC PC

Published by Uniform
An imprint of Unicorn Publishing Group
5 Newburgh Street
London W1F 7RG

www.unicornpublishing.org

A catalogue record for this book is available from
the British Library

5 4 3 2 1

ISBN 978-1-913491-59-8

Cover design Unicorn Publishing Group
Typeset by Vivian@Bookscribe

Printed in Turkey by FineTone Ltd

CONTENTS

FOREWORD BY ADMIRAL LORD WEST GCB DSC PC 6

INTRODUCTION 8

PART ONE – THE FIRST WORLD WAR

Chapter 1   FROM DARTMOUTH TO WAR 11

Chapter 2   HMS *SAPPHO* 14

Chapter 3   HMS *NEW ZEALAND* 29

Chapter 4   THE BATTLE OF JUTLAND 63

Chapter 5   HMS *ASPHODEL* 103

Chapter 6   ACCIDENT 155

Chapter 7   CONVOY OPERATIONS 176

Chapter 8   HMS *TACTICIAN* – 1918 187

PART TWO – BETWEEN THE WARS

Chapter 9   1919–1936 214

Chapter 10   THE EVACUATION FROM SHANGHAI – 1937 .. 217

PART THREE – THE SECOND WORLD WAR

Chapter 11   THE FORMATION OF THE MEDITERRANEAN FLEET 230

Chapter 12   THE ACTION OFF CALABRIA – JULY 1940 .. 242

Chapter 13   TORPEDO ATTACK ON TOBRUK 263

Chapter 14   HANDS ACROSS THE SEA 272

Chapter 15   THE BATTLES OF TARANTO AND MATAPAN .. 276

Chapter 16   THE CAPTURE OF TOBRUK –1941 283

Chapter 17   THE FIRST 10 DAYS AS CAPTAIN HMS *COVENTRY* 300

Chapter 18   POST-1941 YEARS 326

EPILOGUE 334

INDEX 335

FOREWORD
ADMIRAL LORD WEST GCB DSC PC

William Carne was typical of a generation of naval officers that manned the Royal Navy through the German Wars of the first half of the 20th century. It is no exaggeration to say that without the Royal Navy the United Kingdom could not have survived and emerged victorious. We owe these men a huge debt of gratitude for the quiet way in which they did their duty.

What leaps out is the youth of many involved. Carne left Dartmouth to take up his first war appointment in 1914 aged sixteen, a callow youth who had to learn so much on the job in war conditions.

His account of the Battle of Jutland is understated and completely gripping. Aged only eighteen he was in a highly exposed position in the battlecruiser HMS *New Zealand*. His photograph of HMS *Indefatigable* blowing up is iconic. He clearly shows the feelings of elation after the battle which he felt they had won, and then the despondency when the nation held the fleet responsible for what seemed an abysmal result.

The men in the fleet however were correct. Germany never challenged the Royal Naval battle fleet again. The victory at Jutland ensured the winning of the First World War. Germany, in desperation, resorted to unconditional U-boat war which brought the US in on the Allied side. By 1918 Germany was starving, its industries faltering and there was revolution on the streets due to our iron-hard naval blockade.

We glean another fascinating insight into the rather amateurish behaviour of many of the more minor and multitudinous craft that had been manned for a total war. This is well illustrated during Carne's service on HMS *Asphodel* in the Mediterranean. He highlights the almost complete lack of anti-submarine warfare training or expertise – even late in WWI – but also shows how quickly lessons were being learnt. One can understand how the U-boats nearly succeeded in starving Britain into submission.

As with so many of his Dartmouth contemporaries, Carne was a battle hardened highly professional officer by the outbreak of WWII. Despite some setbacks, this cadre of professional officers helps account for the exemplary performance of the Navy throughout almost six years of war. Carne held a key position in the fleet staff during the crucial maritime battles in the Eastern Mediterranean and then as a cruiser captain in the desperate battle for Crete.

An intriguing aspect of his achievements was the use of airborne torpedoes particularly in shallow water, enabling the hugely successful attack on Taranto emulated by the Japanese some months later at Pearl Harbor.

The Navy had rescued our army from Dunkirk, kept our supply lines open and returned a war-winning force to the Continent on D-day. With the European war almost won, the Navy shifted its focus to the Pacific. Carne was promoted to Commodore in charge of the 30th Aircraft Carrier Squadron (the RN had fifty-four aircraft carriers in 1945) with which he supported our Fleet carriers in helping the USN in their operations against Japan.

Captain W. P. Carne CBE RN retired from the Navy in 1950 and there is a wonderful photograph of him with his four sons all Navy lieutenants at one of their weddings. He was a proud man and a classic naval officer of the old school; one of a breed that did so much for the nation they loved. This book is not only a testament to the man but a whole generation of naval officers.

Admiral the Right Honourable Lord West of Spithead GCB DSC PC

INTRODUCTION

My grandfather died when I was eighteen, and I realise now that I did not know him well. I didn't know, for example, that his nickname in the Navy had been 'Silent William', although he was certainly a taciturn man in later life. Like most of his generation, he didn't speak of the wars that he had fought in. Instead, he lived a gentle retired life in Cornwall, far removed from the events in his Naval career.

Fortunately, in the 1960s, he did take the considerable trouble to write down his experiences in the First World War. I remember as a small boy finding a typed copy of these memoirs in a dusty file in the attic, and asking my grandmother about them. She told me that there had been no interest in publishing them at the time as, 'there wasn't enough love interest'.

Some fifty years later these files were rediscovered and, on further searching, exercise books, typed pages filled with memories from the Second World War, letters, photographs and newspaper cuttings were found in an old wooden box. This book is, therefore, a compilation of stories that were never intended to appear together. I have therefore edited this book in distinct parts, each covering a different period and each with inevitably different styles reflecting the material available. Where I found contemporary letters, newspaper cuttings etc., I have included these as I think they provide a different insight into both his personality, and the way in which his loved ones at home found out about his life. Let us remember that they also lived through extraordinary times and endured great hardships.

While the stories may be short in love interest, I hope the reader will agree with me that they represent a fascinating insight into the life of a naval officer during one of the most critical times in our history. Those times may now be history, but I remember my grandparents very well, and I am glad that we now have the opportunity to tell a part of their story.

Mark Carne CBE
July 2021

PART ONE
THE FIRST WORLD WAR

Midshipman William Power Carne – Autumn 1914

CHAPTER 1
FROM DARTMOUTH TO WAR

Victoria Station was chaotic. We six naval cadets had arrived from Portsmouth together with our sea chests, with orders to go to South Queensferry to join our ship HMS *Sappho*. The time was late evening on the 4th August 1914 and, somehow, we had to catch the night train from King's Cross to Edinburgh. But how to get our sea chests across to King's Cross? The station was crowded with army and navy reservists, all more than a little bewildered. Eventually, one of us ran down someone in authority, one of those Railway Transport Officers or RTOs who later became such a familiar feature of all large railway stations. This official produced a horse-drawn waggonette into which we piled our sea chests and, as there was no room in the waggonette for us, we sat perched on the sea chests.

In this manner we started our slow journey to King's Cross. It must have been between 8 and 9pm that we emerged into the area in front of Buckingham Palace, which was filled with a large crowd, quite silent, waiting for the fateful news that the ultimatum to Germany had expired.

Through this crowd the police were keeping open a narrow gangway for the traffic, which, it must be remembered, was still largely horse-drawn. Our waggonette went clip-clop through the silent crowd. Just as we got to the far side a voice at the back called out, 'Up the Navy', and the whole crowd started to clap and cheer.

It was not perhaps astonishing that at this emotional moment, while the fate of the ultimatum was in the balance, that the crowd should have indulged in this hysterical cheering. What was astonishing was that six small boys, we were only sixteen, should have thought it quite natural that at this time of emergency, the crowd should turn to them for help and protection. During our two years at Osborne and one at Dartmouth, the fact that the Navy was the sure shield of the country had been so indoctrinated into us that we naturally thought that, in this moment of tension and danger, the people of England would turn to us despite our youth and inexperience and put their trust in us. Thus, I do not think it was so much pride that supported us on our way to King's Cross, as satisfaction that a self-evident fact had at last been realised.

The events that led up to this scene before Buckingham Palace had started during the previous week when one evening the Captain of Dartmouth addressed the whole college and informed us that in the event of war we should all be mobilised and that when we went to our dormitories we should find lists showing to which ships we had been allocated. He further added that he had informed the Admiralty that he expected to have cleared the college in eight hours from receiving the executive telegram. Not unnaturally this information created a considerable stir amongst the cadets though I think there were few who really believed that it might happen.

The cynics were, however, proved wrong when on Saturday afternoon the telegram arrived ordering the college to mobilise. We were hastily rounded up from the various playing fields and instructed to get into uniform, pack our sea chests and assist in getting the chests out of the dormitories onto the terrace in front of the college. In the meantime, every form of cart, waggon or lorry in Dartmouth had been assembled into which we loaded our sea chests for transport across the Dart to Kingswear, where three special trains had arrived, one to go to each Home Port of Portsmouth, Chatham and Devonport. All my term were to go to Portsmouth and we started our journey about 9pm in a very crowded train, which proceeded with many stops until we reached Salisbury where, to our intense disappointment, the train was turned round and we went back arriving about 7am on Sunday morning. This was a very great disappointment, more particularly as the two trains to Chatham and Devonport had gone on to their destinations. We all went to bed to make up for some of the lost sleep during the previous night.

Most of the officers had left the College to take up their war appointments and nobody knew what to do with us. During the afternoon our sea chests were brought back from Kingswear and we rather languidly got them back into our dormitories.

In the evening the music master put on an organ recital in the Chapel. I can't remember why there was no evening service, I suppose the chaplain had already gone to his war appointment. In the middle of the recital a further telegram arrived for us to proceed to Portsmouth forthwith. Immediately all was excitement, noise and activity. Once more we had to get our chests out of the dormitories and load them on the transport which once more arrived in good time. We were getting rather good at getting our chests down the stairs from the dormitories. Each chest was hauled to the top of the stairs and given a gentle push. Gravity did the rest and if a few banisters were carried away or the paintwork damaged, who cared? Weren't we going to war?

This time our train went right through to Portsmouth and we were accommodated in the Officers' Mess in the Naval Barracks. As there were no cabins available for us, we were each given a mattress from a sailor's hammock and a blanket and told to doss down in the library. Here we remained throughout Monday. On Tuesday various detachments departed to ships in Portsmouth and after lunch we got our orders to join HMS *Sappho* at Queensferry. It was not long before we were on a train to London and, as I have already described, making our way to King's Cross to catch a train to Edinburgh.

While at Portsmouth I drew from the library a book whose title was I think "Rasplata" which was a personal account by a Russian Naval Officer of the destruction of the Russian fleet by the Japanese at the battle of Tsushima. As I was quite certain a similar fate awaited the German fleet, I was not particularly perturbed, it was quite inconceivable that the British fleet could suffer a similar disaster.

We duly made our way to Edinburgh and thence to South Queensferry. Sometime during the night, we heard that the ultimatum had expired and that therefore we were at war.

CHAPTER 2
HMS *SAPPHO*

We joined *Sappho* just before lunch, to find that the ship had recently arrived from Scapa having brought Admiral Callaghan, who had just been relieved as Commander-in-Chief by Admiral Jellicoe. Almost as we stepped aboard, we were informed that we were going to coal ship that afternoon and that we had better dig out some overalls from our sea chests.

The next few hours were very confused. Nobody knew what to do with six naval cadets in a ship with no gunroom. Eventually we were put into a small mess down aft, that had been the Admiral's stewards' mess. It was a small space, curtained off from the after-cabin flat, eighty percent occupied by a mess table with a bench running around the outboard and after side. Our chests were stowed in the cabin flat, and two marines told off to draw hammocks for us. We were to be fed from the Wardroom as there was no other organisation.

In the meantime, we were best getting into our oldest clothes, as we should be required to assist with the coaling. The ship had a much-reduced ship's company, as in peacetime she had been employed as a sort of Admiral's yacht. Until her complement was completed by reservists, it was hoped a number would arrive during the day; the assistance of six cadets to help with coaling would be welcome. The ship was to sail again at 5am the next morning for Scapa.

I don't remember much about the rest of that day, except that I was more tired than I had ever been before. We started coaling about 4pm and continued long after dark on that fine summer evening. The coal was hoisted in hundredweight bags, each bag lifted onto a trolley and rolled away to a chute down which the bag was emptied. My job was to collect the empty bags, drag them back to the gangway, and from there throw them back on to the deck of the collier. The bags were of heavy reinforced canvas with steel gromets, through which the hoisting strops were rove.

The bags had been used many times before and were impregnated with coal dust, and consequently both heavy and awkward to throw. I soon grew weary, and I fear more than one bag went into the sea between the two ships instead of on to the collier's deck.

One of the hazards of coaling ship was caused by the chutes, which were holes in the deck about eighteen inches in diameter. After a few bags had been emptied down a chute, the whole deck was covered in loose coal and, particularly in the dark, the hole in the deck was not easy to see. Many sailors struggling with a heavy bag of coal have put their leg down a chute and ended up with a broken leg. Late at night, when dragging a pile of sacks back to the gangway, I put my leg down a chute. However, my lucky star, who has looked after me on many occasions, was working full speed that night and I put my leg down a chute that was choked with coal only about a foot below the surface of the deck, so I came to no harm.

Soon we were black with coal dust, black faces and black clothes with coal dust in our eyes, up our noses and caked around our mouths. Being inexperienced we had not tied scarves tightly around our necks, so that soon the dust was working down under our clothes. There was coal everywhere, inches deep on the deck, and everything one touched was covered in coal dust. As the light failed, yardarm groups, large brass reflectors, each with half a dozen lamps, were switched on. Each illuminated part, but only a part, of the deck so that the figures of the working men passed alternately from darkness to light. Any clothes were permissible for coaling ship, so that as a reaction to the uniform the sailors were required to wear every day, many of the men were inclined to adopt somewhat bizarre garments, but very soon they were all a uniform black colour from the all-pervading coal dust.

After interminable hours, the bunkers were all reported to be filled and the collier cast off. The last of the coal dust on the decks was swept down the chutes, the deck plates replaced, and a hose rigged from every rising main in the ship. Each armed with a broom, the tired sailors proceeded to scrub the decks while the petty officers directed the hoses and made sure no part of the deck was left unscrubbed. At this late hour no attempt was made to deal with the paintwork, boats, equipment etc. Of course, everything required washing, but this was left for the next day.

In this water picnic we cadets were rather lost, not knowing what to do. Fortunately, the First Lieutenant came along and saw that we were merely in the way, and dismissed us to get clean and turn in. In the after cabin flat, a tired and dirty marine produced two cabin baths, tin dishes about three feet in diameter and six inches deep, and a couple of cans of warm water. Each can held enough to produce a depth of about one inch of water in each bath. In this meagre supply of water, we endeavoured, without complete success, to rid ourselves of our coating of coal dust and then to climb into our hammocks, which had also been slung in the cabin flat.

We had no difficulty in getting to sleep that night, nor did the sound of the ship getting underway at 5am disturb us, although the cabin flat was immediately over the propellers, and was a very noisy place at sea. The marines told to look after us called us about 7 am, and we made a further effort to remove the traces of coal from our bodies in the inadequate baths. By this time there was a little motion on the ship, and the water in the baths was slopping out onto the cabin flat deck. However, that did nothing to curb our appetites for breakfast.

The ship was now well clear of the Firth of Forth and heading for Scapa. Immediately after breakfast the ship went to action stations. I found myself posted to the starboard waist, where there was a battery of three 4.7-inch guns. I felt completely lost and did not know what was happening. However, after about an hour the hands fell out from action stations and got back to their interrupted work of cleaning the ship, and the First Lieutenant directed

HMS Sappho. Ref IWM ©IWM(Q75413)

a Chief Petty Officer, who combined the duties of Chief Bosun Mate and Chief Gunner's Mate, to show us around the ship. This Chief Petty Officer, whose name was Cotton, combined the qualities of a good petty officer with the manners and methods of a good old-fashioned nanny, being quite respectful to us in our capacity as junior officers, but at the same time being quite firm and allowing no skylarking.

Under his tutelage we learnt that the *Sappho* was an old-fashioned, out-of-date second-class cruiser whose armament consisted of two 6-inch guns mounted on the fo'c'sle and poop respectively and six 4.7-inch guns, three in each waist. The high poop on which the after 6-inch gun was mounted allowed comparatively capacious cabins to be built under it. It was largely due to the fact that the ship had these good cabins that she had been retained as a tender to the fleet flagship as a sort of yacht for the benefit of the Commander-in-Chief. The 6-inch guns were very ancient pieces trained by two trainers, one either side, laid by another man while the actual gunlayer stood in rear of the gun and laid it over open sights, giving verbal orders to the trainers and layer respectively. The gun was actually fired by the gunlayer, who carried a pistol switch on a long wandering lead, the power being supplied by a battery of Leclanché cells. At a later date we did some gun practice, firing at a barrel supporting a short flagpole with a red flag. Practice was carried out at a range seldom exceeding half a mile as we steamed around the target. The fo'c'sle 6-inch gun resisted all attempts to fire, as we had had heavy weather a few days previously and the box containing the Lechanché battery had not resisted the onset of the saltwater. The after 6-inch succeeded in getting off two rounds, neither of which pitched even approximately close to the target.

But our main strength was in the 4.7-inch guns in the waists which actually had telescopic sights; though, it is true, they still had three motion breech blocks. But they were the same type of gun as had been taken to Ladysmith during the Boer War, where they had rendered good service, so why shouldn't they do just as well against the Germans? During gun practice, each gun fired two rounds separately and there was tremendous competition between the various gunlayers as to who should obtain a direct hit. There was no attempt to fire salvoes, each gunlayer banged off in turn judging his own range and deflection.

Between the sponsors of each 4.7-inch gun, the ship was fitted with high bulwarks so that seen from outboard the ship appeared to be flush decked from fo'c'sle to poop. In each bulwark was fitted the hammock nettings. As the gun sponsons were by no means watertight, in heavy weather the deck of the waists was awash and the air filled with spray, so that a man getting his hammock out of the netting was almost certain to get it wet before he could get it down to a messdeck and sling it. Above each waist were stowed the boats, we were each told off to a boat and I found myself midshipman of the Captain's galley, a six-oared gig of which I was very proud. Cotton showed us how each boat was hoisted and secured while at sea, and where its gear was kept.

We completed the passage to Scapa in fine weather and on arrival were directed to anchor as a guard ship for Holm Sound, as at that time there were no defences to Scapa Flow. That night I kept my first night watch as a lookout on the After Bridge. I had absolutely nothing to do or anyone to speak to except stare into the darkness. I found the hours quite interminable and the effort to keep my eyes open almost unbearable. On the other hand, if anyone had suggested that I should be much better off if I went back to Dartmouth and was tucked up nice and comfortable in my bed in a dormitory, I should have been most indignant and would have replied that the naval life was just what I wanted, and under no circumstances would I change it.

During the next two months we spent most of our time in or around Scapa Flow, acting as guard ship at night and occasionally patrolling outside. The summer of 1914 was a very lovely one, and Scapa Flow, which in after years I learnt could be a very unpleasant place as regards weather, treated us royally. The First Lieutenant, who thought that the ship was likely to be used for commerce protection duties and would therefore have to be proficient at boarding merchant ships at sea, was very insistent in getting the boats' crews thoroughly efficient. Thus, we cadets found that we spent a lot of time away in our boats, which was excellent training both in handling boats and in taking charge of sailors.

During this time a number of reservists joined the ship to bring her up to war complement. Included amongst these were two RNR lieutenants, good seamen but as ignorant of anything to do with guns as we cadets. But they relieved the officer situation considerably as previously the only executive officers in the Wardroom had been the First Lieutenant and Navigating Officer. On the outbreak of war these two officers were extremely busy and could spare no time for half a dozen cadets, but with the arrival of the RNR lieutenants they began to give us a little desultory instruction, but of course our real instructor was the active service conditions under which we were living.

On the 28th August we were patrolling to the westward of the Orkneys and I, for one, was very seasick when the CPO telegraphist came down with the news that three German cruisers had been sunk by our battle cruisers

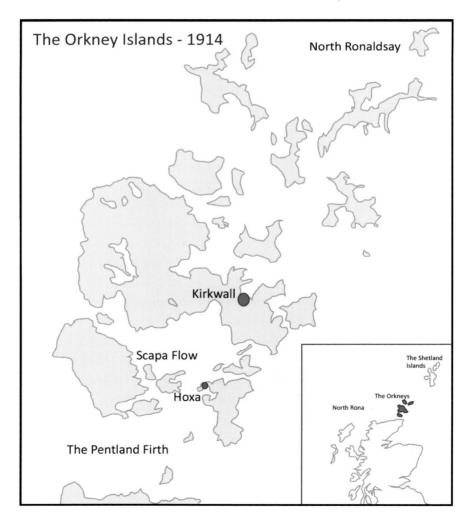

at the Battle of Heligoland. He went on to ask if that news make me feel better, and wouldn't I have liked to be in one of the battle cruisers? I should indeed have liked, at that moment, to be in a battle cruiser; but chiefly I think because in such a ship the motion would be less, and I shouldn't feel quite so ill.

During the periods when we were in harbour, we usually anchored a long way away from Scapa pier, so that there was no opportunity to send the stewards ashore to buy fresh provisions in Kirkwall, nor had the organisation for supplying the fleet with fresh provisions been as yet completed. On several occasions, therefore, the First Lieutenant landed the cadets close abreast the ship, with instructions to visit every farm within walking distance and buy anything in the way of fresh food that they had to offer. I found these expeditions in the fine summer weather most enjoyable. We were always well received at the farms who were avid for news. I doubt if many of the farms ever saw a newspaper, certainly not a daily one. We, however, had the benefit of a wireless bulletin every morning. We soon found it was worthwhile to get a few extra copies of this made out, and take them round the farms where they were eagerly received. In return they sold us goods at very reasonable prices, such eggs, chickens and ducks as they could spare. It was still very early days in the war; I am afraid it was not long before prices rocketed when the whole Grand Fleet started combing the islands for fresh food.

In the autumn of that year, the German submarines had several successes. This new type of ship, never used in war before, started to spread a certain degree of consternation. The range at which the German craft were operating was greater than had been expected, and the first reaction in naval thought was that they must have secret bases from which they could refuel. The *Sappho,* amongst other ships, was sent to examine various remote lochs and harbours in the Outer Hebrides. We crept into all sorts of little holes and corners, somewhat to the alarm of the navigating officer who was of the opinion that the Captain's zeal for hunting submarines was bringing various unnecessary navigational hazards to the ship.

Having drawn a blank in the Outer Hebrides we were sent to examine North Rona Island, an uninhabited island, or rather a deserted island – it had been inhabited once – some forty miles northwest of Cape Wrath. The island was not much more than a large rock some two miles long. We steamed around it close inshore, and from there we could see the ruins of a cottage and a large flock of sheep. There was no harbour, but there appeared to be a small cove at which it looked possible to land.

The Captain decided that the island must be more carefully examined, for which purpose he himself would go ashore, and he would take four cadets with him. The ship was duly anchored as close to the cove as was reasonably safe, but steam was kept on the engines as the island afforded no protection from the weather, which was not looking too good, with a falling barometer.

The Captain very shortly appeared on deck in his shooting clothes and with his gun. It then appeared that the main object of the expedition was to shoot a grouse and the cadets were to act as beaters. The First Lieutenant then bobbed up and said, "What about some fresh mutton?". During our cruise of the Hebrides, we had expended all our fresh meat, and were down to corned beef. The First Lieutenant's proposal was approved, and the Navigating Officer and Cotton were added to the expedition, each armed with a service rifle and pockets full of ammunition.

We landed at the cove, but not without some difficulty as there was an appreciable sea running. From there we scrambled up the cliff, each cadet in turn offering to carry the Captain's gun but he, wise man, kept his precious weapon in his own hands.

When we arrived at the top of the cliff, the sheep took one look at us and proceeded at full speed to the other end of the island. A scramble up to the top of the highest hillock soon showed that North Rona Island as a base for submarine operations lacked any natural facilities, thus confirming the opinions made from our circumnavigation of the island. Further that, as there was little or no heather, it was hardly worth wasting time looking for grouse; nor did there appear to be any other bird worthy of being shot.

Most of the island was covered with lush grass upon which the sheep, who we estimated to number at least two hundred, appeared to flourish. We therefore decided to shoot a couple of the sheep who, however, had different ideas and kept well out of range using their local knowledge of the terrain to outwit all our attempts to approach them.

Eventually the Navigator and Cotton took cover behind some rocks, while the Captain, with the four cadets, gradually drove a portion of the flock towards them. The sheep went past the 'guns', leaping from rock to rock and taking full advantage of any cover. A considerable fusillade ensued, in which one sheep was killed. I think both riflemen claimed to have hit the animal, which may well have been the case as it was certainly hit twice.

It was then necessary to get the beast down to the boat. The Captain refused to allow any further pursuit of the sheep, as the weather had begun to look more menacing and he was anxious to get back onboard. Cotton handed his rifle to one of the cadets, hoisted the sheep on his shoulders and carried it to the boat, but by the time he had got it down the cliff and onboard he was saying that nothing would persuade him to volunteer in future for any sheep-shooting expeditions.

When we arrived onboard, we found a rather anxious first lieutenant as, owing to the depreciating weather, he had doubts about getting the boat back before he would have had to weigh and stand-off. We were soon on our way back to Scapa, with a cold wind rapidly rising to gale force and producing a heavy sea. I think this expedition to North Rona Island may be described as completing the picnic side of the war for me; the mobilisation from the College had been a picnic, joining the *Sappho* and coaling ship had been a picnic, so had early days at Scapa, with foraging trips to the farms interlarded with trips at sea around the islands. But now the weather had broken, the sea was cold and rough, and most days I was seasick. The war was still a very great adventure, but it had ceased to be a picnic.

Looking back with the advantage of hindsight. I think it may be said that this expedition to North Rona Island epitomised the casual way in which the Navy took up the First War. If Wellington could hunt foxes behind the lines of Torres Vedros, obviously the captain of one of HM ships sent to look for submarines at North Rona Island, and not immediately finding any, could go ashore and shoot a grouse. But he had been sent to look for submarines. Surely, he should have borne in mind the possibility, if not the likelihood, of there being a submarine in the vicinity, and therefore it was surely unwise of him to anchor his ship, thus making her a sitting target?[1] But it took a large number of rude shocks before the Navy woke up to the fact that this was the twentieth century, and that we were fighting a war against professionals. We were professional seamen, we had learnt that from our forefathers and our

---

[1] It is recorded that the German U-Boat U-90 used to stop at North Rona during their patrols, where they would also land a party to shoot sheep.

traditions; what we had to realise was that not only must we be professional seamen, but also professionals at sea warfare, which was not the same thing.

I cannot pretend that I, or for that matter, anyone else in the *Sappho* had begun to realise that we had to readjust our ideas; but a succession of disasters which occurred during the autumn of 1914 gave us certain twinges of uneasiness. The loss of the *Cressy, Hogue* and *Aboukir* followed by the *Hawke* and *Formidable* in home waters, and the sinking of the *Good Hope* and *Monmouth* at Coronel, in all of which ships were cadets who had been at Dartmouth with us, brought home to us the fact that this war was not going to be a walk over, and that we were in it up to our necks.

It was about this time that the Admiralty promoted us all to midshipmen with seniority from the time we joined our ships. This was a great day and we hurriedly wrote away to Gieves for the white patches of our new rank, which we sewed onto our collars. What is more, it meant that we got paid as midshipmen. It is true that our pay packet only amounted to some £6 a month, but that was a vast increase on the shilling a week pocket money we were allowed at Dartmouth. With patches on our collars, money clinking in our pockets, and being addressed as midshipman, we were now convinced that we had finally said good-bye to Dartmouth and were indeed part of what we called 'The Service'. Before this, I think we had always had an uneasy feeling that we might suddenly be sent back to Dartmouth again to restart our studies at our desks.

The German submarines having proved that they could operate at greater ranges than had previously been thought possible, the Grand Fleet was forced to lead an uneasy existence, as at this time no harbour had yet been made safe against attack by submarines.

The *Sappho* was in Scapa when occurred what was subsequently called the Battle of Scapa Flow. At this time there had built up a large number of ships in the Flow, mostly colliers and tankers. The only ship of first importance was the *Iron Duke*, which for some reason was not at sea with the rest of the fleet. Early one morning, some destroyers who had been patrolling off Hoxa Sound, the main entrance, came into the Flow at high speed firing at something in the water and a submarine was reported to be in the Flow. *Sappho* went to action stations and hurriedly weighed anchor to steam slowly around the Flow looking for the reported submarine.

Two colliers were hurriedly berthed either side of the *Iron Duke*. In the meantime, the destroyers were dashing about the Flow at high speed, at intervals opening fire at something in the water, which, apparently, they did not damage, nor fortunately did they damage any of the other ships in the Flow. Eventually the excitement died down and nothing further happened. It was believed that this was another false alarm, possibly caused by a school of porpoises, of which there were many about at this time.

The Grand Fleet moved round to the West Coast of Scotland to Loch Ewe, until the defences of Scapa could be improved. But their mail had been despatched to Scapa and, as it was not known when the fleet would return, the *Sappho* was directed to embark the complete mail for the fleet and take it around to Loch Ewe. This duty completed, we returned to Scapa Flow and prepared to carry out a more important operation.

The time was now well into October 1914, and the first convey of Canadian troops was due to cross the Atlantic to the United Kingdom. To cover this movement, various forces were sent to sea. The *Sappho* formed part of a rather heterogenous collection of ships detailed to carry out the Muckle Flugga patrol. The ships of this force were stationed in line almost ten miles apart in a bearing roughly northeast from Muckle Flugga, which is the northeast corner of the Shetland Islands. We steamed roughly southeast by day until we were about fifty miles south of our line of bearing from Muckle Flugga, turned sixteen points at midnight and steamed on a reciprocal course until noon the next day, when we were about fifty miles north of our line, and then repeated the operation. We seldom exceeded ten knots and must have been an easy target for a submarine. Any neutral ships we encountered, we stopped and boarded. We were in fact the beginning of that force which was known as the Tenth Cruiser Squadron, which throughout the war maintained the blockade in northern waters. But later the force consisted of armed merchant liners, far more suitable ships for the prevailing weather conditions.

Throughout the ten days that *Sappho* remained on the patrol, the sea was rough, the wind seldom blew at less than gale force, the visibility was much reduced by rain, sleet and hail showers and the poor old *Sappho* went through almost every antic that it is possible for a ship to perform, during which she almost rolled her masts and funnels out of the ship. I, in common with most of the ship's company, was cold, wet and miserable and, in addition, I was very seasick.

Any form of comfort disappeared. Fresh food rapidly ran out, and the cooks had great difficulty in keeping a fire alive in the galley sufficiently long to cook a meal. Washing became unpleasant and hazardous. The motion in the after-cabin flat was tremendous and unpredictable; the water slopped out of our little tin dish baths, making the deck slippery, and then the baths took charge and careered around the flat. To an onlooker it might have appeared rather humorous to see a naked boy crouching in a tin dish which was careering madly about the deck, coming to rest at intervals with a loud bump against the bulkheads, while the boy collected a number of interesting bruises from collisions with the rifles which, in common with all HM ships at that time, were stowed in racks against the bulkheads of the cabin flat. But I was long past seeing any humour in anything.

Each forenoon we reported by signal to the senior officer the percentage of fuel remaining. Fortunately for us, the *Sappho* was not designed for long periods at sea and our percentage of fuel remaining dropped rapidly. We midshipmen eagerly scanned this signal each day and tried to calculate when we should be released. At last, the eagerly awaited signal arrived and we were ordered to leave the patrol line in time to enter Scapa at dawn the next morning. Thus, our ten days of purgatory came to an end. I have endured heavy weather mixed up with cold and rain and snow on many occasions since, including a couple of Russian convoys, but I don't think the conditions were ever quite so unpleasant as they were in the *Sappho*, a very old ship quite unsuitable for the duties on which she was employed.

The morning we entered Scapa I had the watch as midshipman of the watch. After ten days of the *Sappho's* unpleasant motion, my seasickness had abated a little and I hoped I was getting over it. In this, however, I was unduly optimistic; while I could more or less get used to the motion after a few days at sea, after a few hours in harbour the next experience of bad weather would produce the same unpleasant symptoms. As we approached Hoxa Sound in the unpleasantly rough waters of the Pentland Firth, which were even worse than usual, we met Commodore Goodenough in the *Southampton* leading the 2nd Light Cruiser Squadron to sea. As the *Southampton* came in sight, her signal light started winking at us. But the light was frequently hidden by the ship's smoke, which was being blown straight towards us, and the motion on the *Sappho's* bridge was so violent that the seasick signalman could not keep his glass on the light and was unable to read the signal. This was made rapidly and repeated several times by the Commodore's efficient signal staff, who were probably being cussed by the Commodore for not getting an answer. I was hanging onto the bridge rails trying to prevent myself from being thrown about the bridge, and dodging down behind the bridge screen each time we buried our bows in a wave and a cloud of spray shot up over the bridge. The Captain told the Officer of the Watch to read the signal, but he was one of the RNR officers and could not make head nor tail of it, so the Captain turned to me. By reading a word here and a letter there, I made a guess that the Commodore was asking for a weather report on conditions outside. The Captain told the signalman to make back 'Rough'. I think he was going to elaborate his signal, but by the time our signalman had got his old fashioned 24-inch signal lamp burning and trained on the *Southampton,* she was already well past us and burying her fo'c'sle up to the bridge in the waters of the Pentland Firth, so I think further expansion of the signal was unnecessary.

Later I got to know the hatchet features of the Commodore's face better, as he was a great friend of my second Captain in the *New Zealand* and I frequently had him in my picket boat. I often wondered exactly what he said when he got the signal 'Rough', when obviously what he wanted was the direction of the wind, its force and perhaps more particularly the visibility. Conditions inside Scapa were frequently very different from those outside, and obviously what he wanted to know was at what distance to spread his cruisers and still maintain visual contact.

Goodenough was an excellent seaman and a magnificent Commander of Cruisers, as his subsequent record during that war proved, but he was somewhat old-fashioned as regards some of his ideas. At a later date, about a year after this incident, I met him in Gieves, the naval tailors, in Edinburgh. Recognising me as one of the *New Zealand's* midshipmen who had given him passage in my picket boat, he demanded in a voice that shook the whole shop what I was doing. When I very shyly replied that I was buying some pyjamas, he said with great scorn, "Pyjamas, pyjamas, never heard of such a thing. When I was your age, we wore a sailor's flannel at night. Didn't waste

Midshipman William Carne seated in the front row, far left.

our money on pyjamas". A sailor's flannel is, of course, the square-necked shirt that they wear. It is designed to give warmth, and in those days was made of a material which was definitely tickly, and I cannot imagine a much more uncomfortable garment in which to sleep.

A few weeks later, in November 1914, we were sent for by our Captain who informed us that we had been appointed to the *New Zealand* and that we should be ready to leave at short notice. This information filled us with the greatest excitement, as we were longing to be appointed to a more modern ship and the height of our ambition was to go to one of the battle cruisers.

The glamour which surrounded the name of Admiral Beatty had already penetrated our small minds, and we felt that in his squadron we should get what we called a bar to our medal. In other words, that we should take part in a battle.

A few days later the battle cruisers made one of their infrequent visits to Scapa; they were usually based further south, in order to be in a position to counter raids by the German battle cruisers on the east coast, although up to that time none of these raids had been attempted. Signals were exchanged and we were informed that a picket boat would call for us that afternoon. In next to no time, we were in the boat with our chests waving good-bye to all the officers of the *Sappho,* who came on deck to see us go. I think our departure left rather a gap in the small community in the *Sappho;* no other midshipmen were appointed to take our place.

We had been a nuisance when we arrived, another responsibility at a time of great strain; but we had gradually found our feet, and were becoming quite useful members of the ship's complement and our departure left a gap. As we shoved off, I saw Cotton standing behind the ship's officers, looking even more like a good nanny, wondering whether his charges were going to be a credit to him in their new ship.

CHAPTER 3
HMS *NEW ZEALAND*

Arriving alongside the *New Zealand*, she looked absolutely huge with her two tripod masts and those enormous funnels. She had just completed coaling ship; the collier had just shoved off and the upper deck was awash with water from the many hoses, while what appeared to be enormous numbers of black-faced sailors were energetically scrubbing the deck. The midshipman of the watch, who had more than two years' seniority as a midshipman and who to us was a veteran, escorted us to the gunroom which was situated amidships on the port side. Outside the gunroom was the chest flat, which at that time was occupied by a number of very noisy and dirty midshipmen who were in the process of stripping off their coaling clothes preparatory to bathing. Our guide left us, explaining that the other midshipmen would be there in half an hour or so, and that tea would then be served. The gunroom seemed enormous and most luxurious after the poky little hole we had lived in onboard the *Sappho*.

We were not left long before the gunroom was filled with a noisy crowd demanding tea from the Maltese stewards, and at the same time subjecting the new midshipmen to an interrogation which started with a demand as to who we were, where we had come from and how much we knew. It was made immediately clear that we were very ignorant, untidy and generally a disgrace to any reputable gunroom. It was essential that we immediately improved ourselves and, in the meantime, took over a number of duties from the senior midshipmen who were shortly to be examined for the rank of sub-lieutenant, and wanted an opportunity to work up their knowledge for this exam. To start us off in the right direction after tea, a tour of the ship was organised in order that we should at least begin to know our way about. I was amazed at the size of the ship, the large hatches and broad companionways so different from the narrow and steep ladders of the *Sappho*.

The fo'c'sle deck of the *New Zealand*, as in all the battle cruisers of that date, was continued right aft to the mainmast, with a short after deck abaft the after superstructure mostly occupied by 'X' turret. Contrary to the

HMS New Zealand

normal naval traditions, the officers lived forward. The Captain's quarters were immediately below the bridge from where, going aft, was a cabin flat for the more senior officers, the Wardroom flat with the Wardroom on the starboard side and more cabins on the port side, followed further aft by the gunroom flat with the actual gunroom on the port side while the starboard side was occupied by various officers' bathrooms etc., and finally an office flat before one stepped out onto the after deck. The quarterdeck was therefore forward, actually between the forward superstructure on which was built the bridge, foremost funnel and forward 4-inch guns and the midship superstructure in which was the midship funnel and stowage for various boats etc. The port side of the quarter-deck was occupied by 'P' turret, which could fire from right ahead to right astern on the port side or by training across the deck could fire over an arc of about sixty degrees to starboard. Between the midship superstructure and the after superstructure was the midship deck with 'Q', the Marines turret, on the starboard side capable of being fired either on the starboard side or on a restricted arc on the port side similar to 'P' turret. The fo'c'sle and after turrets were known respectively as 'A' and 'X' turrets.

While we had been doing this quick tour of the ship, 'Cable Officers' had been sounded off on the bugle by the drummer on watch, and all the battle cruisers got underway and, led by the *Lion*, sailed from Scapa. This produced the next surprise, as instead of the bump and thump and noise of the *Sappho's* reciprocating engines, the *New Zealand* seemed to glide through the water, and at ordinary manoeuvring speeds between decks it was impossible to determine that the ship was actually underway. It was not until the squadron was clear of the land and speed increased to 22 knots and course altered every quarter of an hour for the zig-zag, that one realised between decks that one was at sea.

This trip at sea did not last long, as at dawn the next day we entered Cromarty Firth and moored off Invergordon. By this time some rudimentary anti-submarine defences had been established at the entrance to the Firth, but no great confidence was placed in them and all ships lay with their anti-torpedo nets spread. As soon as the ship had moored, a collier came alongside and coaling commenced. Only a short coaling this time, as little fuel had been burnt on the passage from Scapa.

We junior midshipmen went into the collier's holds in the part of the ship to which we were allocated, in my case the maintopmen, and dug coal and filled bags, an exhausting performance, while the senior midshipmen worked the winches. Early the next year, after the senior midshipmen had been promoted to sub-lieutenant and most of them had left the ship, the duty of working the winches fell to us. The method employed was that known as the whip and outhaul. Each hold of the collier was fitted with two derricks, each derrick having its own separate winch. One derrick was rigged to plumb the hold, while the other plumbed the dump inboard. As soon as ten bags had been filled, a strop was passed through the gromets of each bag, the whip hooked on and, at a yell from the hold, the winch of the derrick plumbing the hold hove in at full speed. As the hoist cleared the combing of the hold, the other winch proceeded to heave in, starting the hoist to swing towards the ship. When the hoist was well up clear of the side of both ships, the winch plumbing the hold was reversed, the hoist swinging inboard and as it passed over the dump, the outhaul whip was reversed and, if the operation had been well judged, the hoist was right in the centre of the dump for the inboard crew to get their trolleys under the bags and wheel them away. Everything was of course done at full speed, each gang in each hold raced every other gang and each hold raced every other hold, and each ship raced every other ship. At the end of each hour, a numerical signal was hoisted in each ship reporting the number of tons received in the last hour. It was therefore important that the winches were worked at full speed; when reversing no attempt was made to shut off steam, one simply grasped the lever operating the links and hauled it across. In the case of some of the older colliers with worn winches, this required both strength and agility. The maintopmen to whom I was attached for coaling were usually the fastest hold in the *New Zealand*. We would have about ten gangs in the hold and each gang would fill ten bags in about five minutes, so the winches had to get a hoist inboard once every thirty seconds. This required concentration and good judgment, and heaven help the wretched midshipman who carried away a whip and caused a delay of five minutes or more in the middle of a coaling when the whole squadron were racing against each other. Supplies of fuel in harbour were never allowed to drop below ninety five percent of full capacity, which meant that if we stayed in harbour we had to coal every ten to fourteen days, only a small coaling, a couple of hundred tons or so which would take less than an hour; but the resulting dirt and dust would take the best part of a day to remove.

On this occasion, we remained in harbour for an appreciable period. The battle cruisers had been operating almost continuously since the outbreak of war but, with the exception of the Heligoland Bight action, had not achieved very much. The expected gladiatorial combat between the two fleets in the middle of the North Sea had not taken place; the Germans refused to come to sea, and we didn't know how to attack them in harbour. A pause for thought had become necessary. From the point of view of us junior midshipmen this was very lucky, as it gave us the opportunity to learn our way about our new ship and to settle down to our duties. The First Lieutenant, who was also the Snotties' Nurse, i.e. the officer detailed to superintend the midshipmen's instructions, started us off on an intensive syllabus of instruction but this was frequently interrupted as, at least daily, a portion of the ship's armament was exercised, which the respective midshipmen were required to attend. I and another junior midshipman were detailed for the Transmitting Station, known as the TS, where the gunnery officer had produced a new idea. This consisted of a small table with a roller at either side. Stretched between the rollers was a roll of squared paper, which was wound from one roller to the other by a rating armed with a stopwatch. The paper was supposed to advance at the rate of an inch a minute, but its actual speed depended on the degree of concentration of the rating with the stopwatch which could vary quite a lot over long periods. Across the centre of the table was a ruler graduated in ranges. Along this ruler, the other midshipmen and I plotted ranges received on electrical receivers from the ship's four range finders. Since the paper was moving at a steady speed, at least in theory, the slope of the line of ranges gave a measure of the rate of change of range, and was used as a check on the calculated rate. In actual fact, when the ship was steaming fast, the range finders in the two turrets 'A' and 'X' were blinded by spray and produced no useful ranges, the so-called torpedo range finder behind the foretop was always enveloped in smoke from the foremost funnel, and the only range finder which provided consistent ranges was the foretop instrument. It was from the crude and simple instruments such as this table that we gradually expanded during the war into the complicated and elaborate instruments which were eventually fitted in all capital ships.

Besides our instruction in purely professional subjects, we also had to learn about the traditions and customs of the ship. HMS *New Zealand* had been built at the cost of the New Zealand government, completed at the end of 1912; she had then sailed around the world calling for an appreciable period at each of the principal ports in New Zealand.

The ship was still in her first commission, so that generally speaking all the officers and men of her ship's company when we joined had carried out this memorable cruise. During the time the ship was in New Zealand waters she had been visited by an old Maori Chief, who had prophesied that the ship would shortly be engaged in a great war; shortly before the war she would proceed a long way north. During the war 'X' turret would be put out of action and the foretop damaged, but the ship would come through the war safely provided the Captain, on each occasion of engaging the enemy, should wear two charms, which the old chief donated to the ship, and which consisted of something to wear around the neck and a sort of apron.

As a proof that the old chief knew what he was talking about, we were told that in the early summer of that year, just before the outbreak of war,

the ship, in common with the other battle cruisers of the Home Fleet, had been to Kronstadt where the Czar with all his family had been onboard. The ship's company were quite convinced that the rest of the prophesy would come true and were very insistent that, on each occasion of going into action, the Captain should wear his charms. The ship did survive the war and, as I shall subsequently relate, 'X' turret was put out of action at the Battle of Jutland, but none of the ship's company were hurt.
No damage was ever suffered by the foretop.

The other thing we had to learn was the Haka, the war dance and song of the Maoris. All the officers at least knew the words of the song and, on suitable occasions such as after dinner on guest nights, could perform the dance with éclat, if not with great accuracy. The junior midshipmen had to do physical drill on the upper deck at 7am every morning, which was not altogether a joke in winter in a Scottish firth. We were taken by the physical training instructor, who was also the leader of the ship's Haka team and therefore an expert. He was a big man with suitable facial features and when he turned out with his whole team, dressed in what purported to be Maori war paint, they were a very fierce-looking crew. Actually, while the dance appears to be a fierce war dance, I believe a translation of the words refers more to the delights of love making than of war, though I have never really seen a complete translation.

It was one night in the middle of December that we were called about one o'clock in the morning to be told that 'Cable officers' had already been sounded off, the ship was preparing for sea and the nets, which meant both watches of the hands were coming in in ten minutes. Struggling into some warm clothes, we went on deck to find a beastly night, very cold with sleet showers. With numbed fingers in the pitch-dark – ships were of course darkened and electric torches in the First War were few and far between and rather frowned on – we rove the trailing wires and brought them to the electric winches. At a bugle call all winches hove in together. If all goes well, the torpedo net booms should swing aft on their heel fittings and the topping lift of each boom should bring the boom against the ship's side at an angle of about forty-five degrees. Further heaving in on the trailing wires should hoist the actual net onto the net shelf. But our nets had had much use in the previous four months with little or no opportunity to maintain the equipment. Wire after wire parted, and we were left with the net hanging in bights down the ship's side. The only thing to do was to haul them by hand. This meant getting hook ropes, hooking the net a foot or two below the net shelf, and then with ten or a dozen men on each hook rope, hauling a foot or two of a small section of the net up into the net shelf.

The *New Zealand* was manned from Devonport; she was what is known as a west country ship. At that time the Navy was manned almost exclusively from that part of the country which lies south of the Thames, with the exception of a few Scotsmen, many of whom came from the Hebrides and nearly all of whom were recruited at Devonport. So, a west country ship was manned from the counties of the South West with a sprinkling of Scotsmen. They are apt to be a bit slow and stolid compared with ship's companies from Portsmouth and Chatham, but for a real tough job on a dirty night there is nothing to beat a west country crew. They went about the job with a quiet, determined efficiency. One man would hang down over the ship's side with two shipmates hanging onto his heels until he had the hook rope hooked on, then ten or a dozen would haul away together to the squeaky voice of a small midshipman. Not a grumble from a man as they slipped and fell and tripped in the pitch dark on a deck littered with wires in every direction. And when I came a cropper over some obstruction, I was picked up by a large petty officer who said, "Don't 'ee go falling, Sir, we want 'ee to give the word". And so back to my hammock for an hour or two, to get up again for dawn action stations as by this time the ship was at sea, and of course we always closed up before the first streak of light and remained closed up until we were certain the horizon was clear.

All that day we steamed in a southerly direction until we were off the coast of Yorkshire. It was known that the 2nd Battle Squadron was at sea with us, but no information was available regarding the object of the operation. That night I had a night watch, and was not feeling very fresh when we went to dawn action stations. Daylight came late on that winter morning with mist and rain squalls, poor visibility in all directions and a leaden sea. We checked through all communications and waited, but no order came to revert to cruising stations. In the TS, the atmosphere became very close and it was difficult to keep awake. We speculated as to what was happening; we had in the TS a speed indicator which showed that we were steaming at high speed, and a gyro repeater which indicated that we were making a large number of alterations of course. The morning stretched into the forenoon with no hint of anyone falling out for breakfast. The only reports that came down from the foretop were of rain and mist and falling visibility. In the ship's organisation, there were no arrangements for keeping the ship's company informed as to what was going on. We lived on rumour and speculation. Some signalman had seen a signal from a destroyer, reporting enemy vessels; *Southampton* had reported gun flashes. Then came a definite and surprising report that Scarborough had been bombarded, and we noticed that whereas we had been steaming in a generally easterly direction, we were now making back towards the English coast. But why should the Germans want to bombard Scarborough? No harbour or shipping there. Never mind, they had put their heads in a noose; we were between them and their home ports, shortly we would bring them to action and sink the lot.

The minutes of that long forenoon slowly ticked themselves away. Buoyed up by excitement and anticipation of the battle, we could almost, but not quite, ignore the pangs of hunger. I think it was somewhere about 1pm, when we had been closed up for well over six hours, that a message was passed to all positions to send one hand to collect some sandwiches from the galley. Soon we were munching large, roughly cut sandwiches consisting of two slices of bread with a slab of corned beef between, no butter or mustard to help get them down. However, I found I had no difficulty in getting my teeth into them. We ate hurriedly, thinking that at any moment the enemy might be sighted, though I think that by this time we were all beginning to have doubts as to whether we should meet the Germans. Surely if we were going to catch them, we ought to have come up with them by now? The long afternoon had to be lived through, while a heavy cloud of disappointment steadily descended upon us. Frustrated, annoyed and disappointed, we reverted to cruising stations at dusk and made tracks for harbour.

On this occasion we returned to Rosyth, where some anti- submarine defence had by now been rigged. This harbour remained the base for the battle cruisers throughout the rest of the war, and we always returned here except for brief period at Scapa for exercises. Rosyth was obviously a much better base from which to cut off any German raiding force, should they repeat their raid on Scarborough.

We arrived in harbour, and the inevitable coaling having been completed, we had an opportunity to study the papers. They were of course not very complimentary on the failure of the navy to bring the raiders to action. I think they appreciated that it was impossible to prevent an occasional raid, and they did their best to minimise the amount of damage done but they obviously thought that the raiders ought to have been made to fight their way home, and that at least one or two of them should have been sunk on the way. The opinion of the gunroom was very similar. It was not until we read the papers that we began to have an idea what had happened; we had seen nothing from the *New Zealand*, and such signals as were exchanged by wireless were confidential and not shown to junior gunroom officers. The general sense of frustration which had been building up ever since the outbreak of war was further increased.

But not to worry, here we were in the Firth of Forth with Edinburgh only some ten miles away with good communications by train and bus. If we could get some leave, we could get to Edinburgh for two or three hours, with the possibility of a cinema or at least tea at a restaurant with lots of sweet cakes. If there was any suspicion that the enemy might make a move, we went to short notice, which in the case of the battle cruisers, was two and a half hours' notice. The destroyers were at rather shorter notice and no leave was given. Normally, however, we were at four hours' notice and leave was given to officers from 1pm to 6.30pm. But of course, we junior midshipmen had to do instruction in the afternoon so we could only get the full leave on Saturdays and Sundays. But if we could fix up a rugger match against another gunroom, we were sometimes allowed ashore at 3.30pm. No short leave was given to ratings at this time; it was not until later that a canteen was built in the new Dockyard at Rosyth and a few playing fields laid out. Instead of leave, in order to give the ship's company something of a break at least once a week when we were in harbour, we would land two or three hundred men for a route march on the south side of the Firth. It was usual to march to Kirkliston, some three miles from where we landed with the Marine band, to give an air of jollity when we were marching through any inhabited place. A couple of officers, usually a sub-lieutenant and a midshipman, would walk on ahead and warn the local pub that we were coming. They would then open up and get in a few extra servers. Upon arrival at Kirkliston the party would fall out, nominally for fifteen minutes, during which time the sailors would consume as much beer as possible. At the end of fifteen minutes we would start rounding them up, and half an hour after our arrival we would be on the way back, not always in quite such good order as we had arrived. This wasn't much fun for sailors; a man was very lucky who got a route march once a month. On the other hand they were better off than the men in the rest of the Grand Fleet, swinging around their anchors in Scapa Flow.

We were soon at sea again to back up the attempt to make a raid with seaplanes on Heligoland on Christmas Day. It was hoped that this would bring out some German forces to retaliate. The raid was not a success, as the seaplanes were not sufficiently developed to get off the water in the existing conditions on that day. However, the sailors were not to be entirely done out of their Christmas. They made some attempt to decorate their messdecks, and as the traditional formal visit to the messdecks by the officers headed by the Captain was out of the question, the Captain was on the bridge and a large number of the officers were closed up, they raided the officers mess and grabbed such popular officers as they could find and carted them off to messdecks to be fed on plummy duff – more duff than plum.

The Commander was caught on the quarterdeck, lifted shoulder high and raced around the upper deck by fifty or more cheering sailors. I was grabbed by two large maintopmen, who picked me up in the gunroom and carried me face down with my feet higher than my head to the maintopmen's messdeck where I was plunked on a mess table, fed on various sweets, most of which seemed to be of a vivid green hue, while I shook hands in turn with each member of the gang with whom I used to shovel coal in the collier's hold and endeavoured to reciprocate their good wishes for a merry Christmas.

All this occurred while we were manoeuvring within a short distance of Heligoland. It was the last time that I remember scenes like this occurring with the ship at sea. Nobody was the least bit drunk; the sailors had had only their usual tot of rum, and strict orders had been issued that no officer was to stand a rating a drink. But it was the excitement of the occasion and the momentary relaxation from tension. At that time, for about an hour, the sailors were ready to fraternise with the Germans, as on that day the soldiers did in France. For about an hour they felt themselves freed from restraint and let themselves go. But only for an hour. By the time we were halfway through the afternoon watch, we were back to the grim realities of war and thinking that as we had been steaming hard for a long time, we should have a big coaling when we got back to harbour.

Back in harbour, the First Lieutenant changed around our duties from the beginning of January, and I found myself running the second picket boat. I was very proud of my boat; as well I might be, at 16 ½ to be running a boat fifty foot long driven by powerful engines with a crew of a petty officer as coxswain, two bowmen and a sternsheetman, a stoker petty officer for the engine-room and a stoker for the boiler room. Above the hatch to the forepeak was a mounting for a 3-pounder gun. The boat was steered from a position just abaft the engine-room casing, the coxswain and midshipman getting a little protection from the elements from a canvas screen, but steaming fast in the sort of sea which a moderate gale whipped up in the Firth of Forth was liable to be a very damp business. In addition, the smoke from the low funnel beat down straight into one's face. In the early days of the war, when ships lay with their torpedo nets spread, the only accommodation ladder that could be rigged was a small ladder right aft on the quarter. The peacetime formality, when the midshipman, having put on his dirk, received his orders from the officer of the watch and manned his boat by the gangway, had gone by the board. We got our orders, manned the boat over the boom, usually a stern boom if the nets were out, and proceeded on one's mission. Manning the boat over the boom in the open waters of the Firth with a westerly gale and a sluicing ebb tide taught one to be reasonably agile.

The submarine defences of the anchorage consisted of a net hung from the railway bridge, at that time, of course, the only bridge across the Forth. The net could be lowered to the bottom whenever it was necessary for ships to pass in or out, and therefore by its very nature, it was a comparatively light net and it was thought that a really determined submarine might be able to force its way through.

Early in January there was a report of a submarine having been sighted in the lower waters of the Forth. All ships were ordered to provide a picket boat to patrol the net during the night; *New Zealand* and another ship each to provide one boat during the middle watch. The 3-pounder gun was hurriedly hoisted into my boat, a box of ammunition was provided, and my boat's crew was augmented by a torpedoman equipped with a 16¼lb tin of wet guncotton, the necessary primer and detonators, and an electric battery with which to fire the charge. At a quarter to twelve I left the *New Zealand* to relieve the boat on patrol on the northern span of the bridge, while the other boat patrolled the southern span. On my way I tried to work out what action I should take if we did sight a submarine, but once I arrived on patrol, I was so busy avoiding the various navigational hazards that I hadn't time to worry about submarines. To start with, we nearly rammed the boat we were to relieve; we were both without lights and the night was very dark with squalls of cold rain. Then the tide was running out very fast and the boat was in continual danger of being swept into the net. Fortunately, I had a good phlegmatic coxswain, a big man who topped me by a whole head. He had a golden beard and wore little gold earrings in his ears. He seldom spoke, and then only in direct connection with the boat. Except on one occasion at a later date, when we were ordered to sea and I was sent into the Hawes Pier at South Queensferry to land a mail and told to get back quick for the boat to be hoisted before we sailed. For some reason the postman was delayed in getting his receipt for the mail, so I had to shove off and make back at full speed. One left Hawes Pier on a course parallel to the bridge until in the centre of the Firth, and then turned towards the anchorage passing to the north of the destroyer trot. The destroyers had already sailed, but their mooring buoys lay in our path deep in the water; very difficult to see in the dark but quite large enough to stove in a picket boat driven at speed and to sink her. I had a bowman looking out forward, but he saw nothing. The first thing I knew was looking over the port side to see a large buoy in the boats wash within few feet. In the relief of the tension, for once we had passed a buoy I knew where we were and the rest was plain sailing, I laughed. But my coxswain didn't approve at all; he told me that it was the hand of the Lord that had insured that we should not hit that buoy that night, and that it was very wrong of me to laugh. I accepted the reproof, too astonished at hearing the coxswain speak on a subject not connected with the boat that I had nothing to say. Of course, I was not a very talkative chap myself; it was long before I earned the nickname of 'Silent William', but even in those days, I don't think I talked very much.

To return to the patrol on the net, my idea was that if a submarine attacked it would have to do so at periscope depth in order to navigate in those narrow waters. In which case it might be possible to lasso the periscope and let the submarine tow the boat. One would then have time to rig the explosive charge and lower it over the side, until one calculated that it was somewhere near the bottom of the submarine and fire it in this position. I have very little doubt that had my experiments got to this stage I should have ended up by blowing up my own boat so from every point of view it was just as well that no submarine appeared that night.

Looking back over the past it is difficult to understand why so little progress had been made before 1914 in designing a weapon with which to attack a submarine. It was some time before the first depth charge was produced, and that was a very crude weapon. Even in 1917 I was in a sloop doing convoy escort duty in the Mediterranean with only a single depth charge with which to attack a submarine and, as I shall relate, that didn't go off when required.

THE BATTLE OF DOGGER BANK – 24TH JANUARY 1915

There was considerable enemy activity during January 1915, and we were at sea about the middle of the month to support a reconnaissance which however did not lead to any action. A few days later on the 23rd January we raised steam and hurried to sea. It was fairly obvious that something was in the wind as all forces at Rosyth set sail, which included the 3rd Battle Squadron as well as the 3rd Cruiser Squadron besides the battle cruisers with their attached 2nd Light Cruiser Squadron.

The next day dawn came late that winter morning, and there was little light when we made contact with the forces from Harwich at 7am. As the light increased it was seen to be a fine morning, with a light breeze from the northeast and a calm sea. It was 7.15am when *Southampton* reported gun flashes from an engagement taking place between *Aurora* from Harwich, who was a little late at the rendezvous having been delayed by fog, and a German light cruiser. During the next hour several reports came in and it became clear that the enemy consisted of their Battle Cruiser Squadron together with a Light Cruiser Squadron and a considerable number of destroyers. At the first alarm the enemy had concentrated and altered course for their base, which put us practically right astern of them. As soon as the enemy had been identified we began to work up in speed, as the Admiral signalled for 26 knots which was a knot more than the designed speed of either the *New Zealand* or *Indomitable*.

In the TS the excitement was intense when the foretop reported the enemy in sight. In the clear morning air they were sighted at a range of about fourteen miles, well outside our maximum gun range, which in the case of the 12-inch guns of the *New Zealand* was only some ten miles though the 13.5-inch guns of *Lion*, *Princess Royal* and *Tiger* could fire a little further. The enemy were going for home as hard as they could steam. The Admiral signalled for more speed and eventually the signalled speed was 29 knots. *Indomitable*, the oldest of the battle cruisers, started to drop astern and *New Zealand* though close up, couldn't quite keep in station. It took time to increase speed to this extent, all the ships were coal fired so additional speed could only be obtained if the stokers could burn more coal faster which meant harder and harder stoking. The engines of the *New Zealand* were designed to give 44,000 hp at full power. On this occasion the torsion meter on the propeller shaft indicated that we were developing well over 60,000 hp. In the TS we watched with anxiety the speed indicator while the

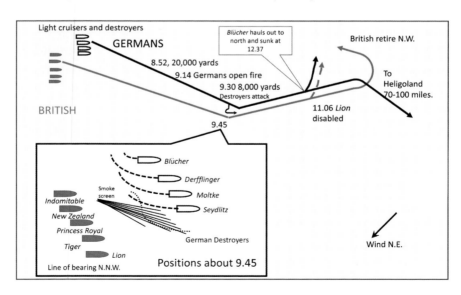

Fleet movements during the Battle of Dogger Bank 24th January 1915

foretop range finder transmitted ranges fairly consistently that indicated that we were gaining on the enemy.

It was after 9am and we had had the enemy in sight for over an hour when the *Lion* tried a single ranging shot that fell short. A few minutes later she tried again, and the shot fell over the rear ship in the enemy line which subsequently proved to be the *Blücher*. *Lion* then started to fire salvoes and *Princess Royal* and *Tiger* joined in, but New Zealand was still out of range with the *Indomitable* still further astern. Excitement in the TS was intense as we eagerly watched the range receivers, quickly plotting each range as it was received and so calculating the rate. The result varied between 50 and 100 closing. How true it is that a stern chase is a long chase.

Then the order came down 'Salvoes' and we waited on tip-toes of excitement for the fire gong. When it came it was a bit of an anti-climax, as only one gun caught up the salvo. The *New Zealand* had not yet been fitted with director firing; in fact, at that time I think the *Tiger* was the only ship to be so fitted. Consequently, we were in gunlayers firing, i.e. each gun was fired individually by its own gunlayer. At the speed at which we were steaming there was much spray; this, smoke from the next ship ahead and the long range made it very difficult for the gunlayers to see the target. In addition, the enemy's smoke was being blown by the light breeze towards us frequently obscuring individual ships. In these days of the universal oil-fired ship it is not easy to remember the vast quantities of smoke which a coal fired ship steaming at full power could make, particularly battle cruisers whose three large funnels seemed hardly big enough to allow all the smoke to escape. It came out of the funnels almost like toothpaste out of a tube and then started to spread, the cloud getting wider and wider as the distance from the funnel increased, obscuring more and more of the horizon.

As the range slowly decreased, we began to fire more and more steadily, with more guns picking up each salvo. It was difficult to tell in the TS which gun had fired; each one shook the ship and there was a dull boom, but as we were near the bottom of the ship with all the watertight doors firmly closed, we were very isolated from the actual battle, only able to follow at all by watching our instruments. In fact, I remember very little about this, my first battle. When I think of it, the clearest memory I have is of the look of intense excitement on the face of the rating who was working the stopwatch on our improvised plotting table, and the look of almost stunned surprise on the face of the ship's chaplain whose action station was also in the TS, to be well under cover, but where he had nothing to do to keep himself occupied.

The gun range was now decreasing considerably, and we were firing steadily. We counted each gun in each salvo with growing excitement. Although we must have realised that since we were firing at the enemy, the enemy must also have been firing back at us, I don't remember experiencing any feeling of fear or anxiety. In fact, the *New Zealand* was not hit; very few rounds came near us. Our target was the *Blücher*, but by the time we opened fire on her all the other three ships of the squadron had engaged her in turn as they overhauled her. They had treated her pretty roughly so that by the time they had moved on to engage the other enemy battle cruisers, the *Blücher* was not in condition to put up a very effective resistance. Though she must be given credit for the fact that she continued firing up to almost the very end, but her shooting became very wild.

About this time, we received a report in the TS that the *Lion* was slowing down and leaving the line. We then made several large alterations of course while the gun range decreased very rapidly. This was followed by a report that the *Blücher* was sinking and we ceased fire.

What had happened was that, when the *Lion* dropped astern, the command of the squadron was automatically transferred to Admiral Moore who was flying his flag in the *New Zealand*. He decided that he would make certain that the *Blücher* was sunk and altered the course of the whole squadron to close her and finish her off. By the time the *Blücher* had been sunk, the remaining German battle cruisers had got out of range and as they were already within some eighty miles of Heligoland, he did not consider that it was worthwhile to continue the pursuit any further. This is no place to argue the rights or wrongs of Admiral Moore's decisions, but it is almost certain that had he continued the pursuit and left the *Indomitable* to finish off the *Blücher*, the German battle cruisers would have suffered considerably more damage. They had already been heavily hit and one or more of them might have been sunk. On the other hand, the extent of the damage to the *Lion* was unknown and Admiral Moore must have been anxious about her safety. We now know that she was in no danger of sinking and therefore the verdict of history must be that an opportunity to deal the German battle cruisers a really hard blow was lost.

As the action was clearly at an end, we fell out from action stations early in the afternoon. We who had been shut up in the TS hurried up on deck in an endeavour to see something of what had been going on. I think the first thing that struck one was how dirty the ship looked. Each gun was black, with cordite smoke from the muzzle to halfway down its length; the concussion of the guns had dislodged large quantities of soot and dirt from the funnels which had settled all over the upper deck. Between decks, large numbers of fittings had been shaken adrift and were lying on the deck. Several joints in the fire main and fresh-water pipes had been started with the result that the decks were awash with dirty water. Although there was no sea to speak of, at the speed we were steaming every time the wheel was put over, the ship heeled appreciably so that the water was continually on the move. Most of the Gunroom crockery and glasses had been broken by 'Q' turret firing across the deck just above the Gunroom. We appeared to have suffered considerable financial loss, as most of the Gunroom's small stock of wine had been broken, but the suppliers subsequently replaced all the broken bottles free of charge.

On deck we could see the *Lion* slowly limping homeward already surrounded by a number of destroyers, as it was thought that the German submarines would make a dead set at her by day and she might well be attacked by destroyers after dark. Soon after we came up with her, she broke down altogether and the *Indomitable* was directed to take her in tow.

On deck the guns were being unloaded. When in the loading operation the shell is rammed home and driven into the chamber sufficiently hard for the driving band to grip on the lands of the rifling. It is therefore not easy to get the shell out again. The first method of unloading is to elevate the gun at full speed with the breech open until it comes up with a bump against the stops, in the hope that this will shake the shell clear and that it will slide back onto the loading tray. If this fails one is reduced to using the extractor, which consists of a large lump of wood shaped to the bore of the gun and bound with brass, which is passed down the muzzle on the end of a number of extension rods, made on the principle of a chimney sweep's equipment, with which the gun's crew bump the shell back into the chamber. In the case of 'Q' turret this was not possible, as the guns were loaded with lyddite shell which are nose-fused, and on which it is therefore considered dangerous to use the extractor. Having failed to bump the shells back by elevating the guns, we were left with the only alternative – which was to fire the guns. I remained on the upper deck when these two guns were fired, as I was anxious to know what it was like to be near a big gun when it was fired. I was nervous about this; in fact, I think I was much more frightened of the noise that the guns would make than I had been throughout the whole battle.

The following night was one of considerable anxiety for those in authority in the fleet for, with the *Lion* in tow of the *Indomitable* well over towards the German side of the North Sea, it appeared highly probable that the enemy would make an effort to interfere with our slow retreat to harbour. As a zeppelin had been in evidence as the *Blücher* sank, in fact she had dropped bombs on the destroyers endeavouring to rescue the survivors, it appeared probable that the enemy had good information of our position and slow advance. For us midshipmen however, it was an evening for self-congratulation; hadn't we taken part in a full-scale battle? Surely we would now get a bar to our medal? We patted ourselves on the back and thought we were tremendous chaps.

The squadron covered the *Lion* and *Indomitable* all that night and the next day and then, when the tow was close to May Island, we went into Rosyth to be greeted by the inevitable collier and of course we were faced with a big coaling after all our hard steaming. Just as we completed coaling the *Lion* came up harbour; the I*ndomitable* had towed her nearly to the bridge where the Dockyard tugs took over. As she came to rest in her usual berth, she was cheered by all the rest of the squadron. The cheering was quite spontaneous. Our collier was still alongside; the sailors climbed out of the holds and cheered and cheered again, with their faces black as coal dust and the pale winter sunlight lighting up the whites of their eyes.

A few days later, an opportunity was given to us to visit the *Lion* and to see the extent of the damage. She had been hit a number of times, but most of the damage was very local. Very lucky in two respects. Firstly, she had had very few casualties; only one man had been killed and, secondly, although a shell had passed very close to a magazine, she had not had a cordite fire. The good fortune which stood by the *Lion* on this occasion had unfortunate repercussions since; as there had been no cordite fire, the extreme danger that this may present to a modern ship was not realised, and no additional precautions were taken to safeguard the magazines. It was this danger, from a cordite fire, that subsequently caused such appalling disasters to the battlecruisers at Jutland. On the other hand, the *SMS Seyditiz* had been hit and her after guns put out of action by a cordite fire, which had done much to alert the Germans to this danger, with the result that at Jutland their ships were able to stand up to a tremendous hammering without blowing up.

Questions of the design of ships were however beyond the purview of midshipmen. We were pleased with our ship and still more pleased with ourselves – an opinion which we were encouraged to believe was correct by the daily papers who spread themselves over our little battle. The war in France had descended into the morass of trench warfare, which gave the papers little on which to bite; our battle provided them with a chance to spread themselves, which they proceeded to do for several days.

Some lucky man in one of the destroyers had obtained a remarkable photograph of the *Blücher* bottom up with many of her crew still clinging to the ship. Reproductions of this photograph appeared in several papers, and obviously provided the lucky owner of the negative with considerable financial reward. I made a mental note of this fact; in future, I always kept

SMS Blücher capsized, 24th January 1915 during the Battle of Dogger Bank

Thursday
Feb 5th

Dear Daphne,

Thanks very much for your interesting letter. I had a letter
the other day from Aunt Janet saying she was going down to
Falmouth at the end of this week so I suppose she will be down
there by the time this reaches you.

I suppose you would like to hear about our little scrap though
there is not much of interest that I can tell you. You see my
action station is in the Fore Transmitting station which is
right at the bottom of the ship so that I was unable to see
much. We went to action stations at 6.55 am as we knew that
we were in the vicinity of the enemy. The enemy were sighted
at 7.45 and our destroyers and light cruisers were ordered to
chase the enemy's destroyers while we went at full speed for
their battle crusers. As the day was fine we sighted them at
about 16½ miles away which of course was at much too great
a distance for us to open fire. As we were going faster than
them we gradually closed them. They opened fire at 8.45 and
the Lion at 9.00. The Princes Royal and Tiger opened fire
soon after but as our guns are slightly smaller we did not open
fire until 9.40. Owing to the long range (a matter of some 10
miles) the firing at first was not very accurate but by 10.40
we had closed to about 6 miles and then we gave them a bad
time. During the action we got little driblets of news from the
conning tower such as "the enemy's rear most ship is hauling
out of line". "The enemy's rear most ship has had her foremast
funnel shot away." "The enemy's leading ship is on fire." "The
Blucher is sinking." All this of course was very exciting. The
Blucher sank about 11.45.

my camera loaded and was determined that if the opportunity of a picture of newsworthy value came my way, I would not waste my chance.

As January stretched into February and March, the question which arose in all our minds, Wardroom, Gunroom and ship's company alike, was the possibility of a little leave. The ship had not given any long leave since Easter of the previous year and we midshipmen of course had gone back to Dartmouth in early May and had had no opportunity to visit our homes since. Rumours and conjecture about leave filled the air. The *Lion* was still away in the Tyne having her damage repaired but the *Queen Mary*, who had missed the recent battle because she had been in dockyard hands and giving leave, had rejoined the squadron, so surely it was now the turn of the *New Zealand*. But it was not until after the *Lion* had re-joined the squadron and the *Princess Royal* had been away to a dockyard for her direct firing to be fitted that the turn of the *New Zealand* arrived. It was well towards the end of May when one night we slipped out of Rosyth and arrived in Cromarty Firth at Invergordon the next day. Here a floating dock had been established, and sufficient dockyard facilities to enable routine dockings to be carried out and emergency repairs. Practically the whole of the ship's company were to be sent on ninety-six hours leave together; only a small party were left onboard during docking who would be given leave after the main body had returned.

Special trains had been ordered for early the next morning and we were allowed to draft telegrams to say that we were coming on leave, but they were not despatched until the next morning. As my home was in Cornwall, it seemed a great waste of time to attempt to go all that distance, so I telegraphed to my parents that I was going to London and would go to the hotel at which they usually stayed when in town. Our train got away on time in the morning and should have arrived in London about midnight, but owing to a serious train accident near Gretna Green involving a troop train, our train had to be diverted and it was 4am before I arrived at the hotel.[2] There I found a telegram from my father to say that they would arrive at the

---

[2] The Quintinshill rail disaster occurred on the 22nd May 1915. Over 220 people were killed when a southbound troop train struck a stationary local train that had been positioned on the southbound mainline to allow the passing of two late running northbound sleepers. The two signallers then overlooked the presence of this local train and cleared the troop train to proceed. Both were later convicted of manslaughter, but served only a year in jail. This remains Britain's worst rail disaster.

hotel that morning so, worn out with the long journey in a very overcrowded train, I went to bed and was immediately asleep.

It seemed that I had only just got to sleep when I was woken up to find my father looking at me and explaining that he and my mother had travelled up from Cornwall during the night, and that they were in a room on the same floor. Jumping out of bed I ran along the corridor to greet my Mother; there didn't seem much to say, we just clung to one another until my father suggested that some breakfast would be a good idea. I thought so too. We hadn't been able to get much to eat on the train the day before. Kipling, in his book *Captains Courageous,* tells us that great joy induces a good appetite. From practical experience I can confirm this opinion.

Immediate hunger having been satisfied, I was not above swaggering a little; after all, wasn't I a full-blown midshipman who had taken part in a battle? Naturally I thought myself a bit of a chap. My parents deferred to me. We went to the theatre, the choice of play being mine. I wanted to see the latest musical shows whose tunes were being constantly ground out on the very battered gunroom gramophone. I don't think my parents were very interested in the shows and my mother, who had a bit of a musical ear, thought nothing of the early jazz tunes which were invading the London stage.

Ninety-six hours' leave sounds a lot when written down like that, but when two long train journeys are cut off from either end of the period, the remainder seems to disappear before one has time to turn around. It seemed that I had hardly started my leave before the time came for me to hurry to King's Cross to catch a special train late at night back to Invergordon.

I said goodbye to my Mother in the hotel; it was no good pretending I was a smart midshipman, I was a small boy going back to school and I hated it. I couldn't prevent the tears pouring down my face.

My father accompanied me to the station where one of my cousins also turned up to see me off. He was in the uniform of the OTC, being still at London University. He was over three years older than I, which made me feel rather superior again – to see him still in a training corps when I had actually taken part in a battle. I felt much better, and managed to put on a good face when I said goodbye to my father.

Without the excitement and anticipation of going on leave, the journey north proved to be long and tiring and it was well into the next afternoon

Midshipman William Carne with his mother, Annie Carne
(1872–1942) at Garras the family home in Falmouth

before we arrived in Invergordon. As the train ran into the station, we saw
that our ship was already out of dock anchored in the Firth and – oh horror
– a collier was just going alongside! As we crept onboard, we were told to
get into our coaling rig as coaling would start in ten minutes time. A greater
contrast from the flesh pots of London could not be imagined. As soon as
we had completed coaling we sailed for Rosyth where, on arrival, we were
again greeted by a collier.

The remainder of 1915 was a comparatively quiet period for the battle cruisers, during which we built up our strength. Those battle cruisers who had been dealing with the enemy raiders in the outer oceans were recalled and joined up at Rosyth. The squadron was then reorganised into the Battle Cruiser Force consisting of three squadrons. The 1st comprised the 13.5-inch gunned ships, that is the *Lion*, flying Admiral Beatty's flag, *Princess Royal*, *Queen Mary* and *Tiger*. The 2nd Battle Cruiser Squadron consisting of the *Australia*, flying the flag of Admiral Pakenham, *New Zealand* and *Indefatigable* and the 3rd Battle Cruiser Squadron of the *Invincible*, flying Admiral Hood's flag, *Indomitable* and *Inflexible*. All ships in the 2nd and 3rd squadrons were armed with 12-inch guns. Attached to the force were the First Light Cruiser Squadron with Commodore Alexander Sinclair flying his broad pendant in the *Galatea,* and the Second Light Cruiser Squadron led by *Southampton* under Commodore Goodenough. Also forming part of the Force was the 13th Destroyer Flotilla which was being formed of the new Admiralty M class destroyers as they came forward from the builders' yards. The whole force was commanded by Admiral Beatty and was based on Rosyth, but usually one squadron was at Scapa exercising as at that time there were no facilities for exercising in the Firth of Forth.

During this period, the newly-formed Battle Cruiser Force spent less of its time at sea which meant that the midshipmen received much more formal instruction; at sea no instruction could be given as we were closed up in watches. The whole ship's company went to action stations before the first streak of dawn and remained closed up for about an hour. From then onwards we went in to three watches manning the secondary armament. At night the turret crews not on watch slept in their turret, with sufficient of them awake to get the turret trained rapidly on any bearing should an alarm occur, while those asleep were waking up and getting closed up.

I was not very pleased with my action station in the TS; it seemed to me that plotting ranges left little chance of showing initiative or skill, and I wanted some more active duty. A chance to get my duties changed came in the middle of this year when six more midshipmen, also members of the same term as ourselves, joined the *New Zealand* from the old cruiser *Venus* to which they had been sent when we mobilised from Dartmouth. One of these new midshipmen took over my duties in the TS and I went as midshipman of 'A' turret, the lieutenant in charge of the turret being an officer known by the ships company as Mr. Battenberg, but the more formal Navy List described him as Lieutenant His Serene Highness Prince George of Battenberg. He was the eldest son of Prince Louis of Battenberg who had been First Sea Lord at the outbreak of war and who on more than one occasion came and visited his eldest son and stayed on board for the night as a guest of the Captain. The younger brother of my turret officer came to sea during the latter part of the next year, and joined the *Lion* as a junior midshipman thus starting a career during which he succeeded his father as First Sea Lord.

I met him very briefly when he first joined the *Lion* when I was a midshipman with some two years' sea experience and thought myself rather superior. Subsequently we only met twice, once for an hour or so in the thirties when we were both commanders and again in the fifties when he was First Sea Lord when he astounded me with the depth of his memory, being able to tell me the names of many of the officers of the *New Zealand* which I had long ago forgotten.

But 'A' turret did not remain my action station for very long. Up to this time the only position from which the *New Zealand's* torpedoes could be controlled from was the Conning Tower. It was thought that in the event of the Conning Tower being damaged or the communications cut that there should be a secondary control position. A small compartment at the after end of the after superstructure on the 4-inch gun deck was adapted for this purpose. The position was two decks above 'X' turret, in other words about level with the muzzles of 'X' turret when the guns were at maximum elevation and when the guns were on their extreme forward bearing on either beam they almost looked into this small space which was now known as the secondary torpedo control position. It was built of one-inch armour plate and also served as a protected position for the officer controlling the 4-inch guns in action. As the secondary armament was completely unprotected, the 4-inch gun crews went below to the 4-inch ready use handing rooms during a big gun action. If a destroyer attack threatened, the control officer had to summon his gun crews from below. I was already becoming interested in torpedoes and wondering if I would not one day try to specialise as a torpedo officer. I was therefore very pleased when I was selected to become the secondary torpedo control officer. The somewhat irascible Scottish torpedo officer did his best to instruct me in my duties, but he was a clever man himself with a quick brain and not very patient at explaining details in simple language to a rather dull schoolboy. However, I liked him and admired him and became in time very much his faithful servant, and very proud of my position as the secondary torpedo control officer.

Towards the end of this year, we had an addition to our gunroom in the form of another member of our term. D.H. Barton had been sent to one of the old battleships when we mobilised from Dartmouth and in due course his ship had been one of the first in the attack on the Dardanelles.

He had been in charge of the ship's launch at the original attack at Anzac, and during his second trip to the beach had been wounded by a

Scene on the quarterdeck of HMS New Zealand. Left to right, Assistant Paymaster Birch, Midshipman L.G. Pennington*, D.H. Barton (holding the ship's mascot, the bulldog known as Pelorus Jack, so called after a famous dolphin that escorted ships through a stretch of water in Cook Strait, New Zealand), Midshipman W.P. Carne and Signal Boatswain Lewis.

*Lionel Pennington was killed during commissioning of submarine N25 HMS Thetis when it sank during commissioning on the 1st June 1939 with the loss of 99 lives.

rifle bullet. When he had recovered from his wound he was sent to the *New Zealand* and became the after 4-inch control officer in action. It therefore came about that he and I shared the amenities of the secondary torpedo control position during the Battle of Jutland, a terrifying experience which did much to cement the friendship that was was growing between us.

Barton was a most charming personality, and was rapidly developing into a most competent officer. I have little doubt but that he would have gone as far if not further than any one in our term had he survived. He specialised in submarines after the war and was doing very well in them, when unhappily he was lost in the L24 when she was accidently struck and sunk by HMS *Resolution* during an exercise off Portland Bill in January 1924.

At this time, it was the Admiralty's policy that all officers, ex-Dartmouth, should do some engine-room training. It was intended that a certain percentage should volunteer to specialise as engineers to be known by their substantive rank, with the letter (E) after their rank, as opposed to the older officers of the branch who were distinguished by the title Engineer in front of their substantive rank.

It was during this year, therefore, that we each did some three months Engine Room training. During this training period we joined the Engine Room branch being attached to one of the Engineer Lieutenants as his assistant. At sea we kept watch with him, and in harbour tagged around behind him while he attended to the maintenance of that portion of those installations for which he was responsible. Every fortnight or so we changed around, thus getting an insight in turn of the problems involved in maintaining the boilers, main engines and auxiliary engines in turn. I found this instruction very interesting; I have always had a slight bent towards things mechanical. My Mother used to tell a story of how I was taken to an agricultural show when I was aged about five, with a number of other boys, to see the horse jumping. After a period, I was missing and was only discovered after a considerable period of time talking to a very grubby gentleman whose duty it was to attend a steam engine which was driving a number of agricultural machines of various sorts. But even with this bent towards things mechanical I never had any ambition to become an engineer officer; I had joined the Navy to command a ship. That was my ambition and I was not going to be deterred from it. In the meantime, however, I was prepared to enjoy a little engineering training, and since I enjoyed my training a number of details which I learnt have stuck ever since. For instance, even today I could tell you how many of the *New Zealand's* 31 boilers were fitted in each of her five boiler rooms and I could tell you which of her Babcock and Wilcock boilers had 29 headers as opposed to those which had 30 and 31. Quite useless bits of information which stuck because I enjoyed finding out about the boilers and knowing about each individual one.

During our training we were made to share the actual work of the stokers, including both stoking and trimming coal. The *New Zealand* had bunkers for 3,000 tons of coal which, as I have explained, were always kept well topped up. But she was built during the period of transition from coal to oil and in addition to her coal she had tanks for 800 tons of oil fuel. Over the door of each furnace was fitted an oil fuel burner which could be switched on to supplement the coal fire. This auxiliary oil fire in each boiler enabled increases in speed to be made comparatively rapidly as compared with ships which only had coal fired boilers. Each boiler was fitted with four furnaces

Midshipman William Carne, on the left, on HMS New Zealand

and each furnace was cleaned once a watch, so the crew of a boiler had to clean a furnace once an hour. To do this the whole fire had to be stirred up with an enormous poker called a slice. This was much too heavy for me to handle and when I had to clean a furnace, I had to get a stoker to help me handle the slice. Breaking up the clinker at the far end of the furnace necessitated standing close up to the furnace door, where the heat was blistering. The stokers' working kit consisted of a singlet and pair of roughly cut trousers of a rough woollen material called dreadnought cloth. They were cut very high and held up by a wide leather belt. Around their necks they wore a sweat rag which, when they were close up to the furnace door, they picked up the end and gripped between their teeth, thus protecting a small portion of their faces from the heat.

The coal was stowed in bunkers abreast each boiler room. In order to maintain the watertight integrity of the ship in the event of damage, individual bunkers were kept small. Thus, between the boiler room and the ship's side would be two bunkers separated by a watertight bulkhead, the outer one being known as the wing bunker. As coal was expended from the inboard bunker it had to be replaced by trimming coal from the wing bunker. Trimming was a very unpleasant, dirty job in an atmosphere almost solid with coal dust. During coaling to ensure that the maximum amount of coal was stowed, it was necessary to trim from where the chute entered the bunker to fill up all the corners. A well-trimmed bunker was filled with coal to within ten inches of the beams overhead. To do this the trimmers had to lie on their stomachs to work the coal across into all the vacant spaces. During one coaling I was attached to the double bottom Chief Stoker, whose duty it was to make certain that every bunker was filled to capacity. We entered each bunker in turn and crawled around on our tummies making certain there was no space left which could be filled with a little more coal. When we had finished, I felt as though an appreciable quantity of the 3,000 tons of coal carried by the *New Zealand* was lodged in my mouth and nostrils.

Our double bottom Chief Stoker was a big chap called Lake with a sense of humour. Normally he had a rather lonely job wandering around all the many compartments in the bottom of the ship, and I think he rather enjoyed having a midshipman to take around with him. He didn't let us off going into all the most awkward holes and corners, but he always played fair and went first himself. Amongst other duties he had to estimate how much coal we had expended, and he developed a wonderful eye for calculating just how much coal was in a particular pile. He would go into a bunker and say the capacity of this bunker is 250 tons and there remains 135 tons and he would be right within a ton or two.

Two colleagues of William Carne on the deck of HMS New Zealand, Midshipmen Baker and Sub-Lieutenant Bowlby 1916. (Photo W.P. Carne)

Philip Baker left the service in 1923 and re-joined in 1938. He was awarded an OBE for 'bravery during enemy air attacks' in North African waters and retired from the service as a commander in 1945. He died in 1952.

Cuthbert Bowlby was awarded the DSC in 1918. He gained the rank of Captain in the Second World War and was appointed a CBE in 1945. He was in the Foreign Service from 1946 to 1955 and died in 1965.

To get the coal from the bunker into the furnace for burning it was shovelled into a steel box called a skid, hauled along the floor plates to a position in front of the next furnace to be fired and tipped out into the plate. Two stokers were required to actually stoke the furnace, one to shovel the coal into the furnace, the other to open the door at the critical moment as the shovel came forward to discharge its load of coal. As soon as the load had left the shovel the door was closed again. The boiler room was, of course, under air pressure to create a forced draught, if the furnace door was left open the draught rushed into the furnace tending to cool the fire and only causing the coal to burn on top of the pile. The correct route for the draught was through the ash pan, and so up through the fire to the uptakes so that the whole mass of coal on the fire bars was kept burning. In a well-stoked furnace, the fire was six to eight inches deep and burning fiercely throughout the whole depth. To keep each furnace pulling its full weight required skill, attention and hard work. We were taught the golden rule of good stoking, i.e. quickly, lightly, evenly and often.

Each group of boilers was in the charge of a stoker petty officer, or a Chief Stoker in the case of the after two larger boiler rooms, each of which held eight boilers. The petty officer attended personally to the adjustment of the fan engines maintaining the draught and kept an ever-watchful eye on the water level in the boiler gauges. We had automatic feed regulators, but they were not quite a hundred per cent reliable and of course if the water level started to drop, quick action was necessary.

I learnt most of my stoking technique from an enormous Chief Stoker who spent the whole of his watch singing Moody and Sankey hymns[3], but who could correct a stoker whose furnace was not perfect in language more reminiscent of a dockside area, and was not above emphasising his remarks with the aid of the wheel spanner which he always carried. But he could also be helpful. When I and a small stoker were endeavouring to clean a badly-clinkered furnace, he came along, thrust us both to one side and, picking up the slice as though it was a feather, he proceeded to break up the

---

[3] Dwight Moody (1837–1899) and Ira Sankey (1840–1908) were American evangelists who attracted vast audiences to their revivalist meetings in the USA and on their visits to Britain.

clinker in all directions. A few rakes with the rake and all the clinker was out of the fire; he then took a shovel and proceeded to place a couple of hundredweight of coal in exactly the right place to build up the fire again. That done, he handed the shovel to the stoker, started the next verse of his hymn, and walked away without a word or a change of expression.

The peace time complement of the *New Zealand* comprised sufficient stokers to steam the ship at more or less full power in two watches, i.e. four hours on and four hours off. But this limited the total time the ship could be steamed at full power as the stokers became worn out. It must be realised that although the ship had engines of 44,000 hp, her ultimate mobility depended on the muscles of her stokers and the rate at which they could be trained to shovel coal into her furnaces.

Unless they were given a reasonable stand-off between watches, they could not keep up the necessary effort to keep the ship steaming at full power. On the outbreak of war, the stoker complement was gradually increased to enable the ship to steam at full power in three watches i.e. only a third of the stokers would be below at a time. Under these circumstances the ship could steam at her designed full power as long as her bunkers contained any coal. But it meant that the stokers' mess decks and rather primitive bathrooms were very crowded.

The confined, monotonous conditions under which the stokers and, indeed, the whole of the lower deck lived proved an excellent breeding ground for every sort of rumour. One of the favourite rumours about this time was the date on which the ship would sail to go 'Up the Straits' i.e. to the Dardanelles, where the Navy was being actively employed assisting the Army. But this rumour ran a poor second to rumours of leave or, as the sailors would say, 'a nice drop of leaf'. It is frequently said that the lower deck knows about the movements of a ship long before anyone else in the ship. The truth is, of course, that the lower deck has so many, and such diverse rumours floating around at any one time, that whatever orders are received they can always turn-round and say, 'There, we told you that was going to happen'. The various rumours that didn't come to fruition are of course conveniently forgotten. However, in November of 1915 a favourite rumour did prove itself to be true. One night, the *New Zealand* sailed from Rosyth escorted only by two destroyers, who also left us when we had passed

Cape Wrath. As we sailed well out into the Atlantic, the wildest rumours circulated but an old favourite turned out to be true. After passing down the west coast of Ireland well out in the Atlantic to keep clear of the submarines, we turned easterly and, passing south of the Scillies, entered Devonport before dawn one cold November morning, there to have director firing fitted and, more important, to give eight days' leave. For our turn to have director firing to arrive was a great thing, but that we should actually go to our home port, where a large percentage of the ship's company had their homes, was a bit of luck that could only have been granted by the gods themselves.

We were all owed to go on leave immediately after breakfast; hurriedly writing out a telegram, I rushed to the station. I suppose our Marine postman was a bit overwhelmed with all the telegrams he had to despatch as, after a two-hour train journey, I got home before the telegram arrived. I was a bit surprised that there was no-one at the station to meet me, but I found a horse-drawn cab to take me home. I had known the cabby all my life, as his stable was not very far from my home and, in the days before taxis, he was much in demand. He gave me a warm welcome and drove me up the hill as fast as his old horse would go. Bursting into the house, I found a strange parlour maid in the hall, and it was with some difficulty that I extracted from her the information that my Mother was still in bed suffering from a slight cold. When I rushed upstairs to my Mother's room the parlour maid followed, evidently thinking that I was some interloper, and was not satisfied until she heard my Mother's surprised greeting as I burst into her room. At least my surprising unannounced arrival had one good result; it cured my mother's cold immediately. Eight days' leave may be twice as long as 96 hours, but it seems to disappear just as quickly. My leave was up at noon; I arrived back at Devonport dockyard to find that the ship was already out of the basin and alongside the outer wall preparing – to coal! It was too much to hope that the sailors would all get back strictly on time from their home port; they dribbled back during the afternoon one hour, two hours, three hours late. So, we started coaling seriously shorthanded and, as we had steamed all the way around Ireland at high speed, we were some 1,700 tons of coal short. We coaled all that afternoon and evening and far into the night and sailed again early the next morning back to Rosyth, but stopping at Scapa en route for an exercise period to try out and get used to our new director firing system.

H.M.S. "_____ " Cash Account for _____ 191 . Voucher No._____

NAVY PRIZE.

No. 14A. M.C.

11926

ADMIRALTY,

30 april 1918.

SIR,

~~With reference to your application of the~~

I have to request that you will cause payment of the sum shown on the other side hereof to be made to the person named in respect of ~~their~~ *his* share in the Prize Bounty awarded for the destruction of the Enemy Ship *in The* *Destruction of the Blücher 24th January 1915.*

The amount should be brought to account under the head "Naval Prize Remittances."

~~Payments to men should be noted on their Service Certificates.~~

I am, SIR,

Your obedient Servant,

Accountant-General
of the Navy.

To

The Commanding Officer,

H.M. Ship *Asphodel.*

Certificate of Prize Bounty of twelve shillings and one penny for the destruction of the Blücher.

CHAPTER 4
THE BATTLE OF JUTLAND

In the early months of 1916, the war at sea began to hot up again, and we made several sweeps into the North Sea. The German submarines were becoming ever more ambitious, and much thought was being given to counter and thwart their attacks. It had become the accepted principle that during the hours of daylight ships should zig-zag. Alterations of course were made regularly every quarter of an hour by signal, an equal amount either side of the mean line of advance. The more sophisticated zig-zag diagrams of the later years of the war had not yet been introduced.

It was thought that ships steaming in line abreast made a more difficult target for the submarines than if they were in line ahead. The battle cruisers adopted this cruising formation. It was not very popular with Captains as the problems of keeping accurate station were considerably enhanced, and therefore unless the Officers of the Watch were thoroughly experienced, the Captain had to be about continually on the bridge. The policy at that time was to employ the more experienced lieutenants in controlling the armament in watches, thus the duties of Officer of the Watch were usually carried out by sub-lieutenants and RNR Officers. The Captain and Navigating Officer were of course always near or around the bridge to give a helping hand if the ship got out of station, but it was a considerable strain on them. Further, the cruising formation had been adopted hurriedly without giving full thought to all possible eventualities. This led to an accident which might have had very serious repercussions.

We were in single line abreast, the *New Zealand* being on the starboard beam of the *Australia*, when we ran into one of those dense banks of fog for which the North Sea is notorious and which are extremely difficult to detect. One moment we were in comparatively clear weather, the next it was almost impossible to see the fo'c'sle. Should we remain on the present course until the fog cleared, continue the zigzag or turn to the mean course? A difference of opinion occurred in the *New Zealand* and the *Australia* and the two ships sheered in towards one another. Fortunately, they both realised what was happening and reversed their rudders but not in time to prevent the two ships coming together broadside to broadside at 22 knots. The bump and resulting damage were considerable.

I was in the gunroom when the collision occurred, which being on the upper deck, we were allowed to have our deadlights up during daylight hours. Suddenly all daylight was cut off, followed immediately by a tremendous grinding noise; all three gunroom scuttles were blown in and a considerable quantity of water forced up between the two ships shot across the gunroom from the scuttles. Jagged bits of glass from the burst scuttle glasses made unpleasant missiles and the sub of the Mess received an appreciable scalp wound.

A rapid examination of the damage soon showed that both ships could continue to steam; in fact, the damage to the *New Zealand* was comparatively slight. Most of the shock had been taken by the torpedo net booms, several of which were missing, and the remainder were hanging down the side with their lower ends crushed looking rather like giant pieces of asparagus which had been sucked. Forward on the port side, rather further forward than the gunroom, was a hole in the ship's side where the *Australia's* sheet anchor had penetrated into the Paymaster Commander's cabin just as he had opened the safe to count the available cash for the next payment of the ship's company. This hole was well above the waterline, was soon patched temporarily and in no way affected the sea-keeping ability of the ship. The *Australia* had not fared so well and was damaged below the waterline but again not too seriously.

The sweep was called off and the fleet returned to harbour. We arrived in Rosyth and an immediate decision was taken not to attempt to repair the torpedo net defence but to remove it altogether. Now that our harbours were reasonably well defended against submarines, we had ceased to use our torpedo nets; in fact, they had not been streamed for many months. We were pleased to see the nets go, which were unsightly and untidy and required much labour to maintain them. A further advantage in getting rid of them was that the removal of this large weight of equipment went a long way to compensate for the additional equipment which the experience of the war had shown was necessary.

We were then moved into the basin of Rosyth dockyard, which was now sufficiently advanced to carry out repair work, as strenuous efforts had been made ever since the outbreak of war to complete this important dockyard. As nearly six months had elapsed since we had docked at Devonport, it was decided to dock the ship, repair the hole in the side and carry out certain other maintenance work necessitated by all our hard steaming. Since this was going to take an appreciable time eight-day leave was given to the ship's company. Taken by and large, the ship's company did not think our bumping match with the *Australia* was a very serious disaster. On this occasion I did not feel justified in asking my parents to meet me, so I made the long journey to Cornwall. One afternoon we went to Edinburgh by train, had a good dinner there and caught the night train to London. I might mention that at this time Edinburgh was known as Grad. The Russians had decided that St. Petersburg had too Germanic a sound so had renamed it Petrograd. Obviously, Edinburgh became Edingrad or, for short, just Grad.

That leave, like all other leaves, passed all too quickly. I don't remember anything particular about it except that I had an argument with a railway official who thought that, on my railway warrant from Edinburgh to Falmouth, I should have travelled by a slow train with many changes down the west coast, instead of taking the fast train via London. I managed to travel the way I wanted to go.

I arrived back in Rosyth again and we were soon out in the stream once more, ready for sea. As the *Australia* was still away being repaired, Admiral Pakenham transferred his flag to the *New Zealand*. It thus happened that when on the 30th May the whole fleet were ordered to sea in a hurry, the *New Zealand* wearing the flag of Admiral Pakenham, led the 2nd Battle Cruiser Squadron into the biggest naval battle of the war.

On the following morning, nearly one of the longest days of the year, we went to dawn action stations before 4 am. The sun rose in a clear sky with a gentle breeze and a calm sea; a nice summer day, in fact, but with those patches of thin mist which are typical of the North Sea. We continued our sweep to the southward throughout the forenoon with the 2nd Battle Cruiser Squadron on the port wing and the cruisers spread well ahead. At 2pm we turned to the northward to rendezvous with the Grand Fleet in accordance with the programme. It was at 2.20pm that the *Galatea*, the

William as a midshipman at home with his family. Standing: George, Mona, James, Daphne, Ruth. Seated; William, Annie and George Newby Carne.

James became a soldier and joined the Gloucester regiment. He was awarded the VC for valour in the Korean war.

George served in the Second World War in Burma, on both of the Chindit expeditions, and was awarded the MC.

easternmost cruiser on the screen, reported two enemy cruisers. Actually, these were destroyers, but *Galatea's* original signal was rapidly followed by others indicating that there were considerable enemy forces at sea and that she was already in action. The course of the battle cruisers was immediately altered to the eastward and speed increased. The 5th Battle Squadron, who were in company and had been five miles ahead when the course was altered to the north at 2pm, did not confirm immediately to the battle cruisers with the result that they opened their distance to nearly ten miles.

In the *New Zealand*, the afternoon calm was shattered by the stirring call of action stations on the bugle and the pipe that enemy forces had been sighted by the *Galatea*. I was off watch in the gunroom so, hurriedly collecting my

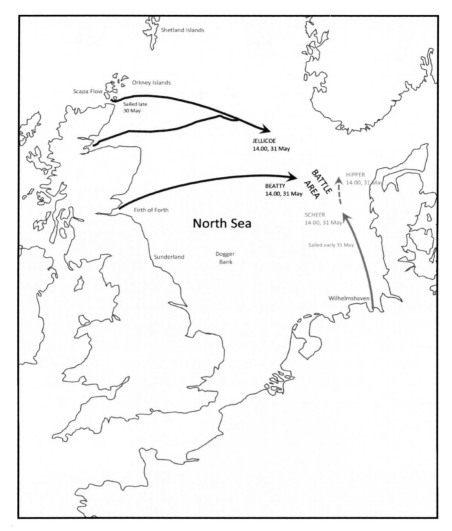

The Battle of Jutland – Movements on 30–31st May 1916

camera, I rushed to my action station in the after-torpedo control station. My first duty was to make certain my voicepipe man had checked through all communications; nothing had been touched since dawn action stations, so that a quick check through was a matter of moments.

From the submerged flat came anxious inquiries as to what was happening. I climbed up to Barton in the after 4-inch control position on top of the after superstructure. He had just completed checking his communications with his guns and was wondering whether he should keep his crews closed up or send them down to their protected position, on the assumption that the forthcoming action would be a big gun action. Together we surveyed the scene.

The 2nd Battle Cruiser Squadron was now in line ahead and having been on the eastern wing during the sweep was, since the turn towards the east, in the van. The 1st Battle Cruiser Squadron had formed a single line ahead and were some two miles astern of us. The battle cruisers were increasing speed and raising steam for full speed, causing them to belch smoke which was rapidly reducing the visibility to leeward.

At this time, we hoisted our battle ensigns, five of them, two of which had been presented when the ship was in New Zealand and were already a little battered from having been flown at both the Heligoland Bight and Dogger Bank actions. They were in addition to two white ensigns painted on either side of the foretop in case the bunting ensigns got shot away. In those days, we still liked to go into action with a certain panache.

We were straining our eyes towards the eastern horizon, that is more or less right ahead, and therefore not easy to see through the smoke pouring from our three funnels, when a burst of flags from the *Lion* ordered the 2nd Battle Cruiser Squadron to take station astern of the 1st Battle Cruiser Squadron. I remember thinking at the time that it was a pity that the *New Zealand* was not to be allowed to lead the fleet into action, but in fact it was an excellent thing that we were not allowed to become engaged without the support of the other battle cruisers, as I feel convinced that we would have been overwhelmed. With two sixteen-point turns Pakenham brought the 2nd Battle Cruiser Squadron into station astern of the 1st, making the *New Zealand* the fifth ship in the line. Then a small turn to starboard and as we followed round the next ship ahead, we sighted the German battle cruisers looking large and menacing.

In the heated controversy that developed after the battle and went on for some fifteen years it was maintained by several experts that much should have been done in the interval between the original enemy report and the sighting of the enemy, to concentrate the British forces and engage under conditions more favourable to ourselves. They are possibly right if the concentration could have been affected without the enemy, who were not going to wait, escaping without being brought to action at all. What no one who was not present seems to be able to appreciate was the extraordinary excitement which caused that interval of some eighty minutes to pass as though it were only five minutes. We had waited for nearly two years for this moment, we had been frustrated again and again, we had practised and thought and dreamt about this battle. We knew that it was going to be a great ordeal, but we longed for it, prayed for it. Was it a surprise that we rushed into it? We knew that ships would be sunk and many would be killed, but of course at my age (I was just six days beyond my eighteenth birthday) I didn't for an instant think that I should be killed – that was something that happened to other people. We had waited so long and then suddenly, in the middle of a summer afternoon, there were the enemy. It was a moment of incredible excitement.

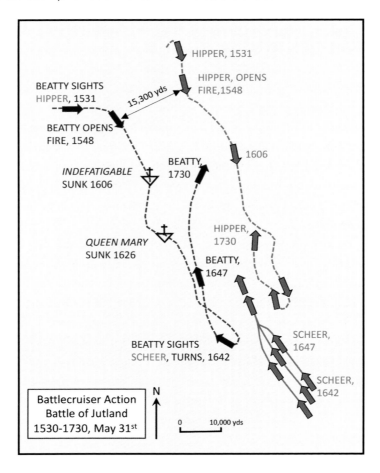

It was obviously going to be a big gun action. Barton hurriedly sent his gun crews below while we stood together as high as we could get, and stared through our glasses trying to count in the smoke and haze how many of the enemy were battle cruisers. Had the sun gone in, or was it only smoke that seemed to make the whole scene darker? Was the sea really greyer and colder looking? What was it that suddenly made the whole scene look so incredibly menacing?

All turrets were trained on the enemy, the muzzles of the guns moving slightly as the elevation was adjusted for the slight roll of the ship. A large section of the eastern horizon was a cloud of smoke in which from time to time the enemy battle cruisers appeared. Then suddenly a lurid flash; the *Lion* had opened fire. Almost immediately, a flicker of light along the horizon – the enemy were returning her fire. We strained to spot the fall of shot of *Lion*'s salvo when we were blinded by the flash and stunned by the roar of *New Zealand*'s first salvo. Cordite smoke blew past us through which we saw the flash of the rear ships of the enemy line opening fire.

All the British ships were fitted with director firing in which all guns in a salvo, normally four, were fired at once making a big flash. The Germans used a different system called Peltravic in which all guns in a salvo were fired in rapid succession so that in place of one big flash a normal salvo consists of four flashes with a small fraction of a second between each. Being on the receiving end, I could not help feeling that the German flicker of flashes was much more menacing than the British big flash.

As we were pulling ourselves together from the shock of *New Zealand*'s first salvo, the German opening salvoes started arriving with that horrible increasing sound that projectiles make as they pass overhead. Actually, they were all over, both fleets had considerably over-estimated the range. Beatty had intended that we should open fire at about 18,000 yards or about the extreme range of the 12-inch ships. But actually, the opening range was little over 15,000 yards so rapidly had the two fleets closed each other.

The German salvoes fell well over but still looked unpleasantly close. Looking down from the top of the after superstructure the ship seemed to dwindle in size as these enormous columns of water shot up where each projectile fell.

Suddenly Barton and I realised that the battle had actually started and we were not in our action station. We bolted for the ladder down two decks to the after 4-inch gun deck and aft into our little rabbit hutch. Just as we were entering with the door open *New Zealand* fired her second salvo; the hot scorching blast from 'X' turret was terrific, blowing us sideways through the door and scattering signal pads and papers in all directions. We hurriedly closed the door and hammered up the clips, it was a good solid watertight door. Inside there was just room for the four of us, Barton, myself and our two voicepipe men, to stand athwartships. To look out we had three narrow slits each about four inches wide, one long one across the after bulkhead through which one could see out astern and two shorter slits each side which enabled one to see out to about forty degrees before the beam each side.

The blast from 'X' turret was devastating. We tried to calculate when the next salvo would be fired, and ducked our heads down out of line with the slits through which came the blast. Some stray back draught filled the compartment with cordite smoke after every round, making us cough and our eyes water. By this time all exaltation had left me and I was frankly terrified and numbed and deadened by the appalling noise. There were upwards of a hundred great guns, more when the 5th Battle Squadron joined in firing and each getting off at least one round a minute. Quite apart from the noise of the actual discharge, each of our own salvoes made a roaring noise as it went away for many seconds, while the German salvoes made a noise as they approached, rising to a crescendo of sound as the projectiles struck the water.

The German projectiles seemed to arrive in an almost continuous stream; they seemed to be firing much faster than ourselves and we had the feeling of being overwhelmed. That they were firing faster, at least at the beginning of the action, was true. Under the British spotting rules, a salvo was fired at the best estimated range and deflection and then the spotting officer waited for the salvo to fall before passing a corrected range and deflection to the TS. At the ranges at which we were engaging the time of flight of the projectiles was of the order of thirty seconds, so that by the time the salvo had been spotted and the correction passed to the TS and so to the guns, there was an interval of about a minute between salvoes. On this occasion, an interval of four minutes twenty seconds elapsed between the *New Zealand's* first salvo and her fourth. The Germans employed a different technique. They used what was called the 'Ladder' system, in which one salvo having been fired from one gun of each turret, the range was immediately corrected by a fixed amount and a second salvo fired from the other gun of each turret, resulting in two salvoes being in the air at the same time. The spotting officer then waited to correct on both salvoes. This speeded up the rate of fire very considerably, so that it is believed that the first four German salvoes were discharged in one minute forty seconds. This very rapid rate of fire, which was also astonishingly accurate, was extremely disconcerting. It wasn't until we had found the target, that is, that we had seen that our salvoes were straddling and we went into what was known as 'Rapid Salvoes', that our rate of fire became comparable with the Germans.

In this hell of noise, I was endeavouring to answer the telephone from the Conning Tower where the Captain and Admiral were trying to control the ship. but whose lookout astern was strictly limited. I eventually made out that they wanted to know if the 5th Battle Squadron astern of us was yet in action. But our view was blocked by the *Indefatigable* astern of us, whose funnel and cordite smoke were blotting out the horizon.

Not only was the horizon blotted out, but the very sky seemed to come down almost to the mastheads. The sun had gone, the sea had lost all its sparkle, the very wash normally white and sparkling for half a mile astern of the ship steaming at that speed had gone a dirty grey. One's eye was attracted too and held in horror by those black shapes on the horizon which were being continuously illuminated by their flickering flashes, each one of which heralded another salvo on its way to our destruction.

It was as though we were in a cavern, a long, low dark cavern at whose mouth was a terror always advancing towards us leaving no possibility of escaping. It was just then, about quarter of an hour after the action had commenced, and I was staring at the German battle cruisers trying to make out which was which when a gasp from one of the voicepipe men attracted my attention, and I saw he was staring at the *Indefatigable*. Turning towards her, I saw that she had been heavily hit aft and was she sheering off to starboard and rapidly dropping astern. As I looked, there seemed to be an explosion aft and some large object was thrown up on end just forward of the main mast. Could it have been a picket boat?

I stared in stunned amazement, and it was some time before I realised that I was letting the chance of a photograph slip me by. Hurriedly opening my camera with trembling fingers, I suddenly realised that the lookout slits were too high for me to be able to see into the viewfinder of the camera. The camera was old-fashioned, even in those days, and one had to get one's head over the viewfinder to make certain that the lens was pointing in the right direction. So, just holding the camera up to the slit, I pressed the shutter release and hoped for the best. As I did so another salvo fell. I was just in time, as almost immediately the ship was rent by a tremendous explosion and the *Indefatigable* disappeared in an enormous cloud of smoke. A cloud which took that form which I have noticed is common to all very large explosions, a comparatively thin column of smoke which goes vertically upwards at high speed while vast volumes of smoke belly outwards from the point of the explosion in a horizontal direction, so that after a few seconds the form is that of an inverted mushroom.

As soon as the *Indefatigable* had been hit, Barton tried to pass the information to the Conning Tower by telephone. But the telephone was that instrument fitted in all ships in those days known as a Graham navyphone. It was what is known as a 'direct acting' phone designed to give loud speech but difficult to keep in proper adjustment and at the best of times it distorted speech, so that to get a message through correctly, very clear annunciation was essential. In the noise, confusion and nervous strain of battle the navyphone was not an efficient instrument. By the time Barton had got his message through he had to correct it to report that the *Indefatigable* had sunk. Even so, we were not sure that the message had got through when, the smoke from the wreck of the *Indefatigable* lifting slightly, we saw a flash from the 5th Battle Squadron which indicated that at least one 15-inch gun ship was firing at the enemy. Appreciating the importance of this information to the Admiral,

Barton said he would make his way forward to the Conning Tower while I took over the telephone.

Opening the door of our rabbit hutch, endeavouring to choose a moment between salvoes from 'X' turret, Barton ran forward along the after superstructure and down an external ladder onto the upper deck where he was able to run forward under the guns of 'Q' turret to the forward superstructure and so up an external ladder to the Conning Tower deck.

Standing on the disengaged side and shouting through the Conning

Imperial War Museum version of a photograph of HMS Indefatigable taken by William
Carne from the after-torpedo control position in New Zealand.
© The rights holder (IWM Q 64302)

A photo from William Carne's album clearly showing the ship outline and the fall
of four shells. Printed by RN School of photography, Portsmouth 1938.

Tower slit, he attracted the attention of the Captain and Admiral where his information that the 5th Battle Squadron were in action was well received. Actually, I had just got the message through by phone. Barton confirmed my message and was also able to inform the Captain that during his passage along the upper deck he had not seen any signs of damage to the ship. The Captain was much relieved as the dozen or so navyphones in the Conning Tower were all making noises, but few of them were producing any coherent messages.

The Captain told Barton to return to his station but not to go via the upper deck as he had come. He was to go down a deck and go through the cabin flat, Wardroom flat and Gunroom flat and so climb up again to the after superstructure. On the way he glanced into the gunroom and saw that the blast of 'Q' turret firing across the deck just overhead, had burst open the tobacco cupboard and a number of tins of cigarettes were rolling about in the two or three inches of water on the deck. Keeping his head, he quickly picked up a sealed tin of fifty cigarettes and brought them back with him to our action station.

He yelled to us to open the door. Helped by the voicepipe men I opened the door hoping 'X' turret would not fire while it was open. Just as Barton stepped inside, 'X' fired a salvo and the resulting blast slammed the door and it jammed so that from inside we were unable to open it.

With white faces and trembling lips, we discussed the situation as we realised that if anything happened to the ship, we could not help remembering what had just occurred to the *Indefatigable*, we were trapped like rats in trap. Barton and I were close to one another; had we been alone, I think we might have flung our arms around one another in an effort to get some comfort from sheer physical contact. But, of course, we were officers in the presence of two sailors, one of whom was reduced to crouching on the deck and quietly sobbing to himself.

By this time the *New Zealand* was well into her stride and was firing steadily and rapidly. At each salvo, if our heads were in line with the lookout slits, our caps were torn from us and we felt as though our heads had been driven down between our shoulders. So, we took to taking a quick lookout immediately after each salvo and then ducking down until the guns had fired again. I remember making some remark to the effect that we must be hitting them hard, but my teeth were chattering so much, the words would hardly come out.

I had ducked down to avoid a salvo and had not looked out for perhaps half a minute when on once more bringing my eye up in line with the lookout slit, I was astonished to see that we were steaming past a ship at a distance of two to three cables (400 to 600 yards). She was partly obscured by a large cloud of smoke, but I was able to identify her as the *Queen Mary* by her distinctive large midship funnel. She had evidently been heavily damaged forward; her fo'c'sle was under water to the fore turret and she had a heavy list to port, that is away from us. The submerged forward had brought her stern out of the water so that her starboard outboard propeller could be seen still revolving quite fast. Men were climbing out of her turrets, and from doors in her after super-structure and trying to climb down her side which, with her list to port, was now far from vertical. As I looked, a man lost his grip and apparently fell into the revolving propeller. This was the first time I saw a man fall into a propeller.

The horrifying sight of the *Queen Mary* couldn't have been before our eyes for more than twenty or thirty seconds; she was still well before our beam, when the whole ship was rent by a tremendous explosion, and she immediately disappeared beneath an enormous cloud of white smoke. Out of this cloud came odd bits of the ship; my eye was caught and fascinated by a large sheet of plating which came hurtling through the air towards us, to fall into the sea with a large splash. I mentally compared it in size to a tennis court but I think by that time my powers of judgement were so warped that I probably exaggerated considerably.

The loss of the *Indefatigable* and *Queen Mary* reduced us to one less than the Germans, i.e. four battle cruisers to the German five. It was then that Beatty made his famous remark to Chatfield, the Captain of the *Lion*, to the effect that there was something wrong with our bloody ships that day, and then proceeded to alter course towards the enemy to force the action. The battle then took on what Beatty in his despatch describes as, 'a very fierce and resolute character'. It was during this fierce exchange that the *New Zealand* received her only hit. An 11-inch shell struck the barbette of 'X' turret, just where the barbette and after decks met. Wound around the barbette were the four parts of the 6-inch towing pendant, all parts of which were cut by

HMS Queen Mary exploding

the shell. It seems probable that the towing pendant was sufficient to actuate the fuse of the shell, as it appeared to explode outside the barbette.

It is true that it punched out a roughly circular section of the six- inch armour plate, some three feet in diameter on the inside but less on the outside, that the piece punched out resembled a shallow cone six inches high and roughly three feet in diameter. This piece of the armour fell onto the roller path on which the turret revolves, and jammed the turret. But no section of the shell penetrated the turret.

The position where the projectile struck 'X' turret was below and some fifteen feet from our 'rabbit hutch'. Fragments of shell penetrated the after superstructure both above and below our position, but the one-inch thickness of armour with which we were surrounded prevented the actual position being penetrated.

The noise of the explosion was rather less than that made by one of the guns of 'X' turret, but our attention was immediately drawn to it by the clouds of black smoke, quite different from the cordite smoke from 'X' turret, which whirled around us. We could see that 'X' turret had stopped training. We reported the hit to the Conning Tower and the fact that 'X' turret appeared to be out of action. In point of fact, 'X' turret was only out of action for a short time, mostly during a lull; the turret crew were able to get a tackle rigged on the bit of armour that had been punched out, and to haul it to one side outboard of the roller path where they lashed it up and freed the turret. There it remained, until we returned to harbour when it was hoisted onto the upper deck and mounted on the quarter deck. After the war when the ship was broken up, it was presented to the New Zealand Government, who had originally provided the ship, and it is now in a museum in New Zealand.

The segment of armour punched out of the barbette of 'X' turret at the Battle of Jutland being hoisted on deck (photo by W.P. Carne)

It was shortly after 'X' turret had been hit that a message was received from the Coning Tower to, 'Prepare to repel destroyer attack'. We passed the order to the 4-inch handing rooms. As soon as the 4-inch crews arrived on the 4-inch gun deck outside our rabbit hutch we hailed them to open our door. Three or four of them gave it a good pull and, much to our relief, it came open. Barton ran up to his control position two decks above us. The 4-inch guns crews who came running were full of curiosity to know what had been happening. For the best part of an hour, they had listened to a heavy cannonade without receiving any information as to what was happening. At the same time, a short lull occurred in the big gun action when the German battle cruisers turned away to avoid the torpedo attack of the 13th flotilla which had been developing for some time. To repel this attack, the Germans advanced into the area between the two Battle Cruiser Forces, a strong detachment of destroyers supported by light cruisers. There then ensued a very fierce action between the light forces, the details of which it was almost impossible to distinguish from the *New Zealand*. Ships appeared to be proceeding at high speed in all directions in clouds of smoke occasionally illuminated by the flashes of their guns.

It was to repel any German destroyers that broke through this melee that we had manned our secondary armament. We did not however become engaged with the German destroyers, as shortly after we saw that the *Lion* had turned 16 points to starboard and we followed round and started to steam to the northward. We then very rapidly closed the 5th Battle Squadron, who were still steaming to the south, and did not start to reverse their course until they were already past us. As it took them some time to turn, it thus happened that they were once more a considerable distance astern of us.

We did not know what had happened; we were only deeply grateful for a lull in the action. Thus ended what in the subsequent accounts of the battle, and during the unfortunate controversy which broke out about the battle, became to be known as 'The Run to the South'. Many people wrote many things about the battle and particularly the run to the south, some with knowledge and experience, others with more enthusiasm than knowledge or experience. Many harsh things were said about the standard of gunnery of Beatty's battle cruisers which was compared very unfavourably with that of the 5th Battle Squadron. They forgot that the 5th Battle Squadron were comparatively unhampered at this period of the battle; the German battle cruisers were too hotly engaged with their British opposite numbers to make an effective reply to the 5th Battle Squadron. It is not difficult to hit a man sufficiently effectively to knock him out if he stands still, makes no effort to defend himself, and does not hit back. It is a very different matter to get in an effective blow on a man who not only dodges but hits back hard at any opening.

Throughout the run to the south, the two battle cruiser forces were very heavily engaged with one another. Much play is made with statistics that the Germans made many more hits. Let me quote one statistic. The *New Zealand* took part in all the three battle cruiser actions that day; she was as

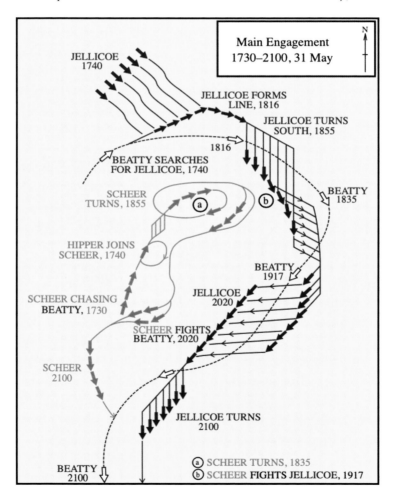

heavily engaged as any ship in the British fleet. She received one hit and one hit only. But she fired more big gun ammunition than any other British ship. The *New Zealand* fired hard and fast and accurately, and so defended herself. Thus she confirmed the teachings of history; that the British fleets of the 18th century won their victories by fast and accurate gunfire. The Admiral may be skilful and develop tactics which place his fleet at an advantage over the enemy, but when the real crunch comes the difference between a partial and a complete victory will depend on the effectiveness of the gunfire.

To return to the scene in the *New Zealand*, the lull in the action was rather like halftime in a hard-played football match. The 4-inch crews were full of fight and annoyed that the enemy destroyers had not pressed their attack, so that they could be greeted with well-directed salvoes from the 4-inch guns. Some of the crew of 'X' turret came and sat on the roof of the turret including the two turret midshipmen in my term, Baker (photo on page 58) and Lovatt[4]. They were very pleased with themselves; they had been hit but they had got their turret back into action again and no one had been hurt. But the turret was full of cordite smoke and smoke from the German shell and they wanted fresh air.

The two midshipmen started shouting questions at me as to what had happened. I tried to be evasive; with the horror of these two ships blowing up still very much in my mind, I did not want to talk about it. But they noticed the *Indefatigable* was not astern of us, where was she? I said she had been hit and dropped astern. But one of the voicepipe men talking to his opposite number in the turret crew gave the game away and admitted that we had seen the *Indefatigable* blow up.

Then someone noticed that the *Queen Mary*, always known as the QM, was also missing and in face of the direct questions the horrid truth had to be told. About this time the news trickled through, I can't remember how it, that the *Southampton* had sighted the German High Sea Fleet and we were

---

[4] Richard Lovatt became Captain of HMS Dunedin in the Second World War. He was awarded an OBE after capturing an enemy ship in June 1941. HMS *Dunedin* was sunk on November 24th 1941 by a U-boat off Brazil. Only 63 men survived out of a crew of 486. They were rescued on 27th November. It is reported that Lovatt gave up a place on one of the rafts for one of his crew.

steaming north to get away from them. There was no news as to the position of the British Grand Fleet.

Just about this time the 5th Battle Squadron started firing again and it was clear that another big gun action was about to commence. 'X' turret crew hurriedly closed up and the 4-inch crews went below again. I can't remember whether we were ordered to send the crews below or whether we did it on our own initiative. I remember feeling lonely as we were left alone again. This time we closed the door carefully in the hope that it would not jam again, and took with us a baulk of timber with which to hit it, should the blast of 'X' turret again cause it to stick.

Soon all four ships of the 5th Battle Squadron were firing steadily and we could see the splashes of the enemy's shells around them. The scene to the south and east was very confused with much smoke and overall was the rumble of the battle, punctuated by the louder crashes of the salvoes of the 5th Battle Squadron 15-inch guns.

Then through the haze we caught a glimpse of the ominous shapes of the German battle cruisers steaming on what appeared to be a nearly parallel course to ourselves. We crouched down in our rabbit hutch so that our heads would not be in line with the lookout slits when 'X' turret opened fire again.

Crouching down, Barton produced the tin of cigarettes that he had salvaged. There was a universal rule in the Navy at that time, under which no-one was allowed to smoke until their eighteenth birthday; though, as a special privilege, midshipmen were usually allowed one cigarette after dinner on guest nights. Barton was not yet eighteen by several weeks, and if found with the cigarettes the result would probably be unpleasant. It was therefore agreed that the cigarettes should be known as mine, as at this date, 31st May, I had passed the critical age by exactly six days. Not that I could claim to be an experienced smoker. I had, of course, smoked the odd cigarette while we were at Dartmouth just to show what a deuce of a chap I was, but I doubt whether at this date I could have smoked more than twenty cigarettes in my whole life.

Further discussion on the ownership of the cigarettes was brought to an abrupt termination by our first salvo, which brought home to us the fact that we might not have the opportunity to enjoy our ill-gotten cigarettes. We were once more engaged with the German battle cruisers, but the 5th Battle Squadron were also heavily engaged with some force further to the south'ard.

This further force must therefore be the High Sea Fleet and, as they were engaged with the 5th Battle Squadron, who were only some three or four miles astern of us, it followed that they could not be far from us; although we could not at that time see them. Where was the Grand Fleet? Unless we could make a junction with them in the near future, it looked as though we were certain to suffer the same fate as the *Indefatigable* and *Queen Mary*.

It was during this period that I was looking intently astern between salvoes at the 5th Battle Squadron, who seemed to be almost hidden in the splashes of the German shells, when I saw an actual shell plunge into our wake, about 100 yards astern of the ship. It must have been in my line of sight for a minute fraction of a second, yet I seemed to see it quite clearly for the last twenty or thirty feet of its trajectory before it was lost to sight in the enormous splash its entry into the sea threw up. So sharply did it register on my mind that afterwards I almost thought that I had actually seen the driving band and markings in white paint on the body of the shell. It was obviously impossible for me to have seen these details, but the memory of this incident has ever since made me very sceptical of details quoted by eyewitnesses of events which have happened at very high speed.

On the subject of seeing the enemy shells, after the battle our director layer told me that on more than one occasion, he saw projectiles approaching the ship. He would be looking through his layers telescope at the target with his cross wires just coming on with the roll of the ship, when he distinctly saw black dots approaching. More than once he was filled with doubt whether he would be able to fire his next salvo before the enemy shells arrived.

It was during this engagement that we first began to feel that we might be getting the better of the enemy. Their fire was not nearly so accurate or rapid and their salvoes were much reduced, frequently only one or two guns. On the other hand, we in the *New Zealand* were firing rapidly and steadily, and as far as we could see the 5th Battle Squadron were firing equally rapidly. With our limited angle through which we could look out, we were unable to see the other battle cruisers; but from the splashes falling around the enemy it appeared that we were engaging them effectively.

I have very few memories of this period of the battle. It was as though my mind had been stunned by the fierce and resolute combat during the run to the south. I can remember having a feeling of waiting, that something was going to happen, and of dreading whatever it was that was being held over our heads.

I have sometimes wondered whether perhaps some feeling of the same sort did not hang over all the British fleet, for it is a fact that very few signals were made during this period. Although both the battle cruisers and the 5th Battle Squadron were in action, none of them made any useful reports to the Commander-in-Chief. I do not remember any demands from the conning tower by telephone for any information from us regarding the 5th Battle Squadron. Jellicoe speaks of this period of silence and his worry and anxiety as the Grand Fleet steamed at high speed towards the scene of the battle, not knowing the exact position of either of the combatants or how they had fared so far.

And then for us another lull in the battle occurred as the enemy battle cruisers turned away from us, although the 5th Battle Squadron were still heavily engaged with the enemy battle fleet. We had been steaming hard and had been opening our distance from them while we endeavoured to place ourselves between the enemy battle cruisers and the Grand Fleet, so that the former should be unable to warn the German Commander-in-Chief of the approach of the British battle fleet.

Although we didn't know it, at the time the 3rd Battle Cruiser Squadron, who had sailed from Scapa with the Grand Fleet, had been sent ahead by Jellicoe at their maximum speed to reinforce the 1st and 2nd Battle Cruiser Squadrons, and had made contact with the German light cruisers ahead of their battle cruisers. The latter fell back on their battle fleet, and the 3rd Battle Cruiser Squadron (having had some success against the enemy light cruisers) followed the enemy battle cruisers and came under a very heavy fire from the High Sea Fleet; during this conflict, the *Invincible*, flying the flag of Admiral Hood, was heavily hit and blew up. It was the third British battle cruiser to suffer that fate that afternoon.

My memory of the succession of events about this time is now very hazy. We had opened out considerably from the 5th Battle Squadron, and they were now difficult to see in the reduced visibility caused by the large amount of smoke, but the flashes of their guns could still be seen. To starboard, where the German battle cruisers had disappeared, the visibility was much reduced though the rumble of the battle still reverberated from that direction. Then, out of the mist and smoke, came a four-funnel armoured

Photograph of the Invincible exploding. From W.P. Carne's photo album

cruiser, obviously British, around which heavy shells were falling in large numbers. She was steaming to pass across our stern between us and the 5th Battle Squadron. She was not one of the ships that had sailed from Rosyth with us and must therefore be a unit of the Grand Fleet; the first evidence we had seen of the near presence of our own battle fleet.

As I looked at her, she was struck by a heavy shell near her after turret. The resulting explosion caused a flash and column of smoke as high as her mainmast head. I particularly remember this incident as it seemed to repeat exactly an illustration in a boy's book that I had been given somewhere around my tenth birthday which purported to portray an incident in the Russian-Japanese war.

The ship must have been the *Warrior* retiring from her encounter with the High Sea Fleet after her flagship, the *Defence*, had been sunk. Shortly after this, as she approached the 5th Battle Squadron, the *Warspite's* helm jammed and she made two complete circles towards the German Fleet, coming under a very heavy fire. It was that short interval in the battle which afterwards became known as 'Windy Corner' when the 5th Battle

Squadron were turning to starboard to take station on the Grand Fleet. The enemy concentration on the 5th Battle Squadron allowed the *Warrior*, badly damaged, to retire to the westward but unfortunately, she sank before she could reach port.

In the meantime, we suddenly saw that the *Lion* had made a considerable alteration of course to starboard and we could see her out of our starboard lookout slit. The other ships of the squadron followed round in succession until it was the *New Zealand's* turn. As we steadied up on our new easterly course, we looked out of the port slits and there the whole horizon was covered with ships coming out of the mist. It was the Grand Fleet just deploying.

We excitedly told one another that it was the Grand Fleet as we tried to recognise individual ships. Almost at once we noticed a ship that we had not seen before, a battleship of the Royal Oak class whose single large funnel was quite distinctive. The sight of the Grand Fleet, further reinforced by this new battleship which we knew was armed with 15-inch guns, gave us tremendous confidence. For us we thought the battle was now over; we led the enemy into the arms of the Grand Fleet, it was now up to them to make the finishing touches.

Almost at once, we were ordered to close up the 4-inch guns crews. The crews came tumbling up, longing to know what had happened and to be allowed to take part in the battle. I left our rabbit hutch and went out onto the 4-inch gun deck. It was good to be amongst lots of chaps again; Barton and I and our two voicepipe men, neither of whom were yet 18 and were therefore classified as boys, had felt very lonely shut up by ourselves.

I found myself standing by a Chief Stoker. I don't know what he was doing there; I suppose he was in charge of one of the repair parties and had come up to have a look around. I pointed out the new battleship to him and we agreed that everything was all right now.

The battle cruisers were steaming at high speed across the front of the Grand Fleet to take up their battle station in the van. Inevitably we were making a lot of smoke and tending to obscure the enemy from the battle fleet. But at our speed we were clearing the front reasonably rapidly. Between us and the battle fleet was an old armoured cruiser who was also endeavouring to take up a station in the van. But she had very little excess of speed over the battleships, and the columns of smoke she was emitting from her four funnels must have done much to increase the difficulties of the gunnery control teams in the battle fleet.

We rapidly drew ahead and had soon passed the van of the battle fleet; the battle ships faded out of sight in the murk. But the whole atmosphere was thunderous with the sounds of the battle, as the two battle fleets came into contact with one another and the Germans twisted and turned in their efforts to disengage.

To avoid getting too far ahead, Beatty at one moment led us around in a complete circle. It was just about this time that the two remaining ships of the 3rd Battle Cruiser Squadron, the *Inflexible* and *Indomitable*, joined up with us so that we were once more a squadron of six battle cruisers.

The summer day was rapidly drawing to a close when we fought our last engagement. This was very different from the first, for we now had the advantage of the light; the enemy to westward of us were silhouetted against the evening sky, and they were apparently incapable of making any very effective reply. We fired hard and fast and, on several occasions, saw the bursts of our shells on their hulls; but their return fire was weak compared to what it had been earlier in the afternoon.

Then the enemy drew away and night fell. We closed up the 4-inch gun crews, checked through all communications and waited. With the enemy so close with his very strong force of destroyers, it seemed impossible that the night should pass without some form of engagement. Obviously there would be a further battle at dawn when the remnants of the German fleet would be sunk.

The uneasy hours of the night passed slowly. The battle cruisers were well ahead of the battle fleet, so that the encounters between our destroyers and the German fleet were a long way from us and were hardly noticed. The regrettable lack of enemy report signals left us with the impression we were still between the enemy and his base and that he could not escape.

Around midnight, the Commander came and collected me to assist him between decks where he was organising some food. Nobody had had anything to eat since midday and the stokers of the afternoon watch had gone below at noon and, backed up by another watch, had remained below until midnight. For most of the twelve hours they had been below the ship had been steaming at high speed; they were worn out and exhausted. With the prospect of the battle being renewed at dawn, they would be required again. We stuffed them with corned beef and hunks of bread and told them to sleep. No question of being able to sling hammocks of course, and the decks were awash with water, so they slept on the mess tables, or in the hammock nettings or any other corner they could find.

Relieved of this duty, I went back to the after superstructure to assist Barton to keep a lookout and, more particularly, to keep both ourselves and the guns' crews awake. We were suffering from the aftermath of the excitement of the afternoon, and I know my eyelids felt like lead. We kept giving the guns' crews dummy runs to keep them awake but there was a slight air of tired despondency. It was now generally known that both the *Queen Mary* and *Indefatigable* had been sunk, and there was a rumour floating around that the *Invincible* had also gone. Nobody was looking forward to tomorrow's renewal of the battle.

During the evening lull Barton and I had sampled our purloined cigarettes and had got some comfort in smoking several; many more than I had ever smoked in succession before. Now I had a sore dry mouth and wanted another cigarette but, of course, it was out of the question to smoke with the ship darkened.

With the first streaks of dawn at 3am we altered course to the north'ard. Now we thought we would soon be at them again, but the whole horizon was clear of any enemy ships. I think it was as early as 4am that a feeling seemed to creep through the ship that somehow the enemy had escaped.

In the clear light of dawn, we all looked dirty, tired and unkept. The ships looked almost worse, with paint burnt off their funnels and streaks of soot everywhere; blackened gun muzzles and *Lion's* 'Q' turret obviously out of action, trained over the side with one gun cocked up in the air and the other depressed. But in the *New Zealand* our battle ensigns were all still intact and were still making a brave show.

We steamed in a northerly direction all the morning watch and there was no sign of the enemy. How had they got past us in the night? We looked at one another in amazement but I think secretly there were few of us who were not glad that we were let off a repetition of yesterday's ordeal.

Sometime during the forenoon watch, we were back at the scene of the original battle. A shout from one of the 4-inch guns crews drew our attention to something in the water. And there, bobbing about in our wash as we swept by, was a corpse and it was clear to all of us that it was a British sailor. In the next hour we passed several; I cannot remember how many, but the number ran well into double figures. We tried to make ourselves believe that at least some of them were German, but to me they all looked suspiciously British. This sight did nothing to improve our jaded spirits.

Sometime between 8 and 9am we fell out a few at a time to go and grab something to eat. The gunroom was chaotic; all the lockers overhead)we each had a locker for our books, writing material etc.,) had come down due to the blast from 'Q' turret as it fired across the deck. But the Maltese stewards had been released from their action stations, and had prepared some very welcome food.

Closed up again, we waited and wondered. What had happened? Surely the Grand Fleet must have hit the enemy very hard when we had delivered the whole High Sea Fleet right into their arms. But always at the back of our minds was the thought that we had lost three battle cruisers, fine proud ships, and we had no direct evidence that the enemy had suffered any corresponding loss. But if he hadn't been heavily hammered why wasn't he there to fight again? And so the questions went round and round in our tired minds.

It was sometime after noon that we secured from action stations and went to cruising stations as we abandoned the battlefield and shaped course for Rosyth. The afternoon was spent in trying to square off the ship and to prepare for the inevitable coaling the next day. The shipwrights made a rough repair to the after deck where the shell had hit the barbette of 'X' turret. They at least made the deck watertight. Then we got the spare mooring swivel from the fo'c'sle and lashed it on deck across the hole in the barbette. I don't suppose it would have done anything to keep out even a very small shell striking in the same place. But the morale effect was quite good. 'X' turret crew were once more quite happy in the turret, convinced that the heavy mooring swivel would keep out anything.

For the rest, all we wanted to do was to sleep but there were still watches to be kept until we arrived at our usual anchorage in the Forth during the forenoon of the next day, to be greeted by the inevitable collier. But there was no coaling for me that day, as I was doing my turn as midshipman of the second picket boat. Both picket boats and the launch, the only other power boat, had suffered considerably from the effects of the blast from the guns. The second picket boat had suffered least and was repaired before we arrived in harbour, but neither of the other boats were available for several days. As a result, the second picket boat had to do all the boat work, which proved to be very considerable, as there were many calls on behalf of our own ship and the other ships were even worse off for boats than ourselves. So, I spent the day going around the remaining ships collecting stewards and postmen to be landed and correspondence to be distributed.

Such spare boats as were available in Rosyth dockyard had been rigged as hospital boats and were busy the first day or two in landing casualties from the *Lion*, *Princess Royal* and *Tiger;* all had been hit several times, and from the light cruisers and destroyers who had been so heavily engaged in the battle.

I think it was between 9 and 10pm before I had finished all my trips and was told to moor up my boat for the night. Coaling had finished about 5pm, then the ship had been given a quick wash down and the hands sent to supper for a good meal, for they had a lot more work to do. About 7pm an ammunition ship came alongside and we started to embark ammunition to replace the four hundred-odd rounds we had fired during the battle. Each 12-inch shell weighs 850 lb, and with each shell are four quarter charges, each in its own steel cylindrical case about three feet long. Ammunition, besides being heavy, must also be handled carefully so the embarking of this amount of ammunition would be a long slow business for a fresh ship's company and our sailors were all very tired. As soon as I had moored up my boat I was grabbed to go and help with 'A' turret, as I had once been midshipman of that turret, and the proper midshipman of the turret had gone sick.

As the shell rooms of the turrets were right at the bottom of the ship each shell had to be lowered through a succession of hatches including the two in the two armoured decks. As any form of hatch tends to weaken a deck, these hatches were made as small as possible, in fact just big enough for a horizontal shell to pass through if it was lying along the diagonal of the hatch. So, each shell had to be guided down through five or six decks. It was well after midnight before we finished and I was up again at 6am to take the second picket into South Queensferry to fetch the daily papers. Having fetched the papers, I had a quick bath and went along to the gunroom with an excellent appetite for breakfast to find something approaching an uproar. The gunroom newspapers had just been received, they were the first we had seen; I can't remember whether we had had any the day before but, in any case, everyone was too busy and tired to read them. The uproar was caused by the reports in the papers on our battle; they inferred that we had been defeated and what was the Navy doing? We who had fought all day and driven the enemy into his harbours and waited all next day trailing our coat to be told that we had been defeated! It was outrageous; we said so several times individually and as a team. Although, of course, we did not allow our indignation to upset our appetite for breakfast. But between mouthfuls we damned the eyes of every editor in the country. We were so worked up that not a single gunroom argument was started throughout the meal. I should explain that a gunroom argument is defined as a sweeping statement followed by a flat contradiction followed by personal abuse backed up by the threat of physical action. It seldom gets further than threats as anyone taking violent action on his own is liable to be set upon, literally by all his messmates.

I should not wish anyone to think that we were an unduly rowdy mess, but teenage boys must let off steam occasionally. Anywhere in the ship except the gunroom, we were on duty and must behave as officers and, I may say, the standard of behaviour required of us was pretty strict and rigid. But once through the gunroom door we were in our own little world and could let our hair down. We were not the only people who were indignant at the newspaper reports. The whole ship seethed. Eventually the Captain took action and sent the torpedo officer up to Edinburgh to interview an editor and give him some of the thoughts and feelings of a ship's company that had been right through the battle. There was of course strict censorship of all details of the battle, but he was able to talk about the spirit of the ship's company, repeat the story about the Maori chief, and report that the Captain wore his charm around his neck with a result that the ship seemed to bear a charmed life. The editor made a good story of it all. I still have a cutting from his paper, which did something to give the public a better feeling about the actual events of the 31st May. And in the meantime, the Admiralty had done much to correct the unfortunate effects of their original

THE NAVAL BATTLE.

THE NEW ZEALAND'S PART.

HOW THE CRUISER FARED IN ACTION.

[FROM A SPECIAL CORRESPONDENT.]

In the great battle the work of our battle cruisers so magnificently upheld the deathless traditions of the British Navy that any distinction between the parts played by them need not be too finely drawn, but the people of this country will share the gratification of the Colonies on learning something of the place which the New Zealand had in one of the greatest sea fights in history. From a reliable source I am able to furnish some information regarding the splendid ship and her place in the battle. The order of our battle cruisers as they went into action was as follows:—Lion, carrying the flag of Admiral Sir David Beatty; Princess Royal, Queen Mary, Tiger, New Zealand, and Indefatigable. The New Zealand flew the flag of Admiral Pakenham, in the absence of H.M.S. Australia, to which is given as a rule that distinction, and thus in a double sense was the vessel representative of a part of our Empire whose readiness in patriotic effort has been exemplary. In this connection, too, an interesting coincidence may be noted. When the New Zealand figured in the Dogger Bank affair she also carried an Admiral's flag for Sir A. Moore, who was second in command. She sailed into the great adventure off the Jutland coast proudly bearing other evidences of her Antipodean connection. There floated in the breeze of the eventful May evening the White Ensign and Union Jack presented by the women of New Zealand, which figured in her previous engagements also, and is now showing the marks of action, though the Maori emblem on the forepart of the fighting top is so far practically unscathed. Whether the captain shares the superstitions of men "who go down to the sea in ships" I cannot profess to say, but I understand that he fulfilled on this occasion the conditions attaching to a small

NEW ZEALAND IN THE FIGHT

Though the name of his Majesty's ship New Zealand does not appear in the official reports of the North Sea battle, this fine ship was in the action. She was flying the flag of Admiral Pakenham, C.B., M.V.O., commanding Second Battle-Cruiser Squadron, and her position in the line was next astern of the Tiger throughout the whole battle. Some of the reports of the line of battle are, we are informed, erroneous. The first ship was the Lion, the second the Princess Royal, the third the Queen Mary, then came the Tiger, the New Zealand, and the Indefatigable. These were the cruisers which bore the brunt of the battle for half an hour until the battleships came up.

The fire of the New Zealand so punished the ships that engaged her that they were unable to do her more than the most trifling damage. It may be recalled that the New Zealand also took part in the Heligoland and the Dogger Bank actions.

communiqué so that there gradually spread a more balanced view regarding the battle and its effect on the war.

But of the Navy itself, what were the reactions after we had worked off the feelings of physical exhaustion and started to consider the situation? I think perhaps the first and most important feeling was one of bewilderment. What had happened? Why had the enemy got away? We were sad and depressed at the loss of so many fine ships, but we had always known that the battle, when it came, would be a great ordeal and that many ships and lives would be lost. However, we had expected that the enemy would be completely smashed and defeated, and that one result of the battle would be that it was apparent that the end of the war was a big step closer.

Nothing like this had happened. Taking the best view possible, it was clear that there was still a state of stalemate in the North Sea and it did not appear possible that this could be broken without the ordeal of another battle.

Inevitably and no doubt rightly, questions were asked as to why the expected result was not obtained. The controversy worked up over the years and had some unfortunate results, the immediate one being to start a split between the supporters of Admiral Jellicoe and those of Admiral Beatty. I don't think it was ever serious in the seagoing fleet during the war, but there was a slight feeling of jealousy between the Battle Fleet enduring the rigours of Scapa Flow and the Battle Cruiser Force who got all the limelight and who, according to the Battle Fleet chaps, luxuriated in the bright lights of Edinburgh.

I refused at the time to get involved in the controversy which raged for the next fifteen years, but looking back with the perspective of fifty years I think it is fair to say that we learnt two very important lessons from Jutland, both of which we used in the Second War. Firstly, we learnt to fight at night and, perhaps more important, we learnt not to be afraid to fight at night. And secondly, we bred a race of officers who were sufficiently flexibly minded to face up to the advent and increasing effectiveness of air power during the Second War and who, thanks to their flexible outlook, were able to produce solutions which saw us through this particular ordeal.

There were also the short-term lessons in defective material which had to be learnt, and the lessons applied as soon as possible. The mystery of why the battle cruisers blew up so easily was soon proved by an examination of the damaged 'Q' turret of the *Lion*. It was clear that a similar fate would have been suffered by the *Lion* had it not been for the action of the turret officer, with his dying breath, ordering the magazine doors to be closed and the magazines flooded. Immediate action was taken to fit all magazine doors with a flash tight hatch, through which a quarter charge at a time could be passed with the magazine door tightly closed.

The early fitting of these flash tight hatches to the magazine doors did much to improve confidence in the battle cruisers as, until this was done, there was a feeling that the normal risks of naval warfare were enhanced for those who served in a battle cruiser.

Then the whole question of the night fighting equipment of the fleet had to be brought up-to-date and the fleet exercised in its use and much had to be done in studying the problems of both fire control and torpedo control in the light of the experience of the battle. None of this could be done in five minutes, but I think it is fair to say that by 1918 many of the lessons had been absorbed and a great deal of new equipment had been fitted, with the result that the fleet was much more efficient than at Jutland.

But to return to events immediately after the battle. I can't remember whether it was the second or third day after we had returned to harbour when my picket boat was sent into Rosyth dockyard on a trip. As I came alongside the jetty a rather worried Chief Petty Officer, who I think must have been the Admiral's coxswain, came to me saying that the Admiral was just coming down to the jetty and his boat had broken down. Would I take him off to the *Lion*? Of course I would. Just then the Admiral appeared; the Chief Petty Officer explained the situation and the Admiral stepped into the sternsheets of my boat while I gave him my best salute. Shoving off, we went at our best speed to the *Lion*. I had a new and rather inexperienced coxswain, so I was steering the boat myself. As we approached the *Lion*, who still only had a port after ladder rigged, there was a queue of three or four boats waiting to go alongside. I made to cut in ahead of the queue and was waved off by the Officer of the Watch who did not think it was my turn. But, putting all I knew into my still immature voice, I shouted "Flag, Lion", meaning 'I have the Vice-Admiral commanding the Battle Cruiser Force onboard, get out of my way'. And was I proud to be able to give such a shout.

Immediately there was much activity in the *Lion;* the Captain was sent for, all other boats waved off and the quarter deck staff manned the gangway. There was a strong ebb tide running and the wind was causing the *Lion* to lie slightly across the tide, which made the approach not too easy but I took it quietly, swinging my stern in a little towards the ladder so that as I went astern the kick of the screw was just enough to stop the swing and come to rest with the sternsheets abreast the gangway.

The Admiral stepped out of the boat and on the lower platform of the gangway. As he turned to return my salute, I saw how tired he looked. He told me to thank my Commander for him for the loan of the boat, and he added, "You can also tell your Commander from me that you handle a boat well".

Returning to my ship, I delivered the first part of the Admiral's message. I didn't say anything about the second part. Writing more than fifty years afterwards, I shall perhaps not be accused of boasting if I say that I knew that my Commander trusted me with a boat. I was one of the few midshipmen he did trust. But for the next three days I walked on a cloud.

Soon the new dockyard at Rosyth came into its own and the basin was filled with great ships waiting repair. All the four ships of the 5th Battle Squadron had been hit several times, but thanks to their heavy armour their vitals had never been pierced. Nevertheless, there was a great deal of repair work to be done and the dockyard did not stop for a moment night or day. Nor, more importantly from my point of view, did the second picket boat. Being very tired when we got back to harbour and being busy with my boat since, I didn't do much about letter writing. In fact, I didn't write at all for several days until I was brought to my senses by a worried telegram from my family asking whether I was all right. The telegram took an appreciable time to reach me; we normally only sent the postman ashore to collect mail and telegrams once a day. So, by the time they got my reply, they had begun to think that I had met with a disaster.

By the latter half of July, all the battle cruisers were a going concern again and Beatty took us to Scapa for an exercise period; and also for the many technical discussions which the experience of the battle had given rise to. We arrived during the afternoon of a fine summer day. Scapa was looking its best. As Beatty in the *Lion* led us to our anchorage, the ships' companies of all the battle ships turned out and cheered us.

We were favoured with fine weather for our exercise period. I remember that one day the *New Zealand* anchored by herself over on the north shore of the Flow. Half a dozen of us got permission to take away a whaler for a picnic. The sun was so warm that we were tempted to bathe; it was a mistake – the water was much too cold to be enjoyable. Then a destroyer exercising in the Flow passed fairly close at high speed, and her wash picked up our whaler and put it broadside on up the stony beach. We had some difficulty in getting our boat afloat again and, as the paintwork was considerably scratched, we were not popular when we got back onboard.

The next event of importance was the last sortie of the entire High Sea Fleet, on the 19th August 1916. The intention of the German Commander-

Friday

Dear Mona,

Very many thanks for your letter. I hope you have recovered from your swollen glands and are quite well again. You asked me to tell you all about our scrap but I am afraid there is very little that I can tell you. I saw just about everything that there was to be seen which may seem to be an advantage but I am not sure that it was as one not only saw the German ships but one also saw the fall of their shots, some of which came most unpleasantly close. But the worst thing of the lot was our own guns firing. My action stations is quite close to one of our turrets and every time the guns fired my cap was blown off my head. The noise was tremendous as every ship was firing as fast as possible. The flashes from the German guns looked like an enormous giant standing on the horizon and flashing an electric lamp. The German shells were very unpleasant as one could hear them flying overhead and they all sounded just as though they were going to hit you on the nose. We had to remain at Action Stations all that night and the next day so that we were unable to get any sleep or food. As a matter of fact, I managed to get some cake and some bread and butter but that was all the two of us had between us for twenty four hours. Added to which some playful little fellow carefully soaked my hammock for me so that for the next two nights I had to sleep in a chair. Yesterday we went for a picnic and despite some very pessimistic prophesies on the part of some of the Officers succeeded in getting back safely.

Yours
Willie

Jessie Tremona Carne, 'Mona', was William's younger sister (1900–1988)

in-Chief was to bombard Sunderland with his battle cruisers, supported by the High Sea Fleet, and to deploy a large number of submarines who, it was hoped, would cause considerable damage to the British fleet, should we attempt to intercept.

The whole fleet was at sea in good time and on this occasion the battle cruiser force was comparatively close to the battle fleet, not more than thirty miles ahead, so that the *Lion* and *Iron Duke* were always in visual touch through linking cruisers.

Early in the day, about 7am, the *Nottingham* of the 2nd Light Cruiser squadron, being the starboard wing ship on the cruiser line, was torpedoed. At first there was some doubt as to whether she had been torpedoed or had hit a mine. To avoid the whole fleet blundering into a possible minefield, a large alteration of course was made by the whole fleet and the advance to the southward was not resumed for four hours. By this time, an enemy report from one of our submarines confirmed that the High Sea Fleet was at sea and approaching towards us. All that forenoon and early afternoon, great excitement prevailed in the Fleet as it was thought that another action was imminent and, on this occasion, we felt that we were on a much better wicket than at Jutland.

There was therefore very great disappointment when in the afternoon it was learnt that the enemy had abandoned his attack on Sunderland, reversed his course, and was making for his bases without giving us the chance of coming up with him.

The dog watches were, however, not without some excitement as we ran into one of the enemy's lines of submarines and reports of periscopes were coming in right, left and centre. The heavy ships all escaped successfully but the *Falmouth*, of the 3rd Light Cruiser Squadron, was torpedoed and damaged in her engine-room. She was taken in tow but unfortunately was torpedoed again the next morning before she could be got into the Humber.

Thus, we returned to harbour with our sense of frustration still further increased. But for we midshipmen, an ordeal of a different type was appearing over the horizon and already beginning to cast a gloom. Early in the new year we were due to be examined for sub-lieutenant and we should not get our coveted gold stripe on our cuffs unless we passed. Instruction became more intensive and we started making a real effort to learn about our profession. Up to the present, we had been content with learning just sufficient about our ship to enable us to carry out our duties reasonably efficiently. But if we were promoted to sub-lieutenants we should almost certainly be appointed to other ships, probably destroyers or sloops, where we should have to carry out the duties of officer of the watch at sea and of officer of the day in harbour without having anyone at our backs to turn to for advice or instruction. A background of professional knowledge was essential to enable one to bear these responsibilities. At least that was what our instructors endeavoured to impress upon us and at least, up to a point, we listened to their exhortations.

But we did not allow our instruction to interfere with such amusements as were available. By this time, we had built up quite an efficient gunroom rugger team and, with the approach of winter, we challenged all the other gunrooms in the battle cruisers, and I do not think we were ever once defeated. In this game we were much encouraged and instructed by our Major of Marines, who had been a bit of an expert in his day and now enjoyed refereeing our games.

'RING OUT THE OLD THE YEAR IS DONE.
RING IN THE NEW - RING OUT THE HUN'

Christmas card

By this time a Junior Officers' Club had been established at South Queensferry (known as the JOC) where a very charming Scottish lady, assisted by one or two girls, provided large teas for muddied oafs straight off the football field. I do not remember the lady's name, if I ever knew it, but I know she had a large heart because I remember how terribly distressed she was when we returned from Jutland and she found how many of her former patrons were missing.

Our other principal form of entertainment was to organise evening shows which we dignified with the term 'revue', which was much in vogue on the London stage at that time. We never got beyond what is best described as a gunroom sing-song to which we invited the Wardroom. But some ships were more ambitious, and I remember one in the *Lion* to which officers from all ships at Rosyth were invited. What brought down the house at this show was a scene by an officer who took off his captain assisted by a chorus of midshipmen. The captain of the *Lion* was Captain Chatfield, afterwards Admiral of the Fleet Lord Chatfield, a remarkable officer with a manner of speech both concise and incisive and when he made his points, he shot his cuffs. Like many of the senior officers of that day he still wore starched cuffs.

The song about him was to a tune sung at that time in London by Basil Hallam each verse of which started with the line, "I'm Gilbert the filbert, the knut with a K". The parody went, "I'm Chatters, that's all that matters, the Captain of the *Lion*". And on the word *Lion* the chorus all shot their cuffs, which were enormous.

I am not sure that Captain Chatfield's sense of humour altogether appreciated the song, but David Beatty was sitting in the front row of the audience in a wardroom armchair and nearly fell out of it with laughter, so his flag captain could hardly object.

The months passed quickly. A new batch of midshipmen straight from Dartmouth arrived, and early in 1917 we sat our examination for sub-lieutenant. The examination consisted of a seamanship paper which included signals and papers in gunnery, torpedo navigation and engineering. It was necessary to obtain passing marks in all subjects, but the important one was seamanship for which one obtained a first, second or third-class certificate. It was intended that certificates in the other subjects would be awarded on the completion of courses at Portsmouth after the war. The class of certificate one obtained determined one's seniority as a lieutenant, a first-class certificate in any subject giving two months accelerated promotion, and one month in the case of a second-class certificate.

The papers for the midshipmen serving in the battle cruisers were set in the battle fleet, and whoever set the signal paper set a proper stinker. In his book on Jutland, Marder is very critical of the low standard of signalling in the battle cruiser force. I fear that his remarks on this subject are justified, and certainly interest in signals did not descend as far as midshipmen. If we knew the colours and meanings of the various flags and could make and read semaphore and Morse at a reasonable speed, we thought we were pretty efficient. Signals required to manoeuvre a battle fleet, particularly signals to deploy a battle fleet, which were very much in the mind of all the battle fleet officers since Jutland, passed us by. The result was that we scored extremely few marks for signals which was reflected in the certificates we obtained for seamanship. I managed to scrape home with a second-class certificate, but I was the only one in the *New Zealand* who either didn't get a third class or who failed to pass. I had no difficulty with the other subjects, particularly torpedo, in which I was easily top.

However, the great thing was that I had passed and in due course was rated acting sub-lieutenant. Nobody worried much about class of certificates in wartime; there seemed to be more important things to worry about.

It is a very big step forward from wearing a white patch on one's collar to wearing a gold stripe on one's sleeve. The first time I wore my jacket with my new insignia on my sleeve, I couldn't help glancing down at it at frequent intervals and thinking how smart I looked. In fact, for several days, I must have been quite insufferable.

As soon as we had got our stripes, we took over the duties of Officer of the Watch in harbour but only for a few days, as very shortly new appointments arrived for both Barton and myself, he to the *Nigella* and myself to the *Asphodel* – very exciting, as we had never heard of these ships and had no idea what they looked like. We rushed along to the Captain's office, where his secretary produced a confidential publication we had never seen before. This booklet told us that both ships were sloops of the new 'Flower' class, that both ships were in the same flotilla based on Alexandria, and that the *Asphodel* was the senior officers' ship. It seemed a great stroke of luck that while Barton and I were going to different ships, at least we should be flotilla mates and would travel out to Alexandria together.

We were told to pack our sea chests and proceed on leave the next day; instructions for our journey to Alexandria would be sent on to us. So, we said goodbye to the *New Zealand* and while I realised it was time to go and see another side of the Service, nevertheless I was sorry to see the last of her. I had learnt and experienced a lot in her, she was a good ship and a happy ship, with high standards of both professional efficiency and of conduct.

But there was one thing she had not taught me. From the point of view of seasickness, I was still a very bad sailor. For all her 19,000 tons the *New Zealand*, could move about quite a lot in a seaway when steaming at our normal speed of twenty two knots, more than enough to reduce me to a state of walking about with a green face and blue lips, though I had more or less learnt to carry on doing my job, however unwell I might be.

THE BATTLE OF JUTLAND IN RETROSPECT

There remains controversy over the role that the Battle of Jutland played in the outcome of the First World War. In some regards it was considered at the time to have been a victory, of sorts, for the German High Seas Fleet. They suffered fewer losses to both ships and men than the British. The Germans lost eleven ships compared to the fourteen lost by the British. German lives lost were 2,551 compared to 6,094 British. The battle also revealed significant failings in the British fleet. For example, the defective design of the British battle cruisers, including Indefatigable which exploded with only two survivors from her crew of 1,013 (photographed by William Carne on page 74). In addition, the relatively poor performance of British shells, which failed to penetrate German armour and exploded too soon and the inefficient communications which still relied largely on flags, which could not be seen at the distance ships were apart and through the smoke. However, the German's strategic intention behind the Battle of Jutland had been to lure a portion of the British Grand Fleet out and to destroy enough of it to allow German ships to gain access to the Atlantic and to break the blockade that had been in place since 1914. In this, they failed, and the German High Seas Fleet never again sailed in force into the North Sea.

The impact of the blockade on Germany was significant to the outcome of the war. Civilian deaths attributed to malnutrition and fuel shortages are estimated to be over 400,000 – with a further 200,000 deaths due to Spanish Flu in 1918.

Jutland was the last major sea battle involving battleships, as thereafter submarines and aircraft became the dominant technology in naval warfare.

CHAPTER 5
HMS *ASPHODEL*

That leave passed as rapidly as all other leaves, as I waited for instructions to join my new ship. My Mother wanted to show me off in my new uniform; I was only too anxious to get into such old clothes as I could find avoiding uniform for a few days. I had grown out of most of my peacetime clothes, and had to borrow from my Father. My Mother was very worried about my health in my new appointment. She was convinced that Egypt was a very unhealthy country; she was not entirely wrong in this assumption, but of course I should be in a ship. I endeavoured to explain that I should be at sea most of the time, free of all contagion. My arguments were not convincing.

Her solution to the problem was to get out the catalogue of the Army and Navy Stores, not reprinted since before the war and mostly out-of-date, and

Garras, the home of George Newby Carne and Annie Emily Le Poer Carne, William Carne's parents

look up medical supplies. Under this heading she found advertised a 'pocket medicine chest' which she promptly ordered on my behalf. This consisted of a small wallet containing six phials of various pills and tablets whose names conveyed nothing to me except one which was labelled as 'Should be used when the water supply is thought to be contaminated'. I thought it improbable that I should ever want to use such tablets and, in fact, I don't think I ever opened my 'pocket medicine chest'.

But my Mother's generosity did not stop at providing a few pills; she completely overhauled my wardrobe, such as it was, and set me up with a completely new outfit of shirts, underclothes, socks, towels, etc., and topped off her gifts with a nice new silver wristwatch. Eventually, instructions for my journey to Alexandria arrived; they were not very detailed. I was to meet the senior officer of the party going to Malta under the clock on Waterloo station at 8am on the morning of Easter Bank holiday. Neither name nor rank were stated., He would have my tickets and an advance for travelling expenses.

I travelled up to London during the night, and was in the station under the clock long before 8am. Waterloo was a surging mass of people; large numbers of soldiers catching the leave trains back to France, accompanied by many relatives to see them off and a large number of people who, it being a bank holiday, had a few hours of leisure and were trying to get into the country. No-one who might have been the senior officer of our party hove in sight, but Barton arrived from Folkestone, which was his hometown. After the boat train had gone without us, we debated what we should do. Eventually we went to the Admiralty where we found a large number of very busy people; none of whom knew anything about us, but they did tell us that all passages were now arranged by the new Ministry of Shipping who had temporary offices in huts in St. James' Park and we had better try there.

After a good many false starts in that rabbit warren, we ran a woman to earth who said she knew all about us. Our passages had been cancelled for that day and we were to go by the afternoon leave boat the next day. She produced some tickets and an advance for travelling expenses. We found out from her that our passage was definitely arranged from Folkestone.

Barton was naturally anxious to spend his last night at home and suggested that I should go down to Folkestone with him, and that we should see if we couldn't board the leave ship at Folkestone instead of returning to

London to catch the leave train. So, we went to Folkestone where Barton's family, very pleased to see him again if for only twenty-four hours, made me welcome. But they warned us that we should not be allowed near the pier unless we had passes. So that evening we went to see the Senior Naval Officer, who turned out to be a retired rear admiral, and we explained our situation. He made no difficulty about providing us with passes.

That evening Barton, his girlfriend and I, went to the theatre to see a travelling company perform one the Gaiety Theatre successes. I can't now remember the name but the girl who sang the best-known song Widows are wonderful' made quite an impression on me. Folkestone was full of wounded soldiers in hospital 'blue', but otherwise the town did not seem to be much affected by the war.

The next day we sailed about noon, in a very crowded cross channel steamer. We joined up with our draft, which consisted of a couple of RNVR Officers and two very newly-caught RNAS sub-lieutenants. We went full speed for Boulogne and struck an unpleasant southwest gale. What with spray and rain, the upper deck was no place to be, but Barton and I managed to get a corner in the lee of a funnel, where we endured the weather. Conditions below, with hundreds of soldiers being ill in all directions were very unpleasant. Actually, I succumbed before we reached Boulogne, but I managed to hide myself in the 'Gents' and so hoped that I had maintained my dignity.

During the crossing, we drifted into conversation with six newly caught Flying Corps chaps going to France for the first time. They were all dressed up in very new-looking leather coats and none of them had, as yet, very much idea how to wear their uniforms. At that time, April 1917, the life of an inexperienced pilot at the Front was about six weeks. I wondered if any of them would survive to the following Christmas.

Upon arrival, we naval officers going to ships in the Med had quite a lot of luggage compared with the soldiers returning from leave. We had some difficulty in finding a porter and getting our luggage to the station, where we found that our Paris train did not leave until late in the evening and nobody seemed to know exactly at what hour it would arrive for us to get into it. We were somewhat impeded by one of the RNAS sub-lieutenants, who had been terribly ill during the crossing and was quite flaked out until someone found a drop of brandy that put a little life into him.

Sub-Lieutenant William Carne – Circa 1917

Boulogne was very different from Folkestone; it was obviously a town in the hands of the military close behind the front lines. After dark it was completely blacked out and not a soul was moving. We managed to get a meal of a sort at a restaurant near the station, and then hung about waiting for our train. It continued to rain and was unseasonably cold. Later in the evening we were informed that the Paris train was in a siding some distance away. We struggled across the tracks carrying our hand luggage. A very large number of people wanted to travel by that train, and it was more by good luck than good management that Barton and I secured two corner seats. Our next anxiety was to ensure that our heavy luggage was not left behind. Obviously one of us had to guard the seats we had been so fortunate to obtain. Otherwise, in the complete darkness, anyone could have thrown our hand luggage out into the corridor, if not out of the train altogether, and some of our fellow travellers certainly seemed capable of taking such drastic action.

In those days, when one went to Osborne, a term was arbitrarily divided into two halves known, in accordance with Naval tradition, as watches, the starboard watch and the port watch. It then followed that those who joined the starboard watch learned French while those joined the port watch learnt German. I was starboard watch and therefore I was left in charge of the seats on the assumption that my two or three words of schoolboy French would enable me to retain possession of the seats in the face of the most vociferous members of the French nation. Barton, on the other hand, being port watch went to argue with the RTO in English, that official having promised to see that our luggage was put on the train.

We were both successful in our missions and when, some half hour later, the train bumped out of Boulogne, we settled down to sleep. At this, however, we were less successful. The train stopped at frequent intervals with many jerks, sometimes at stations, sometimes in the open countryside. The train was crammed with people; to move along the corridor was almost impossible. Sometime the next day we arrived in Paris, and most of the day was spent in getting our luggage across Paris and getting ourselves washed and fed in time to catch our train to Rome in the evening.

The train to Rome was also crowded, but being further away from the war zone, it ran more or less to time. We had joined up with the rest of the Malta party in Paris so that we were able to fill a compartment, with the exception of one seat which was occupied by a Serbian army officer who was very friendly but spoke no known language. At the frontier at Modane we stopped for about two hours. We all wanted to go to the local hotel for food and a wash and shave. The Serb did not require to wash, but in sign language indicated that he would look after our seats and luggage if we would bring him back something to eat.

Well-fed and comparatively clean, we returned to the train shortly before it continued its journey, with a supply of hard-boiled eggs and sandwiches for the Serb, who we found polishing his knee-high black trench boots. His meagre luggage apparently consisted primarily of a complete boot-cleaning outfit, and he had certainly made a very good job of his boots which had a shine in which one could almost see oneself to shave. In return for the food, he lent us his boot-cleaning outfit, so that we were able to polish up our shoes and look reasonably respectable by the time we reached Rome.

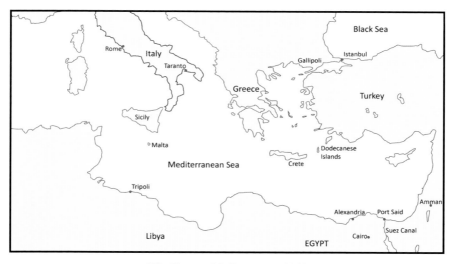

The Eastern Mediterranean 1917

We had nearly a whole day in Rome before our train went on to Taranto. This was the first time I had been abroad and I thoroughly enjoyed the experience. But our travelling allowance proved woefully inadequate and by the evening Barton and I between us could hardly muster enough cash to tip the porter who put our luggage into the train. Another night journey brought us to Taranto where we boarded the *Isonzo*.

The *Isonzo* was a small, fast ship belonging to the P&O Line and designed by them to take passengers from Italy to Port Said. She was intended to run a fast passage for passengers to India who wished to avoid the long sea voyage from England. Taking the *Isonzo* route, they were able to cross to the continent and travel by train to Italy and thence to Port Said in the *Isonzo*, thus saving many days of the passage to India. On the outbreak of war, she had been taken over by the Admiralty and at that time was being used as a ferry between Italy and Malta. Being small and fast, the *Isonzo's* motion in any sort of seaway was considerable. Unfortunately, we ran out of Taranto into a bit of a storm and my introduction to the Mediterranean was most unhappy; I was seasick all the way to Malta. However, the next morning the sun was shining and the day was warm and bright for our entrance into Grand Harbour, Malta.

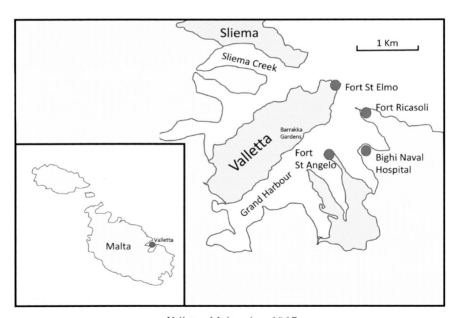

Valletta, Malta, circa 1917

Barton from having been to the Dardanelles knew it well, and as we went up harbour pointed out to me Bighi Hospital, where he had recovered from his wound received at Anzac. Bighi is built on a peninsula with low cliffs sticking out into Grand Harbour. Napoleon is reputed to have stated that he intended to build his Mediterranean Palace on this site. Barton pointed out to me the lift built into the cliffs for the use of patients arriving by sea, the only other approach from the harbour being by a long flight of steps. I was to become more familiar with that lift at a later date.

On reporting at the Admiral's Office in the old Fort St. Angelo, we were informed that there was no transport immediately available for Barton and myself on to Alexandria. We were the only two of the draft going to Egypt. We were directed to turn our heavy luggage over to the Naval Store Officer and, as there was no accommodation available in St. Angelo, to obtain for ourselves rooms at an hotel in Valletta. Once more Barton's local knowledge came in useful. He said quite firmly that the best hotel was the Osborne in Strata Mezzodi and the way to get there was to take a dghaisa to the Customs House, and from thence take the lift to the top of the Barracca. This was my first trip in a dghaisa which is the local Maltese boat, somewhat resembling a gondola, usually propelled by two men, one standing facing while the other sits with his back to the direction in which the boat is proceeding. In those days there were large numbers plying for hire in Grand Harbour, where there was no regular ferry service, as opposed to Sliema Harbour on the other side of Valletta, where there was a regular steam service to Sliema and therefore fewer dghaisas for hire.

The dghaisa men were proud of their boats, which were always spotlessly clean and painted many brilliant colours. In the bright Mediterranean sunshine, the many highly-coloured dghaisas seen against the towering ramparts which surround Grand Harbour look somehow appropriate.

Once we arrived at the Customs House it was not more than a fifty-yard walk to the lift which took us up the cliff to the Barracca where one has a magnificent view over Grand Harbour. From there it was no distance to the Osborne Hotel, where we were soon established. That afternoon we had a quick look around Valletta, met some friends who we had not seen since we left Dartmouth and with whom we had dinner. In fact, we thought we were very comfortably established; the war did not appear to be affecting Malta, and the warm sun was very pleasant after spending the last winter in the Firth of Forth.

Our dream of a nice little holiday in a comfortable hotel in Malta was shattered the next morning when we received orders to report to the Admiral's office. There we were told that we were to go to Alexandria to join our ships in two destroyers; Barton in the *Rifleman* and I in the *Nereide*, and we understood that we were to be onboard by 5pm and that the Naval Store Officer was being directed to deliver our heavy luggage onboard our respective destroyers.

In fact, the destroyers had been ordered to sail at 5pm, escorting a troop ship to Alexandria, and we only just got onboard in time before the ships sailed. We were onboard all right, but there was no sign of our heavy luggage. I reported to the Captain of the *Nereide* but he could not wait for my luggage; the convoy was already leaving harbour. The best he could do was to make a signal asking that our heavy luggage should be sent on by the first available transport. So, I left for Alexandria without any of my nice new white uniforms; in fact, with only a suitcase – which was poor equipment with which to join a new ship.

The ship was in some confusion when I arrived onboard; the ship's company appeared to be both cleaning the ship and preparing for sea at the same time. The addition of an officer passenger to Alexandria was not very popular, particularly when I had to admit that I had never kept a watch at sea and the Captain therefore directed that I was to understudy one of the other officers instead of helping out by keeping a watch on my own. The *Nereide* was one of the older destroyers mounting two 4-inch guns, two 12 pounders, and two torpedo tubes. They were comparatively small ships for this armament, consequently accommodation was very limited. There was no spare cabin, but some sort of bunk and wash basin had been rigged up outside the coxswain's store aft, and I was told to make myself at home there which I did but not in much comfort.

In the hustle and confusion of getting to sea, water and fresh provisions were still being embarked when I arrived onboard, no-one had time to explain in detail the events of the previous forty-eight hours. But over the next two or three days I pieced together the story, bit by bit.

Rifleman and *Nereide* had left Malta, escorting a troop ship to Salonika with something over three thousand troops onboard. Less than twenty-four hours after leaving Malta the troop ship was torpedoed and almost immediately started to take a heavy list to starboard. The two destroyers circled round at high speed, but could see no sign of the submarine's periscope; no doubt she had gone deep by this time and was making her get away. With two destroyers on the spot, she was not likely to risk even a very brief look through her periscope. It was clear to the destroyers that preparations were being made in the troop ship to abandon ship. It was equally clear that owing to the list on the ship it was not going to be possible to lower the port side boats. There was a certain amount of confusion about getting away the starboard side boats, at least one of which was swamped.

The list on the ship increased alarmingly and she was obviously lower in the water. The destroyers closed the convoy to pick up survivors. The intention was to use the troop ship's boats to ferry the survivors to the destroyers, but it was soon clear that there would be insufficient time. The boats crammed with soldiers with only one or two sailors were very unhandy. When the few boats that could be lowered into the water had got away, the increasing list to the doomed ship encouraged many of the soldiers to jump into the oil fuel covered sea. Many were very soon in difficulties. There was sufficient sea running to make conditions difficult for experienced swimmers, and it was obvious that many were not experienced. It was clear that the ship was going to sink very shortly and would take all onboard down with her, and many in the water would probably be sucked down.

The Captain of the *Nereide* decided to take his ship alongside. He told me, when talking about the incident some days later, that he realised in advance that in doing so he was almost certain to chop up a few men in his propellers, or they might get crushed between the two ships before they could be got out of the water. He thought that he was unlikely to kill more than three or four, whereas if the ship sank with all those hundreds onboard, the casualty list would be enormous.

They went alongside. The Captain told me that he was careful not to look aft as he went astern. The troop ship was listing over towards them at an alarming angle; they were nervous that she would roll over on top of them. It seemed that hundreds of men swarmed down the boat's falls and one or two jumping ladders that had been rigged from the bulwarks of the boatdeck. Many others jumped into the sea between the two ships. There was enough seaway to give the destroyer a certain amount of motion which made it difficult to rescue the men in the water many of whom were poor performers at swimming. Two or three of the sailors jumped overboard to help bring men who were struggling alongside the ship, until the First Lieutenant stopped any more from following their example. He explained that a man in the water could only rescue one soldier at a time, whereas a man onboard could throw a line and drag two or three to a position alongside the ship, where they could haul themselves up the ladders which had been rigged.

When they thought they had got all that remained onboard, the Captain went ahead and got clear of the ship, although there were still a very large number of men in the water.

They were only just in time; the ship sank almost at once and they were under the impression that she had taken a large number of men with her. The destroyers continued to pick up men in the water and then to collect the men in such boats as had got away. This was not completed until long after dark. With the wind getting up and a rising sea the destroyers started back for Malta but had to proceed at a comparatively slow speed owing to their overloaded conditions.

I don't think the *Nereide* ever decided how many passengers they had that night. Every corner of the ship between decks was packed and there was only standing room on the upper deck. The First Lieutenant thought they had over a thousand; it was impossible to count them onboard. And when they got alongside in Malta to disembark their passengers, they kept coming out of storerooms and odd corners in the ship in a seemingly endless number.

That night passage was a very unpleasant experience. With the rising sea they were afraid that some of the soldiers would be swept off the upper deck. They used every spare length of rope they possessed to rig lifelines fore and aft and athwartship, but many of the soldiers were exhausted with swimming and others were flaked out with sea sickness. These they lashed to permanent fittings on the deck and hoped for the best. The ship was grossly overloaded and felt quite dead in the water. The sea that got up in the night swept her from end to end. It was impossible to open any hatches, men below had to stay there. They kept the galley fire going, and during the night the First Lieutenant and the coxswain went around the soldiers with mess kettles full of cocoa; that rich rather greasy cocoa made from solid blocks which used to be such a standby of the Navy in those days. They each took with them a basin for every man to drink out of. The First Lieutenant described how they gave a basin of cocoa to every man who was sufficiently a going concern to drink it. But, with successive waves washing around their legs as they fought their way along the upper deck and the air being full of spray, it was impossible to keep the salt water out of the mess kettles, although they kept the lid on except when actually dipping a basin to fill it. Consequently, when they finished their round, there was almost as much liquid in the mess kettle as when they started. However, it kept the soldiers alive, and when they eventually got alongside in Malta the next morning, every single man left the ship on his own legs; though admittedly one or two were pretty groggy.

When I joined the ship, they were still clearing up the mess left by having this large number of men onboard all night. The Captain was a lieutenant enjoying his first command, which he had not held for long. The First Lieutenant was a promoted lower deck officer, and the Sub-Lieutenant was also ex-lower deck, what in those days was known as a mate. I suspect that both the ex-lower deck officers were older than the Captain. They were a good team but not at first very forthcoming. They were of course tired and exhausted by their experiences during the previous twenty-four hours, and I think the sight of so many men being drowned, when they were so helpless to give any effective help, had a considerable depressing effect on them.

It was some days before I got the whole story out of them. When they were together, they wouldn't talk about it, I had to get hold of each separately and hear his version. Although he didn't say so, I know the Captain was inwardly worried as to whether he had done the right thing in going alongside, but both his officers were convinced it was necessary, and that they would not have saved nearly as many men if they had stood off and waited for as many as could swim to come to them.

Our passage to Alexandria was uneventful. I kept watch with the mate for the first two or three days, but after that the Captain let me keep a watch on my own, which relieved the watch keeping union a little. I was still dogged by seasickness and, during a bit of a blow soon after we left Malta, I spent a very miserable twenty-four hours. However, by the time we ran into the nice warm weather off Egypt I was feeling in good form and *Asphodel* was in harbour, so I was able to join as soon as we arrived in Alexandria.

In a small ship such as a destroyer or sloop like the *Asphodel*, with only five or six officers in the wardroom, it is essential that they all work together as one team if the ship is going to be a happy one. It was apparent to me very early on that something of the team spirit was missing in the *Asphodel*.

Arabis-class (part of the larger "Flower Class") sloop HMS Wisteria, *a sister ship to HMS* Asphodel

While the officer complement of the 'Flower' class sloops varied a little from ship to ship, that of the *Asphodel* was typical of the majority of them. The captain was either a commander, usually from the retired list, or a lieutenant commander; two temporary Royal Naval Reserve lieutenants, i.e. straight from the Merchant Service without any Naval training; a sub-lieutenant Royal Navy; an engineer lieutenant RNR, again without Naval training; an assistant paymaster RNR, and a probationer surgeon RNVR. It will be seen that the officers were, in the main, from the Merchant Service and that only the captain and sub-lieutenant were familiar with Naval customs, traditions and discipline. For which reason most captains directed that the sub-lieutenant should take over the duties of first lieutenant i.e. the officer who in a ship is responsible to the captain for the organisation and discipline of the ship's company. But the sub-lieutenant being both considerably younger and with less sea time than either the two lieutenants or the engineer officer, his position vis-a-vis these officers was not too easy, and an appreciable amount of tact was required to make the organisation work at all.

My predecessor, who had commissioned the ship when she was first built, had taken a fairly firm line and had got the organisation working reasonably smoothly. But there had been a little jealousy by both the senior lieutenant, who was an Australian and carried out the duties of navigator, and the engineer officer, both of whom thought that their dignity was a little hurt by the fact that the Captain took the very young sub-lieutenant as his right-hand man.

The Captain had failed to be promoted to commander before the war and had withdrawn from sea service to become librarian of the Naval War College. I don't think he had actually retired. On the outbreak of war he had been made an acting commander, and was in fact the senior sloop captain in Alexandria. He was a dear, kind, charming but very shy man who was very kind to me, and I liked him very much as a man. But it is useless for me to pretend that I thought he was a good officer, and he quite definitely had no ideas of how the problem of overcoming the submarine menace was to be tackled.

My predecessor had hardly stepped over the side when both the navigator and the engineer officer approached me separately, rather on the line that I was young and inexperienced, whereas they now knew all about the ship and that I had better come to them for help and advice. I listened to them both and thanked them very much for their offers of help, but endeavoured to commit myself as little as possible about the future.

One thing I very soon realised was that, while both these officers were jealous of my official position, their jealousy was as nothing to the mutual dislike they had for one another. I had only to suggest a line of action to one of them to curb the actions of the other and I immediately got wholehearted co-operation.

Faced with this awkward situation my every instinct was go very 'softly, softly' and wait to see in which direction events would move. I was therefore very polite to both these two officers and very forbearing when they acted in a manner which I, as first lieutenant, could not approve. In this I think I had the general approval of my Captain who, after I had been in the ship a month or six weeks, dropped a few remarks to the effect that he was pleased at the way I was getting on with the navigator and engineer officer. I realised only too well that he was not the man to want to have a row. Further, if a row did blow up, he might, in fact he probably would, agree with my point of view but his support would only be half-hearted and rather ineffective. Thus, the first three or four months passed in a rather uneasy peace but relations in the mess were unhappy, and I well realised that until the officers were brought together to work more as a team, the ship could never be efficient.

To step ahead four months in my story, events did move in my favour. The *Asphodel* suffered from a defect common to many of these wartime-built ships in that her main engine bearers were insufficiently robust to stand the hard wartime steaming, with a result that the engines became loose on the bearers and vibrated excessively. To cure this trouble, the main engines had to be removed from the ship and the bearers rebuilt, a comparatively long operation. *Asphodel* was taken in hand in Malta dockyard in the following August and, as she was out of action for over two months, the opportunity was taken to relieve several of the officers. The engineer officer returned to England. How much my Captain had to do with his relief I don't know, but I suspect that he had suggested to higher authority that the engineer officer's talents could be better employed in another appointment. His relief turned out to be a Scotsman called Cameron, with all the excellent qualities for which Scottish marine engineers are so well-known. He had been sunk in the *Warrior* at Jutland, so we had shared experience. Professionally we got on well and soon became firm friends.

The navigating officer volunteered for a form of 'Q' ship which at that time was just being introduced into the Mediterranean and his request to exchange ships was accepted. His relief was an older officer, not much older in years, but much more mature. He had been brought up in sail and was, in the best meaning of the term, an old sailor. While he was very much his own master in his own department as navigator, he never questioned my authority as first lieutenant. We soon became very good friends. For some reason best known to himself, he always called me 'Young George', and in course of time the name caught on amongst the other officers. Of course, the sailors all knew me as, 'Jimmy the One' or more usually, just 'Jimmy' amongst themselves.

Then when the ship went into dockyard hands in Malta, the Captain was temporarily taken out of her to help with the administration ashore and, in due course, became part of a new organisation which was being built up to deal with the new policy of sailing all ships in convoy. He was therefore relieved by a much younger officer, a lieutenant commander on the active list. I was very sorry to see my original Captain depart as I had grown to like him very much, but I don't think there is any doubt that when we left Malta after our refit with a new captain and new officers in the wardroom, all of whom were friends, that we rapidly built up to a more efficient team and hence the ship became a much more useful unit. Which was as well, as we then became based on Malta and very much more actively engaged in the anti-submarine war.

To return to my first days in my new ship, to start I had to learn something about the ship, our base and our duties. *Asphodel* was one of a flotilla of twelve sloops based on Alexandria. Also in the port was the old battleship *Hannibal*, one of those relics of the nineteenth century with two round funnels abreast, acting as base ship. Flying his pendant in the *Hannibal* was a post captain as senior officer of the base. My Captain was the senior seagoing officer but as the ships seldom, if ever, operated in company, this fact was of little practical importance. Generally speaking, the ships were employed in patrolling the trade routes; only important ships, which in fact meant troop carriers, were individually escorted. The old principle learnt in the eighteenth century of the importance of sailing all merchant ships in convoy with a strong escort had been forgotten. The Admiralty were just beginning to relearn their lesson but, so far, the new policy had not penetrated to the Eastern Mediterranean.

The sloops were wartime-built ships, part of the programme initiated by Admiral Fisher when he became First Sea Lord in 1914. In order that they should be built as rapidly as possible, they were designed to be constructed by firms which normally specialised in Merchant ships, while their engines, boilers and much of their equipment was of standard mercantile marine design. One of the duties for which these ships were intended was to act as fast minesweepers for which purpose their hulls were staunchly built to stand up to damage from a mine. That the design had been successful in this respect was illustrated by the fact that lying in Alexandria harbour was one of our flotilla, the *Veronica*, who had been torpedoed and the whole of the after end of the ship from the engine-room bulkhead blown off. But the ship had remained afloat and had been towed into Alexandria preparatory to being taken in hand for repairs.

Being powerful minesweepers, they had two distinguishing features; a large 'gallows' aft, and a quarter-deck was much encumbered by a powerful mining winch. This winch was very useful for warping when going alongside or when securing between buoys, but was liable to be a bone of contention between the engineer officer and first lieutenant as it was apt to drip a mixture of dirty water and oil over what a hard-worked first lieutenant was trying to make into a nice clean quarter-deck.

Actually, it was almost impossible to achieve a reasonably clean quarter-deck except after prolonged periods in harbour, which very seldom occurred, as the ships being coal fired and the funnels not very high, the amount of muck that came out of her funnels and deposited itself around the after end of the ship was quite remarkable. There was, however, one fact which I learned with considerable relief; namely that the ship was usually coaled by native labour. In Alexandria, Port Said and Malta the ships were always coaled by a local coaling company who brought the coal alongside in lighters manned by large numbers of natives who carried the coal onboard in baskets and emptied it down the chutes to the bunkers.

Coaling was still a pretty unpleasant business in the excessive heat, as it was necessary more or less to batten down the ship to prevent firstly the ingress of quantities of coal dust, and secondly to keep the coaling team from between decks, as they were inclined to be rather light fingered. And, of course, after coaling the whole ship had to be washed, but we were spared the hard labour of actually humping coal, which was as well as in the heat of Egypt; coaling for our small ship's company would have been very hard labour.

The ship's complement, including officers, was eighty all told, of whom twenty were seamen ratings, which included one chief petty officer, one petty officer, two leading seamen and the rest able or ordinary seamen. When I joined, we were short of one or two seamen due to sickness; there were practically no reserves of ratings in Alexandria to be called upon in the event of a shortage. But most of the ship's company were regulars or

RFR men and fairly experienced. When we went into dockyard hands in Malta, six of my more experienced seamen were taken away to fill vacancies in other ships and when we completed our refit, they were replaced by six ordinary seamen, completely inexperienced, who had to be taught their duties before they became of any value.

The Chief Petty Officer, who combined the duties of Chief Bosun's mate and Chief Gunner's Mate, was my right-hand man. His name was Staples and in appearance he very much resembled Captain Kettle, the hero of so many of Cutliffe Hyne's books. That is to say he was a little man, very spruce, with peaked cap worn hard down over his right eye, and reddish hair and a little torpedo-shaped beard. He spoke with clipped speech and was very conservative. He didn't approve of change; to him anything new was, 'This 'ere noo Navy, and I don't 'old with it'. But he was a very good seaman, and backed me up very well. He had a way of getting the best out of younger men which was very useful to me.

The Petty Officer's name was Carroll. He was a typical pre-First War sailor; he had joined the Service the best part of twenty years before as a boy and hadn't an idea of anything outside a warship. One of the reasons why his ideas of the outside world were so limited was because whenever he went ashore, in the course of a few minutes, he would be drunk and remain so until he fell asleep. Then, having slept it off, he would creep back onboard quite convinced that the shore was no place for a simple sailor and delighted to have a deck under his feet again. But he was a first-class seaman, whose mahogany face never really smiled unless the wind was blowing almost a full gale. Give him a real seamanship job, like splicing an awkward piece of wire, and he was like a dog with a bone; one could almost see his tail wagging. He was Captain of the fo'c'sle and gunlayer of the fo'c'sle gun. As I was cable officer and officer of quarters of the fo'c'sle gun, Carroll and I were always together whenever the ship was carrying out any evolution. His habit of getting drunk was a nuisance but I liked him and when, as I shall relate, he was killed in the accident to the fo'c'sle gun, he was one of the casualties over whom I grieved greatly.

Amongst my other responsibilities, I was in general charge of the maintenance of the armament. This consisted of two 4.7-inch guns, one mounted on the fo'c'sle, the other at the after end of the boat deck. These were very ancient pieces almost as old as the 4.7-inch's in the *Sappho*, but they had been brought up to date to a certain extent by having the three motion breech blocks replaced by single motion blocks. But there was still no separate trainer so the gunlayer was required to train as well as lay. He did this by leaning his shoulder up against a shoulder fitting which was protected by a white rubber protecting piece and pressing with his right hip against a large brass shield secured to the mounting, and so between him and the actual gun as it recoiled.

In heavy weather, the motion at the fo'c'sle gun was considerable and it needed all the gunlayer's skill, strength and agility to keep the gun laid even approximately on the target. On the other hand, the large brass shield could be made to take a wonderful polish which was well set off if the white rubber shield on the shoulder piece was well scrubbed; the result doing something to brighten up the whole ship. Carroll was most attentive to his gun and after any heavy weather, as soon as conditions had eased, he would chase up his gun's crew and, lending a hand himself, soon have the gun a credit to the ship as she went up harbour.

The remainder of the armament consisted of two three-pounder guns mounted either side of the boat deck. These guns were on high angle, or HA, mountings designed to allow the guns to be fired at aircraft, but as no fused ammunition was supplied with them, they were hardly a menace to even the simple aircraft of that period.

On the bulwarks aft was a single chute with what was known in those days as a type 'D' depth charge, with a very primitive pistol. There was an order that these pistols were only to be stripped for cleaning in an organised depot with the proper equipment for testing the pistol to ensure that it would fire at its proper setting. This was rather important, as if the pistol operated at too shallow a depth the resulting explosion could be a menace to the ship. There was no depth charge depot at Alexandria, so the Captain gave orders that the depth charge pistol was to be stripped and cleaned once a month by our one torpedo rating. This was, on the face of it, a reasonable order as at sea the pistol used to get covered with soot and muck out of the funnels. But we had no means of testing, when the pistol was again assembled, that it was in working order. Our torpedo rating was not very clever and, at least once, managed to assemble the pistol incorrectly with most unfortunate results.

Our only other weapon with which to tackle the submarine menace was a sweep known as a 'Modified Sweep'. In effect it consisted of a long wire, nearly 1,000 fathoms, streamed over the stern and kept at a depth by an ordinary mine sweeping kite. Along this wire were secured at intervals a number of high explosive charges which could be fired electrically from the ship.

The idea behind the modified sweep was that in the presence of a submarine, one streamed the sweep, not an operation that could be carried out very rapidly, steamed over the submarine and, when in position, fired all the charges at once. It was not explained how one knew when one was over the submarine.

I was told that the *Asphodel* had streamed her sweep once for exercise soon after she arrived in the Mediterranean. While recovering the sweep something fouled, which was not surprising owing to the lashings of the charges and the electric cables all coming in together with the sweep wire. To clear the foul, the Captain stopped the ship; with the result that the sweep wire hung straight down from the stern of the ship as they were in deep water. When they eventually recovered the sweep and examined the charges that had been on the outboard end of the wire and thus had gone deepest, they found that the detonators had been driven right into the charges by the pressure of the water. It was not possible to get the detonators out without using a tool with some force. In view of the danger of setting off the detonator and thus detonating the whole charge, the Captain ordered these charges to be thrown over the side. We never attempted to stream the sweep while I was in the ship. In fact, the whole equipment was declared obsolete before the end of the year, and we were ordered to land it. I saw it go without any regrets.

The ship remained in harbour for a couple of days after I joined, so I had a chance to enjoy the sun and warmth and easy conditions of service; so very different from those of a battle cruiser in the Firth of Forth. There were few ships in the harbour where the water was beautifully clean, enabling bathing alongside to be enjoyed. All the sloops had by this time made themselves water polo goals and in every dinner hour a match would be in progress alongside one or more ships.

But the most pleasant bathing was to take a boat over to the breakwater before breakfast and bathe before the sun had reached its full power. There were always native boats lying off the ship who could be hailed and which could be hired for an hour or more for a very small sum. These boats, known as dhows, were rather heavily built pulling boats with a large dipping lug sail. During a large part of the year the wind in Alexandria harbour depends on the phenomena known as land and sea breezes i.e. during the day the hot sun heats up the air over the land, causing it to rise, with the result that the cooler air over the sea replaces it, causing a sea breeze. The opposite effect occurs at night. The sea breeze during the day is sufficiently strong to provide a good sailing wind and as the breakwater protects the harbour one has the ideal conditions for a small sailing boat; that is, a strong and steady breeze and a calm sea. The dhows with their large sail area took full advantage of these sailing conditions and provided excellent means of getting about the harbour. And if the breeze died away, as it did sometimes at night, the crew, usually a man and a boy, could make some progress under oars.

The anti-submarine policy in the Mediterranean was still that of patrolling the trade routes, although the idea of sailing all ships in convoy was gradually permeating the Service; the difficulties and extra organisation which this would require were still considered to be too great to be introduced at once. Only 'important' ships were escorted, which in practice meant nothing but troop ships. To carry out this policy, the flotilla at Alexandria worked on a schedule of six days at sea followed by three in harbour. After about six patrols one got an extended stay in harbour of six days in order to clean boilers.

Two days after I joined *Asphodel*, we went to sea to escort a troop ship to Port Said. Leaving Alexandria, the Captain had me up on the bridge and explained to me the system of lights and buoys which marks the passage of the Great Pass; that comparatively shallow and narrow channel through the reefs outside Alexandria Harbour. This was my first introduction to the Great Pass with which I was to become very familiar during the Second War when I had the responsibility of advising the Commander-in-Chief on its defence against submarines, mines, aircraft torpedoes, one-man submarines, and all the other horrors that the Second War brought upon us.

But in 1917 the Great Pass was very peaceful, and our passage to Port Said quite uneventful. We went up harbour for a night and I was much interested in this busy and extraordinarily congested artificial harbour. My predecessor left us at Port Said but the evening before he went we walked out onto the breakwater to get the benefit of the evening breeze and to inspect de Lesseps statue, now alas tipped into the sea by the Egyptians who did not realise what a boon he had brought them.

The next day we left Port Said and spent the remainder of our six day 'sea' period in patrolling the Egyptian coast. During this period my Captain decided that, as he had a new gunnery officer, it would be a good opportunity to exercise the armament. He therefore told me to get a target made, and that at evening quarters that day we would fire two rounds from each 4.7-inch gun. A cross plank buoy was therefore made and decorated with a red flag.

In due course the ship was stopped and the target slipped. The ship then proceeded to steam around it at a range of about half a mile when the Captain gave me orders at the foremost gun to open fire. I gave the sight setter an estimated range and deflection and ordered 'Fire'. The result was a considerable anti-climax. To start with, owing to the roll of the ship, Carroll lost the target in his telescope and it was a good fifteen seconds before he picked it up again. Then when he pressed the trigger nothing happened. He gave the order 'Missed Fire, shift circuit' in a loud voice. The gun was supplied with two firing batteries, but in order to connect the second, known as the auxiliary battery to distinguish it from the main battery, the main firing lead had to be disconnected from the lock and the auxiliary, normally screwed to a fitting close alongside, had to be unscrewed and screwed to the lock.

The gun had recently been painted so that there was some delay in unscrewing the auxiliary battery lead from its securing position. I endeavoured to hustle things on, at the same time answering rather petulant questions from my Captain as to why I did not open fire.

Eventually the lead from the auxiliary battery was connected and the breech worker reported 'Ready'. I again gave the order 'Fire' and, after a short delay while Carroll wriggled about to get his sights on the target, the same thing happened again, the gun missed fire. Carroll ordered 'Missed Fire, percussion firing, shift tube'. The gun was a QF gun, short for quick firing; that is to say, the charge was contained in a brass cartridge case. The charge was fired by a tube inserted in the base of the cartridge case. If the gun was in main or auxiliary electric firing, the tube was fired by an electric current passing from the layers pistol grip, down an insulated pointed rod which made contact with an insulated electrode in the centre of the base of the tube. In electric firing the breech mechanism ensured that the striker did not make contact with the tube until the breech was properly closed. In percussion firing the striker was held back on a spring until released by a jerk on a lanyard when the striker struck the tube and so fired the gun. It was quite impossible for the layer to operate the lanyard so this was done by the breech worker on an order from the layer when his sights were 'on'. The inevitable slight delay between the layer giving the order 'Fire' and the gun actually firing did not tend towards great accuracy in laying.

On this occasion the percussion mechanism operated correctly, and we fired our two rounds; neither of which in any way menaced the safety of the target. The order was then given for the after gun to open fire and, very slowly and deliberately, they got off their two rounds in electric firing, neither of which pitched even approximately close to the target.

As the officer in charge of the guns I expected to be told off pretty heartily by my Captain for the failure of the foremost gun to fire and, generally, the slow drill of the guns crews. However, he took the matter very calmly, remarking that the foremost gun frequently missed fire and that I should look into the question as to whether the circuits were tested sufficiently frequently. Sending for our one torpedoman, whose name was Gale, I proceeded to examine the firing circuit of the foremost gun, and I had no difficulty in bowling out the cause of the failure of both circuits. Each was supplied from its own separate battery. These batteries, which consisted of a number of Leclanché cells, were each housed in their own steel box which was secured low down on the mounting either side. Inevitably, in bad weather both batteries were being continuously submerged as we pitched into a sea which broke all over the fo'c'sle. And, on examination, it was found that both boxes were full of saltwater. The water had entered because the rubber ring which was supposed to make the lid of the box watertight had perished in the hot Egyptian sun.

Cross-examining Gale, I found that he had put new cells in each battery while the ship was in Alexandria. He had put in new cells because the previous outfit had been damaged by saltwater. But he had not taken the trouble to find out where the water had come from, or to take any steps to prevent a similar situation happening again. I found that his orders were to test the circuits daily with an earth lamp and to report if they were not correct. I suspect that he had forgotten to test them that morning, despite the fact that for several hours the previous night we had been washing down forward and, from his previous experience, the efficiency of the batteries and circuits should have been suspect. I promptly altered his orders to the more positive ones that he should test the circuits twice a day and report that they were in good order. Having refitted the batteries and having made certain that the boxes were now watertight, I felt fairly satisfied that on the next occasion of carrying out firing practice we should not put up such a lamentable performance. And in fact, a week or two later, at my instigation we again carried out firing practice, four rounds a gun this time, and got through the practice without a single misfire.

I was not, however, by any means satisfied. There were reports at this time of German submarines lying off merchant ships and sinking them by gunfire. There was also a report, never I think confirmed, of one or two of their largest submarines being armed with 6-inch guns. I foresaw the possibility of a situation developing in which the *Asphodel* might have to engage a submarine on the surface and, if we could not improve our gunnery efficiency, we might well have the worst of the encounter.

I thought that the armament would never be used effectively if both guns were in local control. My solution to the problem was to control both guns as a battery from the bridge, from where it would be much easier to spot the fall of shot, and the control officer would not be blinded by the flash of the gun, nor subjected to the showers of spray which enveloped the foremost gun if we were steaming into a seaway. To enable this form of control to be carried out it was essential to provide efficient communications between the bridge and the guns. As a system of electrical transmitters for range and deflection on the bridge connected to receivers at each gun would obviously be expensive and would take a considerable time to fit, even supposing the instruments were available, I proposed that we should ask that a system of voicepipes should be fitted from the bridge to each gun.

But the Captain wouldn't hear of my suggestions. He explained that what I proposed was an 'Alteration and Addition' (known for short as an A&A). An A&A required Admiralty approval; they were only to be forwarded once a year at a certain set time which would not be for another six or seven months. It was therefore quite useless to send one in now. He then revealed the way he had been trained in the Victorian Navy by adding that if the Admiralty thought that the ships required voicepipes, then the Admiralty would order them to be fitted. It was quite improper for young sub-lieutenants or, indeed, any other officer under the rank of Admiral, to think that they could advise the Admiralty.

The fact that we were at war, that all routine matters of administration had long ago given way to getting on with the matter immediately in hand, that we were up against a problem in the anti-submarine war with which no one at the Admiralty had had any past experience, completely passed my Captain by. The Admiralty were in his opinion all-knowing. Our job was to do what we were told, and not to waste time making silly suggestions.

All this was said to me in a quiet gentle voice, reinforced by a nice smile. He went on to say that of course I was very young, only nineteen, too young to be a sub-lieutenant and, of course, much too young to be the first lieutenant of a ship such as the *Asphodel*. It was, therefore, important that I should lean on him and ask his advice on any matters of which I had the least doubt.

After this little homily I felt like a small schoolboy in the presence of the headmaster. I was disappointed that my suggestions, which I still thought were reasonably sound, had been turned down so flatly. However, I realised that if I was going to make a success of my job, I must work with my Captain, so I pigeonholed my ideas about fire control in sloops and concentrated on what the Captain required. And here I had no difficulty in accepting his views and learning much from his suggestions, for he was a first-class man at maintaining a ship. He had much the outlook and detailed knowledge of a good boatswain combined with that of a first-class shipwright. At Captain's rounds on Saturday morning, his eye detected any of those minor defects which ships are always developing and not only would he draw my attention to them but would also tell me exactly how they should be dealt with. And not a single rope or wire in the ship could begin to show the least sign of wear before he would spot it and tell me to have it renewed.

In the meantime, I was finding life very pleasant and interesting. The Eastern Mediterranean in summer is warm and calm and pleasant, and our duties by no means unduly strenuous; six days at sea and then a return to harbour knowing that we should not be required again for three days. I found my duties and added responsibilities as first lieutenant both interesting and absorbing, and when I went ashore the teaming life of the large city of Alexandria was very strange to me and quite fascinating.

At first I was a little nervous of going ashore on my own, as I had no word of any of the local languages. I knew that the notices of instruction on the telephones were in four different languages, none of which were English. I confided my fears to a very old RNR officer who had spent many years at sea. Placing his hand on my shoulder, he said, 'My boy, when you go ashore in a foreign port there are only three things that you need remember. The first is that the word beer all the world over means beer. The second is that the word 'mungy' accompanied with suitable gestures towards the mouth, means something to eat. And the third and last thing a young fellow wants to remember is that a kiss gets a man everything else he requires'.

Whether this rather down-to-earth philosophy is really all that a young Naval Officer requires may possibly be regarded with some scepticism, but in its support, I must record that I have never found it necessary to spend time and energy in making myself proficient in any foreign language.

Each time we went to sea, our engines vibrated a little bit more. The chief spent his time making little wooden wedges, which he pushed in between the bedplate of the engines and the engine bearers and then taking them across to the engineer commander in the depot ship *Hannibal* who did duty as base engineer officer. For a long time our chief didn't get much change, which was partly his own fault. From the day the *Asphodel* had arrived in Alexandria he had sent in innumerable defect lists and complaints about his engines; in fact he had cried wolf so often that now, when he had a genuine major defect, nobody believed him.

At last, our Captain complained to the Senior Naval Officer who directed that the *Asphodel* was to go to sea for a trial at full power with the Base Engineer Officer onboard. We went out to the seaward end of the Great Pass and, having worked up to full power, we kept the ship under helm, zig-zagging hard one way and another, while the Chief took the Base Engineer Officer underneath the engine-room floor plates to note the movement of the engines.

The demonstration convinced the Base Engineer Officer that something must be done. In the meantime, he recommended that our speed should be limited to 130 revolutions which gave us a speed of about thirteen knots with a clean bottom. This of course was a very considerable limitation to our effectiveness, and the SNO Alexandria immediately asked that we should be taken in hand by Malta dockyard as soon as possible.

This suggestion was not popular. Malta dockyard was fully occupied maintaining a considerable fleet of old ships; all the modern ones were at home in the Grand Fleet. They had difficulty in believing that it was necessary to carry out a major repair on a ship that was only a little over a year old, and made various suggestions for strengthening the engine bearers which they thought could be carried out with the facilities available at Alexandria. However, the Base Engineer Officer had been thoroughly frightened by what he had seen when he made his inspection underneath the engine-room floor plates, and continued to reiterate that complete rebuilding of the engine bearers was essential.

Eventually it was agreed that we should be taken in hand by Malta dockyard, but we had to work our passage. The new policy of sailing all ships in convoy was just being implemented, and we were sent round to Port Said to take one of the first convoys to Malta. There we found a heterogeneous collection of some dozen ships of various ages and speeds which we were to escort to Malta.

Up to that time, very little had been issued in the way of convoy instructions. All the ships of this convoy were supposed to be capable of six knots, but in fact several had been a long time out of dock and were undermanned and at least two never exceeded five and a half knots. In accordance with the usual merchant service practice at that time, all ships cleaned fires during the first hour of each watch when the speed of individual ships dropped considerably. Some of the newer ships who were capable of nine or ten knots could maintain the convoy speed of six knots even when cleaning fires, but the older ships dropped back considerably and had not the speed to catch up again when they had cleaned their fires.

The convoy trickled slowly out of Port Said one ship at a time over a period of two hours, and were spread over ten miles of ocean. The rest of that day was spent chasing around the convoy trying to get them into formation.

None of the ships carried signalmen. The officers had some knowledge of morse and semaphore but were without practice, thus the passing of a signal of more than three or four words was a long process necessitating closing each ship in turn.

The Captain's solution to this difficulty was to write out several copies of the message he wished to pass and enclose these in matchboxes with a small lead weight. Then turning the ship over to the navigator, he directed that we should close the merchant ship until the Captain, standing on the fo'c'sle, was able to throw a matchbox with its message onboard the merchant ship. For some reason the Captain always thought it necessary for the actual throwing to be done by himself. Usually, it was necessary to make several attempts before a matchbox successfully landed, and it was seen that one of the crew of the merchant ship had picked it up and was doing something intelligent with it. The crews of some ships were a little slow in appreciating why they should be bombarded in this fashion.

As the sun rose the next day during the morning watch which I was keeping as officer of the watch, it was seen that the convoy was well scattered both in a longitudinal and in a sideways direction. Some ships had not been able to keep up and had dropped astern. The remainder had gradually opened out. The instinct of all merchant service officers at that time was to keep as far away from all other ships as possible. The idea of sailing in a comparatively close formation was against all their upbringing and, inevitably, during the night they had opened out from one another.

All the morning watch and most of the forenoon was spent in chasing up the laggards and trying to get the convoy into a reasonable formation. At noon it appeared that so far, what with the zig zag, we had not made good more than five knots and it was clear that it would be nearly a week before we arrived at Malta.

Considerable arguments arose in the wardroom regarding the new convoy policy. All the ex-merchant service officers were dead against it. They pointed out with reason that the more modern and faster ships were being kept back, that the speed of the convoy was the speed of the slowest ship and with the delays which inevitably occurred when the convoy was formed, owing to some ships not being ready to sail, the overall carrying capacity of the merchant fleet was much reduced. In view of the already heavy losses in ships, this reduction was very serious. Further, they pointed out that we, the escort, could not possibly be of any protection to the convoy; we were doing nothing but run around the rear of the convoy doing a sheep dog act in an effort to keep the ships closed up. Much better they argued, to let the more modern ships sail independently and use their speed as a protection.

While I could not find any good arguments to counter those of my brother officers, nevertheless I felt we were starting on the right lines. It was our job to fight the enemy and we could not do that unless we could get contact with him. As long as we spent our time patrolling, he could always avoid us. By putting the merchant ships in convoy, we were forcing the enemy to come to us. I still didn't see how we were to tackle him when we made contact, but the fact that we were in contact gave us the chance of learning how to deal with the enemy. I don't think I consciously thought back to the defence of trade in the days of sail, but somewhere at the back of my brain was the feeling, which I was unable to put into words, that the same general principles held good, and that we should begin to see our way when we had perfected an efficient convoy system.

The fact that we had not perfected our convoy system was demonstrated when we were about halfway to Malta; we ran into a large convoy on its way to Port Said. If the system is working properly, convoy tracks should be kept well apart so that there is no fear of them running into one another. Fortunately, we met during daylight hours and, having our convoy more or less under control, were able to make a small alteration of course so that the two convoys did not ever become intermixed.

The other convoy was straggling over ten miles or more of ocean in the charge of two trawlers, who appeared to have no excess of speed over the individual ships of the convoy.

It was difficult to believe that the ships of the convoy were enjoying any protection at all. In fact, at first sight it looked as though this convoy was nothing more than a good meal for a hungry submarine. The ex-merchant service officers were very scornful and prophesied early disaster to both convoys. However, in point of fact after six and a half days of shepherding our convoy, we saw them all safely berthed in Malta, and we subsequently heard that the other convoy had also trickled into Port Said without the loss of a ship.

During the passage to Malta I had difficulty in keeping both the electrical circuits to the fo'c'sle gun in an efficient condition. We experienced a certain amount of head wind which was enough to throw up a short sea, that washed down our fo'c'sle at frequent intervals as we thrashed around the stern of the convoy. Gale was coming to me at frequent intervals to report that one or other of the firing circuits was out of action, and would remain so until he had unshipped the battery box, dried it out and fitted spare batteries.

I had a constant dread that we should have one fleeting chance of a shot at a submarine which would be missed owing to the gun misfiring. Eventually I persuaded my Captain to allow me to keep the fo'c'sle gun permanently in percussion firing. I felt that the disadvantages of percussion firing were more than compensated for by the certainty that the gun would fire.

On arrival in Malta, we found that the other sloops with armament similar to ourselves had been having similar trouble and the Admiralty had approved 4.7-inch guns in sloops being fitted with permanent percussion firing. With this objective in view, they had designed equipment to enable the gunlayer to fire the gun in percussion firing thus obviating the necessity for the gunlayer to order the breech worker to fire the gun by a lanyard.

The parts to enable this modification to be carried out were supplied to the ship and we were ordered to fit them. To enable us to carry out this and similar work we had amongst our ship's company an armourer rating, what would now be known as an ordnance mechanic. I cannot now remember his name; he was a particularly nice chap very skilful with his hands who made himself useful in many ways quite outside his official duties of maintaining the guns. As he was the only armourer rating we had, he was always known as The Armourer.

The equipment designed by the Admiralty consisted of a system of rods operated by a trigger under the control of the gunlayer. When the trigger was operated, it revolved a long rod which ran parallel to the gun from the gunlayers position to the breech end of the gun. At the breech end this rod was fitted with a toe, which engaged with another toe on a rod at right angles which ran across the breech block to the lock. Thus, when the trigger was pulled, the long rod was revolved and the toe on it pulled the short rod sideways thus releasing the spring of the lock. Since neither the long rod nor the short one were well supported, there was a certain amount of lost motion where the two toes engaged. In fact, the pull off was nothing like as crisp as it should be for accurate marksmanship.

It was clear to me that if the short rod passed through a bearing so that it could only move lengthways, this lost motion would be largely overcome.

I discussed the problem with the armourer, who thought he could make a bearing on the lines I suggested which would be supported on a bracket. He pointed out that to secure the bracket he would have to fix it to the breech block but he could do this without boring any holes in the breech block, which was strictly forbidden by the regulations, by using the holes which had previously held the clips for the electrical circuit. He added that as we were making a modification to a breech block, we ought, strictly speaking, to obtain approval before going ahead.

I was so certain that my idea would be an appreciable improvement that I told him to go ahead and we would ask for approval when we had proved that the idea worked. So, we scrounged a little brass out of Malta Dockyard and the armourer made a very neat and tidy fitting which restrained the motion of the short rod, making the pull off much crisper and more efficient. I did not officially report this modification until after we had fired the gun with the new equipment and no opportunity occurred for this until appreciably after we had completed our refit at Malta.

To step ahead a bit with the story of this modification, I then got the staff commander in Malta who was looking after the welfare of the sloops to come and see the modification. He was quite impressed with the idea and talked of getting the other ships with 4.7-inch guns fitted in a similar manner. The fact that I had taken this precaution of getting a senior officer to approve what I had done stood me in good stead during the enquiry subsequent to the accident to the fo'c'sle gun.

After we had arrived in Malta there was a delay of a day or two while the dockyard authorities, who were very overworked, decided what they should do about the *Asphodel's* engines. They found it difficult to credit our engineer officer's description of the manner in which the engines were moving, and decided that they must see for themselves. So, we went to sea for a further steam trial taking the Dockyard officials with us. However, a short trial quite convinced them that something must be done and the next day we were officially taken in hand for the engine bearers to be rebuilt, and at the same time the ship was to be docked and refitted. The estimated time for this was six weeks, but we were warned that if more urgent work came along work on the *Asphodel* would have to be deferred. In point of fact it was two and a half months before we were ready for sea again.

The dockyard started pulling the ship to pieces almost at once. To get at the main engines, they had to remove the top of the engine-room casing, which meant an appreciable part of the boat deck. But even faster than the ship was pulled to pieces, the wardroom disintegrated. One of the first letters we received on arrival in Malta informed us that our engineer officer was to be relieved, and his successor arrived a few days later. The engineer officer departed for England within a few days and with him went both the RNR lieutenants and the paymaster on leave, as they had then been out of England for nearly eighteen months. What with delays in travelling etc. they were away for some six weeks. Then the probationer surgeon left to continue his studies and was not relieved.

As soon as the refit had started and the ship was out of action, the Captain started working in the Commander-in-Chief's office. A new Commander-in-Chief, Admiral Gough-Calthorpe, had recently been appointed and he was busy reorganising the Mediterranean station; in particular, he was active in bringing in an efficient system of convoys. He soon found a permanent appointment for my Captain with the title of Commander of Patrols, and a relief was appointed to the ship. This new captain, who was an active service lieutenant commander, did not join until near the end of the refit. Thus, the wardroom was reduced to the new engineer officer whose name was Cameron and myself and, as I was the executive officer, I became temporarily the commanding officer. In view of my youth and inexperience this might have been an awkward situation but, as I have already explained, Cameron and I soon struck up a friendship and we got on very well together.

The next two months while the refit went slowly forward proved to be the most pleasant and easy of any during the First War. I was my own master without very much to do. The weather was fine and hot, sometimes in the dockyard the heat was oppressive, but I was young and didn't let it worry me. Then when work was over for the day it was very pleasant to make a leisurely trip over to the Club bathing place at Tigné where the conditions for diving and swimming were excellent. Then a quiet amble back to the Union Club in Valletta for dinner, where the dinner was nothing much to write home about, but much better than we were used to on board. Of course, the ship was uncomfortable, noisy and dirty and very hot during the day, and in those days there were no adequate precautions against the mosquitoes

Sub-Lieutenant William Carne 1917

and sand flies who invaded the dockyard in large numbers at night. The bite of these insects irritated me quite a lot, and so, in an endeavour to keep them off, I bought myself some mosquito netting which I rigged up over my bunk. This kept the mosquitoes off but was little if any protection against sand flies, and by cutting off any slight draught there might be, made my cabin even hotter. Nevertheless, I enjoyed my period as commanding officer and used my temporary position to agitate for improvements to the ship's armament. I was following up my idea that the two 4.7-inch guns should be controlled as a battery.

I tried to persuade the dockyard to fit permanent voicepipes from the bridge to both 4.7-inch guns. Here I ran up against a brick wall; the dockyard said that if the voicepipes were to be of any use they must be pipes of some appreciable size and well lagged. There was no piping available in the yard suitable for this purpose. I compromised on flexible voicepiping. The dockyard said that over the distances I required, the flexible voicepipes would be useless; nothing would be heard above the sound of the wind and the sea.

I was not convinced, but to prove their point the dockyard lent me a length of flexible voicepiping to try out my idea. I had to admit that they were right; even alongside the dockyard wall it was very difficult to hear, and obviously at sea with the noise of the wind and sea it would be impossible to pass orders etc. by this means.

I was still convinced that the guns must be controlled from the bridge, so I persuaded the dockyard to make me a large board, painted black, on both sides of which were painted two clock faces numbered from nought to ten. Each clock face had a hand painted white. The intention was that the upper clock face indicated range in thousands of yards while the lower the hundreds. I had fixings made so that this board could be rigged either side of the bridge athwartship so that it could be seen by both the forward and after gun range setters. Thus, the same range could be transmitted to both guns. It seemed too complicated to transmit deflection as well, so I decided that each officer of quarters must decide on his own deflection. I thought that at the ranges at which we were likely to engage a submarine it should be possible to spot for deflection from the gun if the bridge, with its better field of view, did the spotting for range.

I showed this gadget with some pride to my new Captain when he arrived and, at least in principle, he liked the idea. He decided that he himself would spot for range and, very roughly, between us we would blow every submarine out of the Mediterranean.

In practice the gadget didn't work so well. It blocked the view from the compass, so it had to be kept unshipped. It was heavy and ungainly and in a gale of wind was difficult to ship, and when in place it fouled the signal flags as they were being hoisted or hauled down. The vibration of the ship when steaming fast caused the hands to move on their own so that they had to be constantly adjusted. However, we persevered with it for some six months by which time I think everyone had come to the conclusion that while the idea was undoubtedly a very clever one, its practical application was not much more effective than the brilliant ideas of Mr. Heath Robinson. When in the course of time I returned from hospital after being patched up from the effects of the accident to the fo'c'sle gun, I found that the board had disappeared. I didn't ask any awkward questions and we went back to the time-honoured method of control by officer of quarters.

With the depth charge equipment, I thought I was going to be more successful. The dockyard promised and indeed did fit three additional chutes making four in all. But when I asked that at least two of these should be fitted with hydraulic release equipment so that the charges could be released from the bridge, I got a very off-putting reply. There might be enough equipment available to fit two of the *Asphodel's* chutes, but they doubted if there would be enough copper piping to enable the equipment to be operated from the bridge. Their doubts were justified; no equipment or piping had arrived in Malta up to the time when we sailed on completion of the refit.

We did have our four chutes but when I came to draw four depth charges it was only to find that none additional were available. We therefore went to sea with the one charge we had landed on deposit when we returned all our ammunition at the beginning of the refit.

Looking back over that period, the summer and autumn of 1917, it is difficult not to be astonished that the build-up of weapons with which to combat the submarine menace had proceeded so slowly. It was partly a reflection of the acute shortage of high explosive. This shortage was partly due to the tremendous expenditure of high explosive on the Western Front which started with the development of trench warfare and had increased month by month until, at this period, hundreds of tons of high explosive were being used to churn the mud of Flanders. This resulted in the Navy trying to break the stranglehold of the enemy submarines with weapons which had been hastily improvised, were uncertain in their action and in very short supply.

Not that I think this shortage worried us at all. We had one depth charge which we were convinced was sufficient to sink one submarine. Let our enemy make one mistake and show himself for an instant, and we would drop our depth charge on his head and that would be the end of him. Submarines did not at that time ever work in company so one depth charge at a time was quite sufficient. Let it be noted that up to this time the *Asphodel* had had no contact with the enemy. Very shortly, we were to have our eyes opened.

Towards the end of September, the two RNR lieutenants and the paymaster returned from leave in England. But the navigator did not stay with us long, a new form of 'Q' ship was to be tried out in the Mediterranean. There were still a number of sailing brigs trading between Europe and the North African coast. The submarines had taken to coming to the surface and sinking them by gunfire. It was proposed to fit out a brig with a concealed 12-pounder gun, with the hope that the unsuspecting submarine would surface sufficiently close to the brig to allow her to deal a mortal wound before the submarine got busy with her more powerful gun. Volunteers were asked for from amongst officers who had had experience in sail. The navigator volunteered and was accepted. I have explained that he was relieved by an older officer, a very experienced merchant seaman, with whom I soon became friends.

The navigator sailed in his brig for their first cruise at about the same time as the *Asphodel* left Malta after her refit. We did not see him again. I did not hear the story of their meeting with the enemy until some time afterwards. I understood that they saw a periscope close alongside, who took a good look at them and apparently became suspicious. Perhaps he thought that there were too many men on board for the brig to be entirely innocent. Anyway, he surfaced over a mile away and opened fire at once. The brig staged a 'panic' abandon ship with some of the crew while the gun and gun's crew remained concealed. But a shell came inboard and killed or injured most of the 'panic' party. The Captain of the brig thinking that his ship was going to be sunk without the submarine coming any closer, then gave the order to open fire. They got the gun up and got off a few rounds from their unstable platform but without obtaining a hit on the submarine who promptly submerged and made off. The brig was considerably damaged and the survivors were lucky to be picked up. The idea was not tried again; the day of the 'Q' ship was over.

Our new captain arrived shortly before the end of the refit. He had at one time been a submarine specialist but for the last year or so he had commanded a 'Q' ship in the Atlantic. His 'Q' ship was a comparatively large and valuable merchant ship. In view of the fact that 'Q' ships had more or less had their day, and to the acute shortage of shipping for normal trade purposes, his ship had been returned to her owners to continue her legitimate duties. He came therefore with certain views on the anti-submarine war, one of which was that sailing ships in convoy definitely increased the submarines difficulties, provided the ships in convoy kept closed up and did not straggle.

On completion of the refit we took the ship to sea for a short steam trial; we had no difficulty in getting our full revolutions without any of the vibration from the engines which had previously been so marked. Everyone reported themselves satisfied with the refit and the dockyard reported that we were now ready for service again. We were also informed that in future we should be based on Malta and as our accounts would be carried out by the Malta base, our paymaster left us and joined the Naval base at Port Said, which was being expanded to cope with the organisation of convoys.

Our first duty on completion of our refit was to escort a convoy to Alexandria. By this time fairly copious convoy instructions had been issued to all merchant ships but the full impact of them had not by any means been grasped by the captains and officers. This convoy proved to be a particularly difficult one to control as one extremely old Greek ship was very slow and dropped astern each night. The whole convoy had to be slowed down each morning to enable her to catch up. Then those ships who had the speed to maintain station kept edging away from each other until there was at least a mile between each ship.

With the picture still vivid in my mind of the efficient way in which convoys operated in the Second War, particularly in the latter years when we beat off the heavy attacks on the Atlantic and Russian convoys, it is not now easy to remember how difficult it was to impose a system of operating in convoys in the middle of the First War.

In 1917, the British mercantile fleet had not sailed in convoy for over a hundred years. Ships had changed from sail to steam, generations of seamen had come and gone, the old rules for convoys had been lost, the stories of convoys had been forgotten, even the very myths of convoy operations had disappeared down the tunnels of time.

Not only had the merchant marine no understanding of what was meant by operating in convoy but the Navy itself had largely forgotten the lessons of the past and, in particular, little or no thought had been given to the new problems which submerged attack posed for the defence of trade. And such was the tempo of the time that there was no question of stopping and thinking out the problem and training the personnel in the new technique. By 1917, the mercantile fleet had been so depleted of ships that every ship must be sailed again as soon as she could be turned around, and so short were we of suitable officers that there was no question of taking them out of their ships and giving them some intensive training; they must go to sea again with their ships and learn the new techniques as they made their perilous way from port to port.

Once again, we brought our convoy to its destination in safety. This was probably due to our good luck in that we did not fall in with any enemy submarine. But I think in some ways at least we deserved our good fortune as our new Captain drove us hard. Day or night we steamed at a speed fifty percent greater than the speed of the convoy, zig-zagging backwards and forwards and immediately bearing down on any ship that showed a tendency to get out of station, with the culprits' pendants flying and our signal lamp flashing as we called attention to her error in station keeping. At first, they were very slow at answering signals or getting back into station, but by the end of the voyage at least their station keeping was improving. Even the Greek ship who invariably dropped astern every night made an effort to keep up; the moment we altered course to close her as the eastern horizon lightened in the morning watch to badger her with our signals, we would see the extra smoke puff from her funnels as she made a further effort to increase the speed of her ancient engines.

It was pleasant to be back in Alexandria again, but it was only for forty-eight hours. The port had changed considerably since we left. The Naval base was much busier and more efficient, and the docks were full of large transports bringing the troops and resources which in a short time were to enable Allenby to carry out his first offensive which resulted in the capture of Jerusalem.

As I have said, we sailed from Alexandria two days later for Port Said, our Captain bringing back from the SNSO our sailing orders with a rather mysterious message that we were required for a special duty. When we arrived at Port Said he hurried ashore for a conference that was to take place that day. He sent back a message which filled us with a certain amount of consternation, as he said that we were not only to complete with coal, but we were also to embark a deck cargo of sixty tons of coal. The only place to stow this extra fuel was in the two waists. Cameron and I put our heads together, and collecting our one shipwright and one or two of his stokers and all available timber, we erected two small bulkheads in each waist to the height of the bulwarks between which we reckoned we could stow sixty tons of coal. It was however difficult to look forward with favour to the prospect of sailing with a deck cargo of coal. Both waists would be blocked to traffic, our newly painted bulkheads would be scratched and dirtied, the whole ship would be covered in coal dust and, in particular, as the deck cargo must be stowed just outside the galley, we could look forward to the pleasure of having all our food liberally sprinkled with coal dust.

On the Captain's return we eagerly asked him what was this special duty for which we were required. It appeared that we were to take a convoy all the way from Port Said to Gibraltar. Up to this time all convoys had stopped at Malta as the escort vessels had insufficient endurance to escort a convoy, making good only some seven or eight knots all the way through the Mediterranean. This stop at Malta obviously delayed the convoy very appreciably.

It was now intended to run some special fast convoys right through to Gibraltar without stopping at Malta. No ship that could not maintain a speed of ten knots would be included in these special convoys. These convoys from the east would be known as Homeward Eastern and we should escort the first which would be known as 'Homeward Eastern Number One' or, for short, HE1. It was intended to provide a strong escort, which in the case of HE1 would consist of two destroyers and two sloops. The two sloops, each with a deck cargo of coal to increase their endurance, would continue right through to Gibraltar, the two destroyers would be relieved south of Malta by two other destroyers from Malta.

The convoy was due to sail in two days' time and arrangements had been made for us to complete with fuel shortly before sailing so that we should commence the voyage with full bunkers. Cameron and I discussed the problem of the deck cargo. The coal was no use to the engineers on deck, they wanted it in the bunkers where the stokers could get at it in order to feed the furnaces. The engine-room complement was short-handed of stokers, we should have to steam hard with this fast convoy and it would not be possible for the stokers to trim the deck cargo into the bunkers in addition to their normal duties of stoking the furnaces. So I had to arrange that such few sailors as I had off watch each day should trim coal from the deck cargo into the bunkers. Cameron calculated that he would be expending rather more than twenty tons of coal a day, so that if we trimmed twenty tons into the bunkers each day, we should get rid of our deck cargo in three days.

I sent for Staples and made out the necessary orders for twenty tons of coal to be trimmed into the bunkers each day. Staples was very gloomy about the whole business; he had never sailed with a deck cargo of coal before and didn't approve of it. 'It was this 'ere noo Navy, and 'e didn't 'old with it'. He was very pessimistic about the whole programme, saying that if we got heavy weather the coal would be washed into the scuppers, which would then be choked with the result that the waists would fill with water. If we then tried to lift the covers off the chutes to the bunkers, we should fill the bunkers with water. I had foreseen this possibility myself and had told Cameron that we could not be certain of trimming down twenty tons on each of the first three days of the voyage; it must depend to a certain extent on the weather.

In the event we had reasonable weather for the early days of our voyage and we got rid of all the coal on deck in three days as we had calculated. But I don't think the idea of relying on a deck cargo of coal to increase endurance is a good one, except in a rather dire emergency and we, in the *Asphodel*, were never asked to do it again.

In due course we sailed from Port Said. All the six ships of the convoy were biggish modern British vessels who formed up reasonably quickly in line abreast with one destroyer zig-zagging ahead of the convoy, the other destroyer astern and the two sloops on either flank. The convoy zig-zagged at ten knots, while the escorts carried out an independent zig-zag steaming some four or five knots faster than the convoy doing a wider zig-zag to prevent ourselves from going ahead. Thus we hoped to confuse and so frustrate the attack of any submarine that might be lying in wait for us.

We sailed from Port Said on a day in early November, typically with a lot of low cloud and a moderate northerly wind which threw up quite a sea, enough to make the *Asphodel* move about very considerably as we buffeted into it. I went to bed early as I had a night watch and was by no means enjoying the rolls and pitches of the *Asphodel* as she zig-zagged into the seaway.

It was towards the end of the first watch, I suppose about 11.30pm, when the alarm rattlers dragged me from my bunk. Hastily grabbing a few clothes, I rushed to my action station at the fo'c'sle gun. The night was pitch dark, it was blowing quite hard and there was a lot of motion on the ship as we drove into a head sea. As I climbed the fo'c'sle ladder, she poked her bows into a big one which broke into a cloud of spray which drenched me as I got to the top of the ladder. I and the gun's crew crouched around the gun holding onto something firm as the motion was considerable and we were constantly being blinded by spray.

The *Asphodel* had been well out on the port flank when the alarm was raised by the torpedoed ship firing a Very light. We closed the convoy at full speed and, passing astern of the port wing ship, sighted the torpedoed ship who had already dropped well astern. The destroyer who had been astern of the convoy had already closed her from the other side. We did a quick sweep around the torpedoed ship and then were told by the senior officer of the escort to re-join the convoy. The destroyer who had closed her from the other side was ordered to stand by her. She sank before dawn, and the destroyer, having picked up the survivors, returned to Port Said with them.

This was not an auspicious start for the voyage of this important convoy. No one had seen the submarine either before or after she discharged her torpedo. We must have blundered on the submarine while she was on the surface; on such a dark night she was of course very difficult to see, but from her conning tower it is probable that she could see the silhouette of a large merchant ship at a range of half a mile or more. She would just have had time to fire a torpedo and submerge before the convoy blundered over the top of her.

The next morning, when we discussed the events of the night, we were a little depressed. This was the first merchant ship we had seen sunk. We had not seen the submarine or the track of the torpedo. We did not know even from which side the torpedo had been fired. It was painfully obvious that despite the fact that the convoy was escorted by what for those days was a strong escort, the submarine had been able to sink a ship of the convoy with impunity. We consoled ourselves with the thought that the submarine must have been extremely lucky, she was just in the right place and we had blundered on top of her. It was bad luck but the pendulum would swing, and next time the luck would be on our side and we would do something effective.

The next three days were uneventful. The ships of the convoy were all reasonably modern and were getting used to operating in company. Generally speaking, their station keeping was reasonably good. We got rid of all our deck cargo of coal and felt happier. Passing well south of Malta, we made a rendezvous with two destroyers who relieved our one remaining one. It blew rather hard that night as we shaped up towards the Skerki Channel.

During the next forenoon the wind eased, but at the beginning of the afternoon watch there was still quite a lumpy sea running. It was early in the watch that the port wing ship was torpedoed. We must have passed quite close to the submarine, but we saw nothing, neither the periscope nor the track of the torpedo. The *Asphodel* and the destroyer astern closed the torpedoed ship at full speed, circled round her searching for a sign of her periscope but we saw nothing. The senior officer of the escort ordered the destroyer to re-join the convoy and *Asphodel* to stand by the torpedoed ship, who was much down by the bows and whose crew were abandoning ship. We continued to circle round for some time, fruitlessly looking for the periscope, when the Captain decided to pick up the survivors whose two boats had by this time drifted well clear of the ship.

He was not anxious to stop longer than was essential with a submarine in the vicinity so as soon as the survivors were out of the boats, we cast them adrift and went ahead. I took the Captain down to my cabin; he was pretty wet, and tried to get out of him what was the state of his ship. He was an oldish man out of whom I could hardly get a word until I had given him some brandy. All he seemed able to say was that the ship was torpedoed forward and he was sure she was going to sink. The chief engineer seemed to be equally pessimistic, but I then found the chief officer who was more optimistic. He thought the torpedo had hit well forward in No. 1 hold, and that therefore the bulkhead between No. 1 and 2 holds should not be seriously damaged although no doubt there was water in No. 2 hold. But if the bulkhead at the after end of No. 2 hold, that is the forward bulkhead of the boiler room held, the ship would not sink, and there was no reason why the ship should not be steamed slowly. The chief engineer demurred at this opinion but one of the junior engineers, who seemed to be a man of spirit, said that he had been in the boiler room when the torpedo struck and he was certain that the boiler room bulkhead had not been damaged.

All this took time. Nearly two hours had elapsed since the ship was torpedoed. The convoy had long ago disappeared over the horizon. The ship, though down by the bows did not appear to have sunk any lower in the water. I felt certain that the ship could be salvaged if we acted quickly and with determination. With this object in view, I hurried the captain, chief officer and second engineer to the bridge to discuss the matter with my Captain. I thought the chief engineer was a pretty miserable specimen who did not appear to wish to make any effort to save his ship, so I left him out.

We found my Captain poised on the horns of a dilemma, he was anxious to re-join the convoy before dark, at the same time he could not leave the torpedoed ship while she was still afloat. I introduced the officers and explained that I had gathered from them that if the forward boiler room bulkhead held it was improbable that the ship would sink and therefore there was a chance of salvaging her. A discussion then took place as to what action we should take. The Captain of the torpedoed ship was very pessimistic about whether the ship would remain afloat and said that as he had cast adrift his boats, he had nothing in which to return to his ship. I chipped in with the suggestion that the boarding party could be sent in one of our sea boats; we had two whalers as sea boats, and that I should go with the chief officer and second engineer. I did not include the Captain in the suggested boarding party as I did not think he was fit either from the point of view of his age, figure, temperament or agility to lead the boarding of a wreck in a seaway. I was anxious to go myself as I felt that a certain amount of determination might be necessary; firstly to effect the boarding, and secondly to bring back a report favourable to putting the ship's crew back onboard.

The ship's captain raised the point that while we could put them back onboard in our boats, they would be left without a boat if the ship sank suddenly during the night. I countered this by saying that we could lend them a Very pistol and lights and arrange an emergency signal, so that if they felt their ship was sinking, we could get a boat alongside in a matter of minutes. It would only be necessary to send a few men back onboard, just enough to steam her slowly to Malta which was little over a hundred miles away.

My Captain listened to the arguments while he made up his mind. He had an intuition, in which he was quite right, that the enemy submarine was hanging about waiting to see if the ship was going to sink. But something had to be done quickly, as the short autumn afternoon was drawing to a close. While the ship's officers were arguing amongst themselves, he turned to me and in a voice addressed to all of us he said, 'I want you to go, Sub'. He addressed me as Sub unless he was being very formal when he called me First Lieutenant. He went on to say that he would close the ship and drop the whaler just to lee of her. He would then steam at high speed around the ship at a distance of about a mile to make any submarine keep his head down and would come back to pick up the whaler in half an hour by which time he wanted us to have finished our examination and be lying off ready to be hoisted.

This was just what I wanted. With a quick, 'Aye, Aye, Sir,' I was down from the bridge and arranging for the second whaler to be lowered. A whaler's crew is five men, as this was a big percentage of our seaman population of twenty, I had to be certain that that I was not taking any man who was vital to the working of the ship, and to leave behind at least one 4.7-inch gun's crew. Then I collected the chief officer and second engineer, equipped them with life jackets and suggested that they should take one other of their crew to assist. One of the quartermasters volunteered to accompany us; he looked an active, intelligent sort of man. I wanted an active man; I felt that boarding this ship might not be too easy. The chief officer was a big heavy man not in his first youth and I thought he might require assistance.

The merchantmen had never been dropped in a seaboat before and viewed the prospect with a little alarm when I told them what we were going to do. However, the mission passed off very satisfactorily. The Captain brought the *Asphodel* up to within a cable of the torpedoed ship and in her lee at a speed of about two knots. Owing to the swell we had to stop lowering the boat when she was still a good six feet above the ship's waterline, but I managed to time our slipping as a big wave came along and we dropped into it nice and gently. Towing on the boat rope for fifteen seconds or so gave us plenty of way to sheer off from the ship's side. We slipped the boat rope and immediately the *Asphodel* went full ahead.

As soon as the boat's crew had got their oars clear and we had shaped up for the torpedoed ship, I looked around for the *Asphodel*, but we were deep in the trough between two waves and she was out of sight. I suppose chaps in the middle of trackless deserts feel a bit lonely from time to time, but I doubt if they feel more lonely than suddenly finding oneself in an open boat in the middle of the ocean.

The ship being well down by the bows, the wind had blown her stern round until she was nearly head to wind but there was a little lee on the port side for which I steered. She was the usual type of tramp steamer of those days with two holds before and two abaft the bridge structure either side of which were the stowages for two boats. I made for the falls of the port foremost lifeboat which were still hanging over the side. Abaft this was the second boat which had been let go with a run and was lying alongside swamped still secured by its falls.

We were soon under the foremost lifeboat falls and, at the sound of our voices, a shrill barking broke out onboard. There was some murmuring amongst my boat's crew at the ship's officers for having left their dog onboard when they had abandoned ship. The quartermaster had no difficulty in swarming up the after fall to the height of the bulwark, then he swung in until he got a foot on the actual bulwark. He then disappeared, only to reappear again very shortly with a jumping ladder which he hung over the side, so the two officers were able to board the ship in comparative comfort. As they disappeared, I sang out to them to be sure and bring the dog back with them.

We passed the boat's painter through the block of the foremost fall, so that the boat lay more or less comfortably a fathom or more from the ship's side. In about ten minutes or a quarter of an hour the boarding party appeared again and, picking up the dog which had continued to bark, without making any effort to carry the animal down to the boat threw it into the sea between the ship and the boat. The wretched animal, a rather diminutive Yorkshire terrier, fell some fifteen or twenty feet and disappeared. This action was not approved by my boat's crew, who tried to fish the animal out on the blade of an oar. There was still an appreciable swell alongside the ship in which the boat was rising and falling some four or five feet. The dog came to the surface more or less winded from its drop and was being swept astern. I told the bowman to pay out on the painter and coxswain to hang onto my legs while I lay across the sternsheets of the boat and, as the animal bobbed up and down, I managed to grasp its stump of a tail and pull it back alongside where one of the boat's crew got hold of it and pulled it onboard. It was a very wet and miserable little dog when we got him into the boat, but it was not long before he started to bark, or rather yap, again.

I re-embarked the boarding party but before shoving off I got their report from them. The boiler room and engine-room were completely dry. The damage was all well forward the starboard side. The forepeak and No. 1 hold were flooded, but No. 2 hold was still dry. The officers were a little hesitant, but could think of no really good reason why they should not go back onboard and attempt to steam her to Malta which was a comparatively short distance away. I was determined to get this opinion out of them, otherwise I was going to board the ship myself and make them point out to me why she could not, in their opinion, be steamed.

Just then the *Asphodel* approached and I shoved off to return to her. They had cleared the lower deck to hoist the boat and had roped in a few of the survivors to help but even so, the loaded boat rose out of the water very slowly. I had taken the precaution of crossing the life lines, but even so, when we were a few feet out of the water we were hit by a large wave which set us swinging dizzily as the bowman had not secured his lifeline adequately and it was torn out of his hands. I told him pretty heartily what I thought of him, but he was one of the HO i.e. 'hostilities only' ordinary seamen who had joined us in Malta straight from barracks. I had trained him in the whaler, but only in harbour. Poor chap; he still had no idea how to be handy in a bit of a seaway.

When we arrived onboard, most of the ship's company wanted to form a committee of welcome for the small dog, who was informing all the world in a most vociferous manner of his indignation at being left behind in a sinking ship. It was clear that he had the sympathy of most of the *Asphodel's* ship's company, but I chased them away to their action stations. I still had the feeling, which I had got from my Captain, that the submarine was in the vicinity.

As soon as the whaler was clear of the water, the Captain had gone ahead at *Asphodel's* best speed and had then turned over the bridge to the navigator while he came down to the charthouse where he had established the torpedoed ship 's captain. He now sang out to me to bring the boarding party to the charthouse to make their report.

We had just got up to the boatdeck off which the charthouse opened, when there were shouts from the fo'c'sle. Most of the gun's crew had sighted the submarine's periscope only two or three hundred yards on the starboard bows. The Captain bolted for the bridge and I went pounding aft along the boatdeck. I was nervous that Gale, the torpedoman, had not got back to his station on the depth charges from having assisted at hoisting the whaler. However, I found him at his station with the safety pin out and watching the hand flag on the bridge, which we used as a signal when to release the charge.

I had not been aft ten seconds when down came the flag on the bridge and Gale released our only depth charge. I started to run forward to the fo'c'sle. I had a feeling that the depth charge might blow the submarine to the surface and enable me to sink it by gunfire. Halfway along the waist I met the chief officer of the torpedoed ship who asked me if we had released a depth charge. I said yes, and stopped to look aft. Surely the charge should have exploded by now? In those days we set our charges for forty feet, and it doesn't take long for a charge to sink that distance. Ten seconds later there was no doubt about it, even if Gale had set the charge to the alternative depth of eighty feet it must have gone off by now. For some reason the charge had misfired.

There was no time for an enquiry. The *Asphodel* had gone ahead at full speed turning slightly to starboard. We must have passed over her or very close to her, but she had obviously seen us and gone deep. We made a large circle and came back over the spot where she had disappeared, but she was not stupid enough to show herself again. Then we made a large circle around the torpedoed ship at a radius of a mile or more and debated on our best course of action. The captain thought the submarine intended to have a shot at us and then finish off the merchantman. He therefore refused to stop the ship to allow us to put a boarding party onboard our charge in order to get her underway again. The short day was drawing to a close, he decided to stand by the ship and try to put the boarding party onboard during the night if the sea moderated or else wait until the morning.

To have one more look at the ship before the last of the light failed, we closed her and went up her starboard side at a distance of two or three cables at our best speed of some sixteen knots. Just as we were abreast the ship, a shout from the lookouts drew our attention to the starboard side where a torpedo had been seen to surface for a moment, and subsequently we saw the track of a torpedo.

If the submarine commander had meant to sink the *Asphodel*, he had badly underestimated her speed for the torpedo passed well astern of us. But he had made certain of hitting something, the torpedo went on to hit the merchant ship amidships abreast her funnel. The torpedo must have flooded her engine-room and boiler-room for she disappeared almost at once with the last of the light.

The problem of whether or not to board the ship was therefore solved and we prepared to follow up the convoy who by now had some four or five hours start and were well ahead of us. But as soon as we reported that the merchant ship had sunk, Malta ordered us to return there with the survivors.

I have always thought that in ordering us back to Malta, which meant calling off the hunt, the authorities made a mistake which was repeated over and over again both in that war and in the Second War. To defeat the submarine, we must make contact with it. That November afternoon we knew there was a submarine in our vicinity, we had actually seen its periscope and the effects of its action, further we knew that the submarine had been submerged for several hours already, it would have to come to the surface sometime during the following night. If we had remained in the vicinity steaming at our maximum speed in ever increasing circles of diameter equal to twice the submarine's submerged speed of two or three knots we must have passed over or close to him at fairly frequent intervals sufficiently close for him to hear our propeller and keep his head down until he had drained his battery enough to make him take the risk of coming to the surface. One then had a chance that one might blunder on top of him. The chance of course would be very small, not one that any sane man would think of taking on a horse, but still a chance. If we didn't take our chances of getting to grips with the submarines, we could never hope to defeat them. It was this necessity to follow up every possible chance that we took a long time to learn in the First War and which we had to relearn in the Second War.

Not of course that at that time I appreciated the necessity of following up every submarine contact. I was not yet nineteen, my thoughts could be summed up by saying that the fact that the submarine had escaped us was bad luck, a pity, but not to worry, another chance would come along shortly and we would get our submarine. But fortune is a jade, if you don't grasp her gifts at the time, she turns her back and you don't see her again. No submarine ever gave the *Asphodel* an opportunity like that again, not in that war, nor, as far as I personally was concerned, in the Second War.

We set course for Malta to arrive early the next morning. On the way we held an unofficial enquiry into the failure of the depth charge. An obvious reason for the failure would be that the safety pin had been left in place. But I had seen it removed and Gale, questioned on this point, produced the safety pin out of his pocket. It would appear that the charge had failed due to malfunctioning of the pistol. Consulting the torpedo log and progress book showed that the pistol had been stripped and cleaned by Gale less than three weeks before, well within the limit of a month laid down by our first captain.

Once in Malta we had to tell our sorry tale. Here was an important convoy on whose organisation great care had been lavished which, despite a very strong escort, had lost a third of its strength when it was only half way through the Mediterranean and, when one of the attacking submarines had shown itself, the resulting counter attack had been a failure. The authorities were not pleased. They were still further displeased when we suggested that the failure of the counterattack was due to malfunctioning of the depth charge as they were putting a lot of faith in this weapon.

Orders were given for all depth charge pistols to be sent to the depth charge testing station for examination and overhaul. We had expended our only type 'D' charge, but we still had two little charges known as type 'G', each containing ten pounds of explosive which were designed, I think, for use from boats. They would have been very useful in the *New Zealand's* picket boat when we were patrolling under the Forth Bridge, but were of little value in a ship like the *Asphodel*.

With such a small charge it would have been necessary to explode the charge practically in contact with a submarine's hull to do any appreciable damage. However, these small charges were fitted with the same type of pistol as the type 'D' charge. On test both the pistols from the *Asphodel* failed to fire. The testing staff then stripped down both pistols, and found that they had been incorrectly assembled and could not under any circumstances have fired.

Then the balloon went up. When had these pistols last been stripped, who had done the work and why? Luckily for me my late captain, who I have explained was now working in the Commander-in- Chief's Office on the organisation of convoy escorts, heard about the enquiry and came forward and explained that he had given orders for the pistols to be stripped monthly, cleaned and lubricated. As there was no means of testing the pistols in Alexandria they had never been tested. Reference to the torpedo log indicated that his orders had been carried out meticulously. Unfortunately, Gale had not been very clever and had succeeded in reassembling each pistol incorrectly. In place of the charge we had expended, we were given two new ones each with pistols, which had just been tested and were guaranteed to be correct. We were also given orders on no account to strip these pistols ourselves but to take them for test at intervals of a month or on each occasion of returning to Malta.

We landed our survivors in Malta, but they left with us their little dog, which they explained would have to go into quarantine in England. The dog, whose name was Vic, soon settled down onboard, making a particular friend of Cameron in whose cabin some sort of bed was rigged up for the animal. This was rather good of Cameron as the cabins were very small and so to have to give up even a small corner to a dog's bed was quite a sacrifice.

We were not long in Malta. The new convoy organisation was getting into its stride and escorts were being worked as hard as possible. Gone was the easy, regular routine of Alexandria. As soon as one convoy had been brought safely into harbour, there was always another waiting for an escort. Mostly we ran to the Eastern Mediterranean but once we went to Gibraltar and several times to Bizerta whose large harbour was now being utilised as a convoy assembly point. The latter port was not very popular with us as in order to coal we had to go inland across the lagoon to Ferryville. The coal was of poor quality, mostly in the form of briquettes and the labour force of Arabs so small that in order to get the ship coaled in a reasonable time we had to put the whole ship's company to assist.

Mails were very irregular, generally speaking we only got a mail when we called at Malta. More than once we went for a month or more without a mail. It was about this time that I received a very useful present. We had not had a mail for some time, when a rather battered brown paper parcel turned up for me with a very well knitted pair of seaboot stockings, blue with a pattern in natural colour wool. Also, in the parcel, was a note from a Mrs Galbraith saying that her son had now written to her and would I accept the enclosed stockings with her thanks. She added that they were the same as she had been knitting for her husband for many years, he being skipper of a trawler sailing out of Stornaway.

I then remembered that while we had been refitting in Malta some six months previously, a letter addressed to the Commanding Officer had arrived from a Mrs Galbraith. She understood that her son was serving onboard the *Asphodel*, but she had not heard from him for six or seven months. Could I tell her whether he was still serving in the ship and whether he was all right?

Galbraith was an ex-trawler hand who had joined up at the beginning of the war to serve in trawlers; he was what in those days we called an AB(T). How he got himself drafted to the *Asphodel* I don't know, but I wasn't going to let him go if I could help it as he was one of the best seamen I had in the ship. The only trouble was that he was almost inarticulate and when he did speak it was with such a broad Scottish accent that I had difficulty in understanding him. But as he could steer a ship, I gave him a job as quartermaster and at once he proved that he could steer better than anyone else in the ship.

All the Flower class sloops to which *Asphodel* belonged were pretty average pigs to steer in a quartering sea. Most of the quartermasters would have the ship veering and yawing twenty-five or thirty degrees either side of her proper course. But Galbraith seemed to feel through the soles of his boots what the ship was going to do and get just that little bit of helm on to check her just before she started to take charge. Cameron, a true engineer upon whose heart every beat and thump of his engines was registered, always said that he knew when Galbraith took over the wheel by the fact that the steering engine then had less than half the work to do. Further, in a quartering sea he could only sleep when the wheel was manned by Galbraith.

Cameron like most Scotsmen was comparatively unemotional but being also an engineer, he was apt to exaggerate and become unnecessarily anxious about his beloved engines. When I received Mrs Galbraith's letter, I sent for her son and asked him why he had not written to his mother. He muttered something about intending to write but he hadn't any writing paper. I told him to get some paper and write a letter by the following morning, as we had just received a signal to say that a mail was going pm the next day. I then sat down and wrote to Mrs Galbraith telling her that her son was quite well, was going to write to her and I added something to the effect that he was proving himself a useful member of the ship's company.

The next morning, I sent for Galbraith and enquired about his letter, which he had not brought to me to be censored. This of course was wartime and I had to censor all the letters. He hadn't written as he had no writing paper and as he was duty the evening before, he had not been able to go ashore and buy any and he had not been able to borrow a sheet from any of his messmates. So, I took him down to my cabin, sat him down at my small writing table, put a pad in front of him and told him to get on with it and I would return in ten minutes to censor his letter.

When I returned, he had written the words 'Dear Mother' in a large and childish hand; but otherwise his letter consisted of two large blots and he was staring at the paper with an expression of complete puzzlement. I then talked to him and gathered that he was genuinely anxious to write to his mother, was sorry that he hadn't written before but simply could not think of any combination of words to express himself. So eventually I had more or less to dictate his letter to him and somehow, we covered two sheets of a large pad with many blots and scratching out of his childish handwriting. And in due course I was rewarded for my efforts with a pair of excellent seaboot stockings which kept my feet warm during many long night watches.

CHAPTER 6

ACCIDENT

Christmas 1917 came and went. We were at sea on Christmas Day, escorting a convoy to Alexandria. It was a rough day; we had had no mail for some time, so nobody had any Christmas letters. It was in fact a dull and dreary day from every point of view. The general feeling of disappointment and frustration at the way the war was going that had been building up all the year in England had permeated to the Mediterranean. The submarines were becoming more and more daring and it seemed impossible to do anything against them. Whenever we met another escort vessel, they had always the same story to tell, of ships being torpedoed without it being possible to take any effective action against the submarines.

We lost another ship early in the new year, under conditions which were rather typical of that time. We were escorting a west-bound convoy from Alexandria to Bizerta. It was a very slow and largish convoy, some twelve or fourteen ships, escorted by the *Asphodel* and two trawlers. They were all slow ships who had great difficulty in keeping even in approximate station in reasonable weather conditions.

When we were somewhere south of Malta, we struck some bad weather and the convoy became very scattered with the two trawlers, who were on either wing of the convoy, barely able to make good the six or seven knots which was all the convoy was steaming. *Asphodel* was doing an independent zig-zag astern of the convoy. At dusk the front of the convoy must have stretched over at least four miles.

When I went up to the bridge at midnight for the middle watch the night was very dark and stormy with a considerable head sea so that as we zig-zagged across the stern of the convoy we were constantly washing down forward and it was out of the question to man the fo'c'sle gun. I wedged myself in a corner of the upper bridge and, in the intervals between being seasick, tried to keep as many of the convoy in sight as possible, but I don't think I ever saw more than three or four at the same time. One went crabwise across the stern of the convoy on a course some thirty degrees different from that of the convoy. I didn't see the trawler on the port wing after about 2am.

She had been dropping back all the watch and I presumed she had dropped astern and would not catch up until the weather moderated. It was after 3.30am and I was thinking that my long watch was coming to an end when, while we were well over towards the starboard wing of the convoy, I saw a streak of light go up from roughly where I thought the port wing ship should be. It was very faint and only appeared for a second or two. It appeared to me to be a rocket.

I rang the alarm rattlers, went on to full speed and altered course to close the point where I had seen the rocket. To do so I had to cut across the bows of one ship of the convoy who had dropped rather astern. The captain arrived on the bridge just as we were rapidly closing her and was rather alarmed, but I was watching her bearing closely and knew that we should pass well ahead of her.

As we went across the stern of the convoy, we examined each ship in turn. As far as we could see, none of them seemed to be damaged. There were no further rockets or signals of distress. We then went well out on the port flank of the convoy but could see no signs of the trawler. The captain asked what the signal looked like. I said a rocket. But neither the signalman nor the lookout on the bridge had seen anything. We then went back into the convoy and called up the Commodore. By this time the organisation of convoys had reached a stage where each convoy had appointed a commodore with, when they were available, a staff of signalmen. But for this slow convoy no additional officer had been available to appoint as Commodore, so the captain of one of the larger merchant ships was given this appointment for the duration of the voyage. However, no additional signalmen were available to supplement his staff. In practice this meant that the commodore's officer of the watch had to read and make any signals.

My Captain never made signals at night if he could help it. He felt that even the most carefully shaded light was a source of danger. But on this occasion, he felt that he must have information. Closing the commodore's ship to within a cable, he made a signal to the commodore asking if he had seen anything, to which, after an appreciable interval, we got the reply 'No'.

We made another attempt to count the convoy, but we could never see more than four or five at a time and they all seemed to be steaming quite happily. By this time the best part of an hour had elapsed since I had given the alarm. The *Asphodel* resumed her station astern of the convoy and we fell out from action stations. The Captain said he thought I had probably been sleeping and had a nightmare. I retired to my cabin and was almost immediately asleep.

Soon after 6am the navigator, who had got up to take some star sights at dawn, poked his head into my cabin and woke me up with the words 'There is one ship and a trawler missing. Perhaps after all Young George you were not quite asleep'.

As the light increased, we eventually saw a cloud of smoke on the horizon right astern of us, which in time proved to be the missing trawler doing her best to catch up. Sometime during the forenoon, she came within signalling distance and reported that she had all the survivors of the sunken ship onboard. In due course this signal was amplified, to inform us that during the night she had dropped astern owing to the heavy weather and poor coal supplied in Port Said. Doing her best to catch up, she came upon the torpedoed ship just as the latter was about to sink and had already been abandoned by her crew who were lying off in her boats. On being torpedoed the ship had fired a rocket, which must have been what I saw, but had then sunk so rapidly that the crew had to abandon ship without making any further signals.

The trawler was one of the older ones still doing service, and had not yet been fitted with a Wireless Teletype (W/T) set. Having dropped astern she was no longer in touch, and had therefore been unable to make any report. Looking back on that night one can only say that the whole affair was very unsatisfactory; a ship had been sunk under our noses, without us even realising what had happened. The only redeeming factor was that the complete crew of the sunken ship had been rescued but that was rather more by good chance than good management.

In an endeavour to stem the tide of submarine sinkings, the convoy system was being expanded as rapidly as possible. Such escorts as were available were worked as hard as possible and an organisation to keep the escorts efficient was built up at Malta. In accordance with this policy, the armourers were taken out of the sloops to form part of the sloop maintenance party. As soon as a sloop arrived in Malta, they came onboard and carried out the maintenance routine on the armament. Although we had lost our armourer, he always made a point of coming onboard as soon as we arrived in Malta and made himself responsible for ensuring that the armament was efficient. He was always welcome, as he was a pleasant fellow as well as being efficient at his job and was popular with all the ship's company.

Thus he was onboard one day early in April when we went to sea early in the afternoon for a firing practice. We and two or three other ships were to escort a convoy leaving late that afternoon. The intention was that we went to sea early in the afternoon for our target practice, returned to the entrance of Grand Harbour to drop our armourer ratings, who were with us to make certain the guns were in every way efficient, and then proceed to the convoy assembly point off Marsa Scirocco at 5pm. We had not had an opportunity to fire our guns for some time. For this exercise we had the use of a proper target towed by a tug, and I was anxious that we should put up a good show.

I think we were the first ship to fire. We approached the target with only the sea watch closed up pretending that we could not see it. When we had closed to a suitable range, the Captain rang the alarm rattlers, we closed up as rapidly as possible and opened fire immediately. We were using my Heath Robinson device for passing ranges from the bridge, so as soon as I got to the gun the sight setter was setting the range transmitted from the bridge. I estimated a deflection and, as the breech worker reported 'Ready' I gave the order 'Fire'. Carroll fired immediately and I was waiting with my glasses to my eyes to spot the fall of shot when I started suffering pain; it was getting worse and worse. Somebody was moving my head and every time it moved the pain got worse and worse. I tried to pull myself together and find out what was happening. I tried to shout or scream but nothing happened. I couldn't see, something was waving about just in front of my eyes. Then I heard a voice say, 'Ee's coming round'. The waving in front of me stopped and I gradually distinguished a face. It was the face of our writer, our one member of the paymaster's department who combined writing up the ledger with issuing provisions etc. When we had a surgeon probationer, he had had the writer as his assistant and had taught him a little first aid; the only man in the ship who knew anything about the subject. He was a perky, rather cheeky little man, who was by no means too popular but on this occasion, he did a first-class job and I am very grateful to him.

He kept assuring me that I was all right and went on winding lengths of bandage around my head. Each time he passed the bandage under my head he had to move it slightly, which was extraordinarily painful. Then someone came and said he was wanted in the fo'c'sle and turning to somebody he told them to look after me. Several people answered and I realised I was the centre of an interested group.

Sometime after that, I don't know how long, I felt a burning thirst. I didn't seem to be able to speak properly but I got out the word 'water'. A voice very close to my head said, 'Get him water quick'. At least two went off and came back with a mess kettle of water. A mess kettle is a metal container in which a mess draws its meal from the galley; it is made sufficiently large to hold the dinner of seventeen or eighteen men and held quite a lot of water.

The basin was dipped in the water and held towards me while my head was very slightly raised. Then I realised that I was lying using a sailor's arm as a pillow, and I realised that it was Able Seaman Chapman, one of our better able seamen who I had always thought of as a rather rough sort of chap. But on this occasion, he looked after me with extraordinary tenderness. I was told afterwards that I continued to use his arm as a pillow until I left the ship; but long before that happened, I had once again relapsed into unconsciousness.

I began to collect myself and realised that I was lying in the starboard waist, but how I got from the fo'c'sle to the starboard waist was beyond my comprehension. Time passed. I kept getting a burning thirst, but Chapman seemed to realise and would very gently lift my head and give me a sip of water. People came and went, I was very confused, but I did gather that we were returning to harbour.

Time passed. Voices murmured but they didn't seem to register. Then I heard my Captain's voice say, 'This is the First Lieutenant'. Through my bandages (I seemed to be completely wrapped in bandages), I saw a serious face that I did not recognise looking at me intently. He must have touched me because I saw an arm covered in stripes and realised that he was a very senior doctor. After looking hard at me he said, 'I can't do anything for this one. Show me the others'. Then he and my Captain went away. I think, not unnaturally, after hearing this remark I reckoned I was on the way out. Soon after this I drifted off into unconsciousness again, and have no recollection of leaving the ship.

And then I was lying on my back in a compartment, there was a deck overhead. I realised that my head was no longer on a pillow and I wondered what had happened to Chapman. I gradually became conscious of another figure beside me. After a time, I can't say how long, I began to realise that I was lying alongside a corpse, very much a corpse. Then I distinguished a figure standing with his back towards me, a white clad figure, dressed in a long white gown, with a dark line down the centre of his back. Was that where he stowed his wings?

The figure didn't move but I became conscious of a sort of rumbling noise and the walls of my compartment started to move. Were they moving or was I moving? Were the walls going down or was I going up? Flat on my back, everything seemed to be out of perspective, but it seemed very important to decide whether I was going up or going down.

Then the rumbling ceased and suddenly I found another figure bending over me, a figure also in a long white gown. But this one was not so tall, rather broader and had red hair. Red hair? Do angels have red hair? But he was very business-like and started asking me questions. What was my rank? What did he want to know my rank for? Surely there were no ranks in whatever place I had arrived at? Anyway, I couldn't remember my rank, my mind was a blank and I couldn't talk. Then he wanted to know my name. But I couldn't remember my name. Still, I vaguely remembered that I had had two names, a Christian name and a surname. But I couldn't remember either and anyway what did it matter? I was very confused and dazed, partly I think because I couldn't hear properly. Although I didn't know it at the time, I was almost completely deaf in my right ear due to the damage I had received, and my head was so wrapped in bandages that I could hear very little with my left ear. And then he asked me what was my religion? At that, the penny dropped, of course, I was C of E, and since they were interested in my religion I must have come to the right place. I managed to tell him I was C of E and got out my name feeling very relieved.

He wrote it all down and then turned to several other white-gowned figures, who appeared and told them to put my stretcher on the trolley and take me to 'Officers' Surgical'. A voice said, 'Yes, Chiefy', and I think it was about then that I began to realise that I had arrived, in the lift that went up the side of the cliff, at the Royal Naval Hospital, Bighi, and that the redhead was a Chief Sick Berth Petty Officer, and his other white-gowned minions were sick berth attendants.

During the next month I saw a lot of redhead, who was the chief regulating petty officer in the hospital, and an efficient chap, but I never got around to telling him that on our first acquaintance I had been unable to decide whether he was an archangel or a high official in hell.

Then I was wheeled away to 'Officers' Surgical', which seemed to be a long way away along a rough path, and my trolley seemed to be singularly devoid of springs. Every bump was a tearing agony until we arrived at a building which, looked at from a horizontal position, seemed to be very tall and dark after the bright sunlight outside. My stretcher was taken off the trolley and dumped on the deck alongside a bed. Then the trolley party stood around looking lost.

Hospital Bighi, Malta, circa 1915

I had been placed on the stretcher with my right knee bent up at a rather awkward angle. One of them asked me if I had broken my leg. For some reason this question amused me; couldn't they see that it was my head that was damaged? He took hold of my leg and gently straightened it out; apparently it worked all right. Then a firm female voice took charge of the proceedings and directed that I should be lifted on to the bed, an operation in which she assisted by supporting my head. Then she dismissed the trolley party while she and a senior sick berth attendant, who had arrived with a trolley covered with equipment, proceeded to undress me. Then a young surgeon lieutenant arrived and he and the Sister kept up a cheerful conversation over the top of me, with a view to assuring me that now I was in hospital I had nothing to worry about and that they would soon patch me up good as new. A quick examination of various bruises and scratches I had received on various parts of my anatomy were brushed to one side as not being of much importance. They kept asking me how I had got hurt and why. But I couldn't give any intelligible reply. I had no idea what had happened. Up to this time I had been in more or less a complete daze. I knew I was in considerable pain, but it seemed to be a long way away, almost as though someone else was in pain and I was suffering a reaction from it.

But when they came to take my bandage off, the pain came right home to me. By this time the bandage put on in the *Asphodel* was firmly stuck and getting it off was no joke. It revealed that I had been struck by something behind the right ear, which had appreciably damaged the scalp and, on the way, had lacerated the ear.

An animated discussion took place between the surgeon and the Sister in which, though I was an interested party, I was unable to take part. It was decided to put four stitches in my head and to trim up my ear which was in rather a mess. The surgeon told me it was going to hurt a bit and that I must not move. The Sister put her hand on my forehead and told me to press up against it. It did hurt and I pushed hard against the Sister's hand. She subsequently told me that her arm ached all night with the effort of resisting the pressure of my head. However, the surgeon apparently did a good job as nobody seems to notice that one of my ears is smaller than the other.

I suppose nowadays surgeons have at their command various means of alleviating pain under similar circumstances, but at that time I was offered nothing. Neither then, nor during the subsequent days, when dressing the wound was a prolonged agony. This was necessary as the surgeon insisted that each day my ear should be thoroughly syringed in order to preserve the hearing.   And, in this, his treatment was successful as, although I was almost completely deaf in my right ear immediately after the accident, I soon recovered my hearing. But it did mean that my dressing had to be removed each day and, as it had invariably stuck to my lacerated ear, the process of getting it off was extremely unpleasant. Then I had to pull the remains of my ear to one side in order to allow Sister to insert the syringe and get a really good stream into the ear.

I can't remember how long all this took but I do know that by the time they had finished the lights were on. The Sister insisted that I should have some supper. The last thing I wanted was something to eat. My head was extraordinarily painful and I didn't seem to be able to move it without all the muscles of my neck objecting very strongly and all my bruises and scratches were coming to life and calling attention to themselves. The idea of being made to eat seemed utterly impossible. But the Sister was brightly cheerful and assured me that I should feel much better after a little food.

I didn't believe her but she arrived very shortly after with a feeding cup and proceeded to pour something, I cannot remember what, down my throat. Some of it went down but quite a lot went sideways and had to be mopped up. I didn't seem to have much control of any of my muscles. Then the surgeon came back and he and the Sister made cheerful conversation and assured me that I should feel much better after a good sleep. I realised that they were shortly going to leave me, and I felt terrified of being left alone. They had put me in a ward with four beds, but all the others were unoccupied. In order to keep the hospital as cool as possible in summer, Bighi is built with very high ceilings. I seemed to be in a large echoing hall with only a spot of light by my bedside, and I couldn't move.

My pride would not let me admit that I was afraid, but I held onto the Sister's hand and would not let her go. I said I could not sleep; I had not tried up to that time. But she looked at the surgeon, who prescribed something which she promptly gave me. I do not know what it was, but I went out like a match and slept all night. Silly to have been afraid of the night, but I was only nineteen and had had rather a trying afternoon so perhaps I can be excused.

Not only did I sleep all night but well on into the next morning. Nobody woke me up. I eventually came to to find a tray of breakfast on a trolley beside my bed which had obviously been there for some time and now looked quite unappetising. With a struggle I managed to find my bell. When the steward arrived, I asked for fresh breakfast and someone to feed me as I couldn't move. This produced consternation, breakfast was long over, and no more food would be available before dinner at noon. Being a Naval hospital, Bighi was manned by sick berth attendants, but at that period of the war many were very young and only semi-trained. The night steward had allowed me to sleep on but had not turned over to his relief that I had not been washed or fed. The one whose job it was to look after me merely stood there dithering. Then the surgeon arrived very bright and cheerful to see how I had slept. Very pleased to hear that I had slept so well. Remarked that my breakfast looked pretty beastly but did nothing about getting any more.

Fortunately, at that moment Sister arrived and in a quiet but firm and incisive voice got the machinery of the hospital working again. I had a bit of a wash and a sort of small davit was rigged at the head of my bed with a short length of chain and a hand grip on the end. With the aid of this, I was able to pull myself up a little on my pillows and no longer felt quite so helpless. Further I was able, more or less by myself, to eat whatever it was that the Sister got for my breakfast.

Fortified by my breakfast my pride began to return. I was very dissatisfied with my one garment, which was one of those awkward affairs with no opening down the front. You pushed your arms into two sleeves and then the garment was done up with tapes at the back. The one I had been given was very short and of a rough sort of flannel which was uncomfortable to lie on. I felt that it was not in accordance with the dignity of the First Lieutenant of the *Asphodel* to appear in such a garment, and that it was not in accordance with good manners for an English gentleman to appear before a lady with a bare bottom. I wanted my own pyjamas. The Sister explained that a signal had been made to my ship asking them to send up some of my clothes but, she wanted to know, why was I in such a hurry for clothes? I must realise that I should have to stay in bed for a good many more days. I was too shy to explain but I think my blush gave me away. I was rather given to blushing at that age. She laughed at me and told me not to be silly. I think it was at that moment that I began to realise that she was not only a Sister but also a person.

My pride did not last long. A white enamelled trolley was wheeled in with all the equipment for dressing my wound. Sister unwound the yards and yards of bandage around my head and then started to soak off the actual dressing. She was infinitely tender about it, and went very slowly, while endeavouring to direct my attention with her conversation. But I was biting my pillow to stop myself from screaming while the tears poured down my face. I was a very small boy in very great pain and I was very sorry for myself. I don't know how long it took but it seemed hours and hours. And this went on every morning. I was in hospital over a month. I am not suggesting the dressing continued to be as painful throughout that time, but the first ten days or so were dreadful, and it wasn't much fun having my ear dressed almost up to the last day I was in hospital.

They used to wheel that beastly trolley into the ward as soon as I had had my breakfast, so that I had a quarter of an hour or so to contemplate my coming ordeal. I was the only officer in the Officers' Surgical Block at the time, so Sister was able to spend lots of time on me and she was certainly generous with her time and did all she could to ease the pain. She never let a

3/4/18

Dear Mrs Carne,

I am very sorry to have to write and tell you that your son was injured in a gun accident onboard and he is now in the RN Hospital, Bighi, Malta. I have just been to see him and found him very cheery and well and in very little pain.

I saw the fleet surgeon in charge of the ward, he says that the wound by the ear is getting on very well and the only anxiety now is as to whether or not the hearing of the right ear will be affected.

I am going up there again tomorrow and the next day and will let you know what the Doctor says then.

I sincerely hope he will be able to rejoin my ship in a few weeks as I would not for the world lose his services as he is so keen on his work and always most cheery.

The other Officers and men have asked me to tell you how sorry they all are that he has been hurt and that you are not able to be with him. Mrs Lyon, the wife of our Commodore, has been to see him and I am sure she will do anything for him, 'I am sorry to say we are going away shortly, but if there is anything I can do for you please let me know.

I hope to be able to give you fuller details when I write in a day or two.

Assuring you how sorry I am that the poor boy should have been hurt.
Yours sincerely
Stanhope, Lieut Co.

steward touch my wound and when she had a Sunday off and another Sister was temporarily in charge of her block, she still came in to dress my wound.

The window of my ward looked out towards Ricasoli fort and the Sister used to be subjected to a good deal of teasing from the surgeon, because he said she spent so much time in my ward pretending to look after me, but really looking towards the fort in the hopes of seeing a certain officer in whom she was supposed to be taking an interest. The surgeon did not get much of a rise out of Sister who was a very reserved person. I rather suspected that the surgeon would have liked to take an interest in Sister himself if he had received any encouragement, but he didn't get any. Her attitude, at least in the ward, was always very strictly correct.

After my wound had been dressed that first day, I was completely flaked out and unable to take any interest in anything. I had no visitors; I don't think Sister allowed anyone in. I vaguely remember that Jessop, the able seaman who looked after my cabin and clothes, arrived with a suitcase. He and Sister stowed the things away in a chest of drawers and, for a moment, Jessop leant over me and said something. I suppose he hoped that I would get well soon. But I couldn't take an interest. I was past caring for anything, even that I now had a pair of pyjamas to wear.

The following day Sister told me that there were two sailors in the hospital who had been injured at the same time as myself, one of whom had been hurt in the right arm and his forearm had been amputated. She also told me that three men had been killed but she did not know their names. That evening my Captain came to see me, and I was allowed to talk to him for ten minutes. He told me that the Commander-in-Chief had ordered an enquiry and that the board had had their first meeting that day. In due course they would want to see me, but the hospital authorities had stated that the board would have to come and see me in hospital, and that I should not be fit for such an interview for several days. He told me that the board were already more or less certain of the cause of the accident. Owing to a defect in the lock, the jar on closing the breech had allowed the spring to drive the firing pin forward so striking the tube and, as it was a percussion tube, it had fired immediately, long before the breech block had started to revolve and so lock itself in the gun. The resulting explosion had driven the breech block out of the gun in one direction while the projectile had gone out of the muzzle of the gun for a distance of two or three hundred yards. In fact, the Captain and navigator with their glasses to their eyes to observe the fall of shot of the first round heard what they thought was the second round and were astonished to see a splash only two or three hundred yards from the ship. It was then they looked over the bridge screen and saw the shambles on the fo'c'sle.

The Captain explained that he had immediately altered course to return to harbour at the same time making a signal to the Castille, the signal station overlooking Grand harbour, asking for immediate medical assistance. Seeing a vacant buoy in Bighi Bay he had secured the ship to it. While doing so he saw a dghaisa going towards Valletta from the hospital with one of the senior medical officers, what in those days was known as a deputy surgeon general. The Captain hailed him and, somewhat unceremoniously, hauled him onboard up the ship's side. It was this officer whose remark that he could do no more for me had somewhat cast down my spirits. Of course, what he meant was that he could do nothing more for me at that moment i.e. until I got to hospital. But that hadn't been very clear to me.

The Captain went on to say that the ship would be sailing as soon as the gun was repaired with the next east bound convoy. A temporary relief was being appointed in my place, but he had applied for me to return to the *Asphodel* as soon as I was once more fit for duty. He expected to return in about a month by which time the hospital authorities had told him that it was possible I might be ready to return to duty. Then Sister arrived and said that time was up so, telling me to get well quickly as he wanted me back in his ship, he departed.

I was very relieved to hear that it was planned that I should return to the *Asphodel*. In the last few months we had become a happy ship, and I didn't want to leave her and be appointed to another ship on the Mediterranean station and have to start all over again. Also, I felt much happier as I felt less isolated and lost. Waking up in hospital amongst strange faces I had felt lost; now that I knew someone was taking an interest in my future, I felt much comforted, though the prospect of a month in hospital seemed rather daunting.

From then on, I was allowed visitors and until the ship sailed some five or six days later, one of the officers came to see me each day and I gradually learnt the details of the accident. When the gun exploded, the brass shield which Carroll had polished and looked after so assiduously was driven into his side and he died without recovering consciousness. The breech block had hit Adams the breech worker and one of the best able seamen in the ship, killing him immediately. The brass cartridge case had been driven out of the breech of the gun like a projectile and had hit the armourer in the stomach. The poor devil didn't die for about twenty minutes.

Of the two injured men, Copeman had his right hand and wrist lacerated and they had had to amputate it about halfway between the wrist and elbow. He came to see me in my ward two or three times before he was sent home in a hospital ship. He recovered very quickly and became mobile long before I did. He was always cheerful walking about the hospital and talking about his stump, of which he seemed to be rather proud. The other injured man, Clark, had only superficial cuts and bruises and recovered very rapidly.

I was informed that I had been found half over the side. Apparently, I had not only been hit on the head by a fragment, but also the blast had blown me off the low platform on which the gun was mounted and I should have gone over the side, in which case I should almost certainly have been drowned; but I came up against a large boom, a foot in diameter, which stowed alongside the port side of the fo'c'sle. This boom, which we used as a lower boom, had originally been supplied for use in conjunction with a form of bow defence gear for protection against mines when mine sweeping, hence its massive strength. It saved me from going over the side, but as I arrived up against it, with considerable vigour, it dealt me several interesting bruises about my back and bottom.

The actual gun was hardly damaged at all. The explosion had occurred before any of the breech threads had engaged with the threads on the breech block. The breech block had been blown out of the gun like a projectile, shearing the hinge pin. All the dockyard had to do was to fit a new breech block, which they did in the course of two or three days.

Having got the breech to a condition which they thought was satisfactory, they allowed the ship to go to sea on service, without having given the gun its ultimate trial i.e. firing it. In fact it was not done until I had rejoined the ship when, upon finding that the gun had not been fired since the accident, I insisted to the Captain that we should do so at once, as I realised that half the ship's company were nervous of the gun and feared another accident.

It meant of course that I had to stand alongside the gun while it was being fired, and I must admit that in the minute or two before we fired the first round, I had a horrid sinking feeling in my tummy. But all was well, and when we had finished everybody said of course they knew the gun was perfectly all right and let's find a submarine and show what we could do with that gun when we tried. In other words, confidence was regained.

A day or so later, the Commodore commanding patrols came to see me with his wife. Actually, he was a retired rear admiral, called back for the war with the rank of commodore while carrying out this appointment. I was still very deaf in my right ear, and with my left ear submerged in bandages I found it very difficult to hear him. Not that it mattered much as he went on talking whether I replied or not. His wife was a very pleasant lady obviously well experienced in the ways of the Service. She got from me the address of my mother, to whom she promised to write and for which, in due course, my Mother was very grateful.

A day or so later the Captain came to see me again to tell me that the hospital had agreed to the Board of Enquiry coming to see me on the following day. He was rather worried as to what report the board would make, as the fact that I had made a bracket for the percussion firing rod and secured it to the breech block had come to light. The captain was afraid that the board might apportion some of the blame for the accident to the existence of this bracket, which was not approved by any Admiralty order. I explained to him that when I had first fitted the bracket during the refit in Malta, I had shown it to the staff commander, who had thought it was a good idea. This information relieved my Captain's mind quite a lot, and he emphasised to me the necessity to bring out this information should the question be raised by the board of enquiry.

The Board arrived the next day, looked at rather suspiciously by Sister, who wondered if I was really fit enough to answer their questions. But she need not have worried. The president was the captain of another sloop, a very old retired lieutenant commander who I had met two or three times before, as his first lieutenant was another sub lieutenant of the same term as myself. He was a charming old gentleman who spent most of the board's time while with me, in commiserating on my accident. They asked what I knew of the accident, but as I was unconscious from the moment of the explosion, I was not able to tell them very much. One of the board started to ask me a question about the bracket, but the president chipped in and said that as they had already decided that the bracket could not possibly have caused the accident, there was no necessity to follow up the question of the bracket any further. So nothing about the bracket appeared in the final report, and my name was quite clear.

A few days later the *Asphodel* sailed with a convoy with the prospect of being away for three weeks or a month, and visitors became few and far between. However, the hospital had a large supply of jig-saw puzzles which occupied a lot of my time. In the evenings I used to inveigle Sister into helping me with them. By this time, I could more or less sit up in bed if well supported with pillows. As Sister had seen the puzzles completed many times before and knew what the completed pictures looked like, she was much better at finding the right pieces and used to laugh at my efforts to fit, almost literally, a square peg into a round hole.

I soon began to lose my awe of Sister and to like her more and more. My only previous experience of Sisters had been the formidable ladies who were in charge, very much in charge, of the sick bays at the Naval Colleges at Osborne and Dartmouth. These starched monuments of feminine respectability were not persons with whom boys could make friends. I don't wish to appear ungrateful; I am sure they carried out their duties very well, but it must be admitted that they were more awe-inspiring than lovable. One took the horrid medicines they dispensed and endeavoured to look grateful, while trying to pour half the obnoxious mixture down the sink when they were not looking. The colleges were rather plum jobs for Sisters who were reaching retiring age, and they were, therefore, generally speaking appreciably older than most of the officers and for this reason rather outside the life of the college.

It was therefore not altogether surprising that my first attitude to Sister was one of rather frightened awe, and that I was all the more pleased when I found that I had made a mistake and that Sister had a delightful personality, a pleasant sense of humour, and was dedicated to her chosen profession of nursing. Compared with my previous experience of Naval Sisters, she seemed to be very young, not more than ten years older than I and probably less, with appreciable claims to good looks. Her youthfulness was explained by the fact that she was not a regular Naval Sister but belonged to the Reserve. She was a New Zealand girl who, having been trained in nursing, felt that she must put her skill to good use and came to England. On seeing an advertisement for nurses to join Queen Alexandra's Royal Naval Nursing Service Reserve she had promptly volunteered – primarily, she admitted, because she thought the uniform was the smartest of the various nursing services, and it was true that she looked very well in her uniform.

As soon as I heard that she came from New Zealand I told her that I had served in HMS *New Zealand*, and the information seemed to forge a link between us. When I repeated to her the words of the 'Haka' she really thought I was someone worth knowing. Ever since, whenever I have met anyone who claims to have come from New Zealand, I have taken an interest in them because without exception I have found that they are pleasant people. Notably, a transport company in the Western Desert in the Second War, all New Zealanders, all with the same Scottish name, all from the same village in New Zealand and all good chaps. I suppose there are a few unpleasant people somewhere in New Zealand, but I hope I shall never meet one as I don't want one of my pet illusions to be dissipated; namely, that all New Zealanders are first-class chaps.

In due course I was allowed up, and convalescence followed its usual slow progress. There were no other officers in the surgical wing and very few in the medical side, none of approximately my own age. I was lonely, but I have never found the company of my fellows essential to my happiness so, though I was a little bored, I was content to let the days drift past. The hospital had a pleasant terrace overlooking Grand Harbour which I usually had to myself. At least no other human beings came to worry me, but if I sat very still the lizards would come out and look at me. We were allowed a small quantity of rather inferior chocolate; this was 1918 and rationing was very strict; not quite as strict as in the United Kingdom, but things like chocolate were luxuries. I soon found that lizards like chocolate. I would put a little bit a foot outside the hole of a very good-looking lizard and then sit absolutely still. After a time, he would come to the mouth of his hole, look at the chocolate for a long time, and then when he was sure that all was safe, he would make a sudden dart, grab the chocolate, and be back in his hole like a flash.

Then I would put out another piece of chocolate, two feet from his hole, and so on until I got him to come ten or twelve feet out of his hole and close to me. Then came the real test to see if I could get him to feed from my hand. I would sit quite still on a garden seat reading a book with a little smear of chocolate on one of my fingers with my hand open on the seat beside me.

Presently I would feel his tongue as he began to lick the chocolate. Without moving my head at all I would allow my eye to turn and look at him. Instantly he would know that I was looking at him and he would freeze. We would stare at one another at a range of two or three feet until he had regained confidence once more to go on licking.

I can't remember how long it took me to train my lizard friend to feed off my finger; I hoped to get him to sit on my hand, but before that happened the *Asphodel* returned to Malta.

The *Asphodel* had been away for a full month. When she returned, she went to buoys in Sliema harbour to boiler clean so we knew she would be in harbour for at least six days. The first day she was in harbour I was allowed out of hospital to visit the ship. My head was still wrapped in yards of bandage and I could only wear a cap by balancing it on top of my head. It was a calm, warm, sunny spring day so I was able to take a two-man dghaisa and go all the way by sea. If one had plenty of time, and I had lots, this was a very pleasant way of going to Sliema, but it had to be a calm day for the trip round St. Elmo point from Grand Harbour to Sliema Harbour.

Everybody seemed to be very pleased to see me when I got onboard. There were many questions about my health, and when I was returning to the ship, but most of their questions worked around to enquiries about Sister, who apparently had made a great impression on every single one of the Asphodels who had been to see me in hospital.

They were all convinced that I must have fallen in love with her. I was astonished. Much as I liked Sister and was more than grateful to her for all that she had done for me, there had never been a suggestion of a sentimental exchange between us. The Captain said that I must play fair and not keep the only pretty English girl in Malta to myself. There were of course very few English women on the island at that time. I replied that Sister wasn't English, she came from New Zealand. All the more reason that she should be entertained, was the substance of the Captain's reply. He would give a small dinner-party; he knew one or two women in the Admiral's Office that had travelled out to Malta with him. He would ask a couple of them and I would bring Sister. I was still very much under the hospital discipline and had to be back by 7pm, while I knew that Sister was on duty most evenings. So, I had to reply that I did not think that suggestion would work. He compromised on a tea party onboard in three or four days' time. I hoped by then I should have got rid of my bandages.

Returning to the hospital that evening I shyly proffered my invitation which, to my considerable delight, was accepted with pleasure. Apparently social engagements for Sisters in Malta at that time were few and far between. I then suggested that for this party I might get rid of some of my bandages. Sister seemed to think that was reasonable and promised to get the surgeon to look at my head and ear the next day. She was as good as her word and next day the surgeon was persuaded to allow me to appear with nothing but a neat plaster patch over my ear. The hair had started to grow where my head had been shaved and now without the bandage, I was able to get the Maltese barber, who came to the hospital several days a week, to cut the rest of my hair and generally make me look a little less untidy.

On the day of the tea party, I had hoped to take Sister round to Sliema in the *Asphodel's* motorboat, as she had never made the trip from one harbour to the other by sea. But there was quite a breeze blowing, and enough sea to stop all boat traffic between the two harbours. So, we had to cross to Valletta by dghaise, go up in the Baracca lift and walk down the other side, where the *Asphodel's* motorboat was waiting to take us off to the ship. The boat's crew expressed themselves pleased to see me, but I think they were much more interested in Sister.

I think the tea party went off all right, although the Captain's friends had not much in common with Sister. I, as usual in company with strange women, I had never seen the Captain's friends before, was overcome by shyness. After tea, as the *Asphodel* was strictly limited for the entertainment of ladies, we all went ashore to the ladies' room at the Union Club. After a round or two of drinks, Sister and I had to make our way back to the hospital. I think she enjoyed her afternoon; she had never been to the Club before and was astonished at the building. She did not realise it had been one of the 'auberges' of the Knights of St. John, as the headquarters of each nationality of Knights was called. I was able to tell her something of their organisation and to point out that the signal station high up over Valletta was called the Castille because it was situated on the roof of the auberge of Castille, one of the largest and richest groups of Knights.

Thus ended the one occasion when Sister and I met, other than strictly professional meetings in the hospital, as a few days later I was discharged fit for duty and returned to my ship. By then *Asphodel* had finished her boiler cleaning and we sailed the next day, and hardly returned to Malta at all until in September I left the ship from Bizerta to return to England.

I never saw her again and completely lost touch. My fault. I should have made some effort to see her. But on the few occasions that we returned to Malta, I was much too shy to go to the Sisters' quarters in the hospital and face the cold eye of the matron while I enquired for her. So, I did nothing, and have regretted it ever since. Not that I suppose I ever crossed Sister's mind again.

I was a patient, discharged, cured, a good job well done, and finished with, now let's get on with the next. But I have always had a horrid little niggle at the back of my mind that I ought to have done something more to show my gratitude for all that she had done for me. I was grateful, very, very grateful, but I couldn't show it.

CERTIFICATE FOR WOUNDS AND HURTS,

These are to Certify the Right Honourable the Lords Commissioners of the Admiralty that

(Name in full)   (Rank or Rating)   (Official or Regimental N°)

belonging to His Majesty's Ship ....

being then actually upon His Majesty's Service in ....

Here describe the particular duty

"Injured" or "Wounded".

Date

was* .... on .... by

Here describe minutely the nature of the injury sustained and the manner in which it occurred:— as required by Articles 1207 1318 and 1354 of the King's Regulations

the .... following injuries:—

lacerated wound over right mastoid region, lobe and lower part of pinna of right ear blown off — Slight contusion of right arm.

* "Sober" or "not sober"

He was* .... at the time.

Personal Description

Age about ... years. Born at or near Falmouth   Height 5 ft 10 ins

Hair dark brown Eyes brown   Complexion fresh

Particular marks or scars

Date 1915

Signature of Commanding Officer of Ship or of Coast Guard or Marine Division

Rank Commander ....

Signature of Person who witnessed the accident

Rank Lieut Comdr. R.N.

Signature of Medical Officer

Rank ....

NOTE — The grant of a Hurt Certificate to a Petty Officer or Man is to be noted on his Service Certificate.

CHAPTER 7
CONVOY OPERATIONS

Back once more in the *Asphodel*, I soon settled down to the routine of the ship. We were kept very busy. The convoy organisation had at last got into its swing which meant that every available escort craft was kept fully occupied. We went from one end of the Mediterranean to the other with occasional diversion to Bizerta and Suda Bay, both of which were becoming important convoy ports.

But despite our efforts, we did very little to prevent the submarines from enjoying their fun and games throughout the length of the Mediterranean. A barrage had been established across the mouth of the Adriatic, but the sea passage was too wide and deep for the barrage to be effective and the submarines went backwards and forwards from the Austrian ports at the head of the Adriatic more or less as they pleased. At the eastern end they could go in and out of the Dardanelles, and seek succour and relief in Turkey, but something had been done with a number of minefields to make this passage rather more hazardous.

We had two other ships torpedoed. The first not far from Malta, slightly to the south and west of the island. The ship was torpedoed late in the evening just as the last of the light was fading. The senior officer of the escort ordered *Asphodel* to stand by her. We made several circles around her but saw nothing. We then closed the ship, by now darkness had fallen and as it was an overcast night it was not easy to see what was happening. The ship appeared to be slightly down by the bows but otherwise normal. There was no sign of the crew wishing to abandon ship.

Eventually the Captain of the torpedoed ship made a signal reporting that he had been torpedoed well forward, he did not think there was any danger of the ship sinking but he was uncertain whether he would be able to steam.

Our Captain then ordered me to prepare to take the ship in tow. Very fortunately I had exercised this manoeuvre that very afternoon. We were provided with an eleven-inch manila hawser for towing purposes, which was stowed right forward under the stokers mess-deck in the mining store.

Getting up this hawser and flaking it down so that it would run clear on the congested deck of a sloop was not a very straightforward business on a dark night with the ship completely darkened. However, thanks to the fact that we had so recently exercised doing just this thing, everybody knew what to do and I was able very shortly to report to the Captain that we were ready to take the torpedoed ship in tow. However, our efforts were not necessary as, very shortly after, the ship reported that she was going slow ahead and we started to lead her towards Malta. At that time two swept channels into Malta were being maintained; one from the southeast leading into the anchorage of Marsa Scirocco and the other from the Grand Harbour along the north coast of Malta and then through the strait between the islands of Malta and Gozo, known as the Comino channel. It was through this latter channel that we approached Malta.

I don't think we made good more than about five knots during the night, but we had not far to go and, as dawn was breaking, we were entering the Comino channel. When we were about halfway through the channel the torpedoed ship stopped and reported that she was anchored. We were rather nonplussed as to why she should anchor in this exposed position, as obviously she must enter harbour if she was to be repaired.

The explanation came shortly afterwards. She had been torpedoed right forward so that the bight of one of her anchor cables had dropped through the bottom of the ship and as she came into shallow water this bight had caught up on a rock on the bottom and brought the ship to a stop. Fortunately, they were able to decide which cable had dropped through the bottom of the ship, unshackle it from its anchor and also get at the slip securing the inboard end of the cable. By letting go this slip, the whole cable dropped out of the ship and so freed her at the expense of losing the cable. By noon we had the satisfaction of seeing her safely berthed in Grand Harbour.

The other torpedoed ship with which we had dealings was sunk before we ever saw her. I can't remember all the details; she did not belong to one of our convoys. When torpedoed she was on her own, I think she had dropped astern from another convoy passing some twenty miles or more clear of our track. When torpedoed she got off a W/T signal reporting her position and that she was in danger of sinking. We were ordered to leave our convoy and go to her assistance.

I think we had about twenty-five or thirty miles to go. Cameron made our engines revolve faster than I think they had ever turned before but we had been sometime out of dock and I doubt if we exceeded sixteen knots. It was a lovely day of high summer, a calm sea and a gentle breeze astern of us, which made the smoke from our two round funnels rise nearly vertically in the air disclosing our position over a considerable distance in the near maximum visibility.

We were at action stations eagerly searching the horizon for the torpedoed ship which, if she was in the position she had reported, should by now be appearing over the horizon. It was not until we were within seven or eight miles of the reported position that we made out three dots on the horizon. Two were easily distinguished as boats, but what was the third one which was moving relative to the others? It was not long before she turned broadside on to us and it was possible to see quite clearly the outline of the conning tower of a submarine.

We were now closing her rapidly and when the estimated range was down to the maximum range of our ancient 4.7-inch guns, which was just over eight thousand yards, I asked permission to open fire. But the Captain refused to grant permission. He was hoping that our approach had not been noticed and that he would be able to get within a range at which we should have a reasonable chance of scoring a hit before the submarine became aware of our approach. This was the period of the war when German submarines, having sunk an unescorted merchant ship, were making a practice of coming to the surface, interrogating the survivors in their boats, and taking the Captain of the torpedoed vessel prisoner.

Our Captain hoped that the submarine would be so busy with the survivors that we would get into effective range before the submarine captain woke up to his danger. The assumption that the submarine had surfaced to interrogate the survivors was correct, but she was also keeping a very good lookout and had seen us almost as soon as we came over the horizon. The turn she had made which had brought her conning tower broadside on to us was the submarine getting into her diving course and she disappeared when we were still a good three miles away.

We were then left with that awkward situation in which one has survivors in boats waiting to be picked up, and a submerged submarine in the immediate vicinity waiting to take a pot shot at the rescuing ship if she stops. As it was a nice fine day with a calm sea, the Captain decided that the survivors could well remain in their boats for an hour or two longer so he proceeded to steam around the area at high speed frequently altering course in the hope that the submarine, if she had remained in the vicinity, would show her periscope and give us a chance to attack her. While doing so we passed more than once through the wreckage left when the torpedoed ship sank. There was a good deal of it, as the force of the explosion had blown the covers off at least one of her cargo hatches with the result that a quantity of her cargo had floated out of the hatch when she sank. Most of the cargo at the top of the hold had been cases of tea, which naturally floated very well. This fact had been realised by some of the more intelligent rats on board, who had each secured for themselves a temporary sanctuary on a case of tea and were distinctly observed from the *Asphodel* as we passed. I need hardly add that we did not stop to rescue them.

The Captain's dilemma was solved an hour or two later by the arrival of a trawler, who had been detailed from another convoy in response to the torpedoed ship's call for help. She picked up the survivors while the *Asphodel* steamed round her to keep the submarine's head down.

This was the only occasion in either war that I saw an enemy submarine on the surface. I was very disappointed that I had not been allowed to open fire on this one. The chances that we might have obtained a hit were microscopic, but I think the effect on our sailors could not have been anything but good. We had been steaming apparently endlessly up and down the Mediterranean, and not unnaturally they were becoming bored and losing interest. If the next time they went ashore they could tell their friends that at least they had opened fire on a submarine, I feel it would have done quite a lot to buck up their morale.

I had seen very little of Barton ever since August of the previous year, when *Asphodel's* base was changed to Malta. His ship, the *Nigella*, continued to be based on Alexandria and was usually at sea whenever we called there. But in the summer of 1918, we escorted a convoy into Alexandria and by good fortune *Nigella* was in harbour and did not sail until late the next day, so Barton and I took the opportunity of dining out together and of bringing one another up to date with our news. The fact that we had both been patched up after receiving damage in Bighi hospital seemed to forge another link between us.

Inevitably, our conversation turned towards the future. We both felt that we had been long enough in the Mediterranean; being first lieutenant of a sloop was very good experience, but we had now had nearly eighteen months of this experience. We felt it was nearly time we went home and had a little leave and got back to the Grand Fleet again. It was all very well to play about in sloops, but we reckoned we had learnt all there was to learn and if we were to get on in our chosen profession, we must get back to home waters and be ready to take part in the final great naval battle to destroy the German fleet, which we still both believed must occur before the war could be brought to a successful conclusion.

It was clear from the lists of appointments that it was the Admiralty's policy to promote the sub-lieutenants who had come to sea at the outbreak of war direct from Dartmouth to acting lieutenant, without waiting for them to do courses, which continued to be in abeyance during the war. The senior term who had gone to sea at the outbreak of war had already been promoted. As it appeared that terms were to be promoted at intervals of two months, we calculated we should be acting lieutenants in January 1919. I think we both had our eyes on the Grand Fleet destroyers. New ships were being turned out at a rapid rate. If we could get appointed to one of them, then after a few months' experience as a sub-lieutenant of a new destroyer, our promotion to lieutenant and with our previous experience as first lieutenant of a sloop, we might well hope for an appointment as first lieutenant of a destroyer. So, with hopes that when we each were appointed to a new destroyer, we should find ourselves in the same flotilla again, we parted.

In this period of the war, even the most optimistic forecasts did not predict that the war would come to an end before the middle of 1919. On the western front we seemed to be only just holding our own; this was before the battle of early August 1918. But even after these battles, I don't think anyone appreciated how close we were to the end. All that spring and early summer we had seen the troop convoys conveying troops back to France from the Palestine front, so we can hardly be blamed for not foreseeing Allenby's victorious advance which knocked Turkey out of the war. We naturally presumed that no further advance would be attempted until once more the additional troops could be spared from France.

While the forecasts of Barton and myself as regards the duration of the war were very much adrift, our anticipation of the Admiralty's policy regarding the employment of ourselves was reasonably accurate and the appointment of our reliefs was published shortly afterwards. We were in Malta when my relief arrived onboard and we expected to be there for another couple of days. I started to turn over to him and to think in terms of getting my gear packed up when the Captain, who had been ashore to the Admiral's office, arrived onboard about noon and, as he came over the side asked me if I could be ready to leave in three quarters of an hour.

Three quarters of an hour didn't give me much time to pack my gear, but with the chance of going home I was prepared to be ready in ten minutes if necessary. Assuring him I would be ready, I ran off shouting for my cabin-hand to come and help me pack. The Captain then realised that I had misunderstood him, and that what he really meant was could the ship be ready for sea in three quarters of an hour, as we were urgently required to take the place of an escort who had just reported that she was unable to go to sea owing to an engine-room defect.

Somewhat disappointed to find that my moment of release had not yet arrived, I busied myself getting the ship ready for sea. The hands had already gone to dinner. I gave them another five minutes to finish what they were eating and then turned them to getting the awnings furled, boats and accommodation ladder hoisted and all the other chores which had to be done to make the ship ready for sea. We were able to get underway so quickly as we still had steam in one boiler. We had arrived in Malta the previous evening and had secured in the dockyard to coal and collect some stores, but had instructions to shift berth to buoys in Sliema that afternoon. Cameron therefore had steam in one boiler and, by the time we had collected the convoy and steamed slowly down the swept channel with them, he had raised steam in the other boiler.

We were to take that Convoy to Bizerta, wait there two or three days and then sail again with another convoy to Alexandria. It looked as though I was going to spend a lot of time wandering up and down the Mediterranean instead of going home to my much looked forward to foreign service leave. I persuaded the Captain to make a few enquiries on my behalf in Bizerta, which much to my surprise proved to be quite fruitful. There was a French transport due to sail the following evening for Marseilles, on which accommodation had already been booked for two junior Naval officers from the Admiral's office at Malta. These two officers had, unknown to us, been passengers in one of the ships we had just escorted from Malta. The French were quite willing to provide accommodation for an extra officer so, provided with an authority to travel by the Senior British Naval Officer in Bizerta, which I hoped would provide me with a ticket from Marseilles to London, I set out the following evening.

There was still one more evening to spend onboard, but the Captain decided that my relief should look after the ship on his own while the remainder of the officers headed by the Captain carried me off to the local hotel, where we had a very good dinner. Although France was in extremities and bled white at this time, the French could still provide a meal far better in quality and cooking than anything it was possible to get in Malta.

The next afternoon I sailed from Bizerta in the French transport. As we left harbour, we passed the *Asphodel* alongside one of the wharfs close to the town. She looked small and insignificant, battered and weary. She had done a bit of steaming and despite my efforts whenever we were in harbour to get the ship's side red leaded and painted, it must be admitted that she was showing a great number of rust streaks. The funnels were caked with salt and the mainmast was black from the smoke from the funnels. But I was a bit proud of her because I knew that within her limits, she was now an efficient ship. I had learnt a lot in her and much as I wanted to go home, I was sorry to leave her.

On board the French transport I found that there were three other Englishmen. The two young secretaries from the Admiral's office who I have already mentioned and an older gentleman who, at that time, was an official of the Sudan government. He was a very cosmopolitan gentleman, with a very charming manner to whom we three younger Englishmen instinctively deferred. He had the gift of getting, in a quiet manner, exactly what he wanted. The French transport was in a pretty depressed condition, she had been running all the war and was short of everything. The gentleman from the Sudan government had a word with the chief waiter, and a table was reserved for the four Englishmen for the rest of the voyage. If we didn't feed very well, at least I suspect that we fed better than anyone else onboard.

It was a most depressing voyage. The ship was full of French soldiers who had been wounded earlier in the war and sent to North Africa to recuperate. Now, once more reasonably fit, they were being bustled back into the front line. They nearly all had either a wife or a girlfriend with them. They walked about hand in hand or sat about on the upper deck on those garden seats which were so typical of French ships of that date, with their arms around one another's waists and seemed to spend all day caressing one another. We were very shocked. We had been brought up to believe that no gentleman caressed a woman in public, certainly not an officer in uniform who of course would not even think of walking hand in hand with a woman.

With the thought of so soon parting from their wives, a parting which might well be for ever, the French were very melancholy and looked askance at us when we laughed and did our best to enjoy being passengers in a ship for once. The gloom was further increased by the fact that they had made no arrangements to darken the ship at night. All they did was to switch off all the electric light so that the interior of the ship was completely black as soon as the sun had set. In this state of blackness, most of the French refused to be caught between decks, should the ship be torpedoed, so they slept in their clothes and great discomfort on the upper deck. I had to share a cabin with a French army officer, but I had the cabin entirely to myself between the hours of sunset and sunrise.

Fortunately, the voyage was of short duration and early on the second morning we arrived in Marseilles in time to get our heavy luggage conveyed to the station to catch an early train to Paris. Despite the chaotic conditions at the station, where it appeared that half the women in Marseilles wished to travel to Paris and were being seen off by the other half, we all four managed to get into the same compartment. We had seen our heavy luggage placed in a van and locked up and we were assured that the van would not be unlocked again until the train arrived in Paris.

Four out of every five French women seemed to be in mourning and, of course, in those days the French did not go into mourning by halves. Such porters as were available should long ago have been relegated to an armchair in the sun. We found an ancient porter with snow white hair and beard who, jockeyed along by the gentleman from the Sudan Government, promised to deal with our luggage. But when he saw our large packing cases, (we were travelling with everything we possessed), he threw his arms in the air and declared it was impossible for him to lift such cases. But we were young and active so, under his directions, we labelled the luggage and stowed it away in the right van. Incidentally, we stowed the luggage of a good many French women at the same time. And then our porter put us into a compartment near the dining car, told us a long story about how his son had been killed at Verdun, shook us all by the hand and wished us 'Bon voyage'. In the end we were off to Paris almost on time.

The train was timed to arrive in Paris sometime that evening, but early in the day it was clear that the overloaded train was losing time and then, during the afternoon, the connecting passage by which one passes from one coach to another gave way; a French soldier fell through, but was caught by one leg and battered until he was unrecognisable before the train could be stopped. The man was quite dead long before he could be freed. Nobody knew what to do with his corpse. The guard went off to find a telephone and came upon a new training camp for American soldiers who, on being asked for assistance, produced a first aid detail with a stretcher who came and took the corpse away. Somewhat sobered by this tragedy, the train proceeded at an even slower speed and it was after midnight when we crept into Paris. It was immediately made clear that under no circumstances was anybody going to do anything about luggage that night. The luggage van was locked and it was going to remain locked until the next morning. The next problem was therefore to find some lodging for the night. The gentleman from the Sudan government was in the habit of staying at a small hotel in the Rue St. Honore, where he was well known. He had written in advance saying that he would be passing through Paris, but had not been able to give a definite date. He thought, however, that they would be able to squeeze him in, and suggested that for a start we should all go there and try our luck. We lugged our suitcases down to the metro, where mine came open and spilled most of its contents on the platform, and then staggered through the streets of a darkened Paris to this small hotel.

When we arrived at the hotel, the gentleman from the Sudan government was welcomed by the proprietor who, however, threw up his arms at the idea of providing four beds. The hotel was full but he might manage a small attic room, quite unsuitable for such a distinguished gentleman as a member of the Sudan government, or a camp bed in a bathroom. But he did some quick telephoning and found another hotel with a room with a double bed to which the two secretaries retired. We were just discussing which of us should have the attic and which the camp bed in the bathroom when along came a tall gentleman with a long grey beard to get his room key. Hearing our discussion, he turned to me and in an American voice said that he had a twin-bedded room, and if I was short of a bed he would be honoured to share his room with a British naval officer.

I immediately accepted his offer and we went to turn in. I was tired after our long journey and wanted to get to sleep but my companion insisted that we made ourselves known to one another. He explained that he was a representative of the American Red Cross, in Paris to arrange facilities for convalescent American wounded, but he had only been in the city a week and was still feeling rather lost. I had difficulty in convincing him that I had been at sea for over four years; he had put me down as aged about eighteen and probably some sort of cadet. As I had taken part in two naval battles and been first lieutenant of a sloop for the last eighteen months, I did not feel very flattered, though at that time I had to admit that I still had a very immature face. He wanted me to tell him my life story, but when he saw how tired I was he relented, on condition that we had a long talk the next day.

I slept very well that night and did not wake up until after my American friend had got up, dressed and gone about his day's work. When I went downstairs, I found that there had been an air-raid during the night, the papers were full of pictures of damaged houses, but I had not heard a sound. Most of that day we spent in getting our heavy luggage across Paris and collecting the necessary tickets for an early start the next morning. Then we all had a good dinner together at a restaurant recommended by our friend from the Sudan government, and subsequently went on, following the tradition of all good Englishmen of that date, to the promenade of the Folie Bergère.

At that time the principal decoration of the promenade was an over life size bronze statue of a woman depicted leaning forward slightly as though to observe or address the main body of the theatre. This being the promenade of the Folie Bergère, she was naturally in the nude. The gentleman from the Sudan government did his best to persuade me to climb up on the pedestal on which she was mounted in order to stroke her bottom. Although I had had a good dinner, I did not feel in the mood to make a fool of myself to that extent. After all, if one is going to stroke a bottom, why choose a bronze one?

Returning to the hotel I found my American friend very indignant, because he had slept all through the air raid of the previous night. How was he going to explain to the folks at home that he had been in a raid and didn't know anything about it? Why hadn't I woken him up? I explained that I had slept equally soundly, but if we had another raid that night, and I woke up, I would certainly call him. So slightly mollified we went off to bed, as I had to make an early start in the morning.

The next day we made the journey to London without incident and quite early in the day we were reporting at the Admiralty. The smoothness of the journey and the efficiency of the Channel passage reflected the improved conditions of the war. But I don't think we realised this. London, with its strict food rationing and shortage of taxis, certainly appeared to be a city still in the throes of a desperate war.

At the Admiralty I was told to go on leave; I should probably get about a month's leave and orders for my next appointment would be sent to me. I took my luggage to Paddington to catch the next train to Cornwall, which was a slow night train. As I had several hours to wait, I went to the West End for dinner, which was foolish as it came in to rain hard. I hung about trying to get a taxi which appeared to be impossible. Eventually, feeling that I must catch that train, I walked to an underground station and got very wet as I had no raincoat. I had, therefore, to sit all night in a very crowded, slow train in my damp clothes and, coming home from the Mediterranean, I not unnaturally caught a chill, and had to spend the first few days of my leave in bed.

CHAPTER 8
HMS *TACTICIAN* – 1918

That leave passed without incident. It was a period of great stringency. There was little food and the rationing system was only moderately successful, not nearly as good as that developed in the Second War. Clothes were in short supply and of poor quality. I had worn out most of my clothes in the eighteen months I had been in the *Asphodel* and was in urgent need of a new outfit. So, towards the end of my month's leave, my Mother and I decided to go to London to do some shopping, stopping on the way at Bath where we had some relatives and my two elder sisters were at school.

Before, however, we could get away for this expedition I was appointed to the *Vernon*, the torpedo school, at Portsmouth to do a short torpedo control course. Largely as a result of the failure of the destroyers to make effective use of their torpedoes at Jutland, the torpedo control arrangements of all the Grand Fleet destroyers had been modified, and all sub-lieutenants appointed to them were first given a short course in these modified torpedo control arrangements.

I have little recollection of this course, except that living conditions were very uncomfortable. There was no room for us in the *Vernon* so we were accommodated in a hulk that had once been an armoured cruiser berthed alongside the dockyard wall. The hulk had been very hastily converted during the war to fulfil a crying need for accommodation and was inadequate in both heating and washing facilities. We had to go backwards and forwards to the *Vernon* in a boat in weather that was both wet and cold and I always seemed to be hungry. However, when at the end of the course I was again sent on leave, I left the *Vernon* with the determination that one day I would return to qualify as a Torpedo Officer.

While on leave, my Mother and I decided that we had better start our expedition as soon as possible as it was obvious that it would not be long before I received another appointment. Hotel accommodation was very difficult; we could only get rooms for two nights in Bath. In London we had to stay at a very second-class hotel which was crowded and very inefficient.

The dining room was staffed by an inadequate number of inefficient girls, supervised by a young head waiter. I suppose he was physically unfit and had so missed the call up. But he knew nothing about waiting or organising the girls and hid his lack of knowledge beneath a manner which was alternatively rude and impertinent. Up to this time I had never seen girl waitresses in a London hotel, and thought they were a very poor substitute for the old-fashioned waiter. Girls had been taking the place more and more of men while I had been abroad. My Father had been reduced to employing a land girl in his garden, as no male gardener was to be obtained. As far as I could make out, she did nothing except eat the fruit before it was ripe.

Eventually my orders arrived, forwarded on to me from my home. They arrived at breakfast time and I had to report at the Admiralty that forenoon. My Mother came with me and sat on a seat in the Mall while I went in to hear my fate. The NA2SL, (which is navalese for Naval Assistant to the Second Sea Lord) who is the officer under the Second Sea Lord, who is responsible for the appointments of junior officers was, in fact, the officer who had been lieutenant of my term when I first went to Osborne. As I entered his large and crowded office, he greeted me with a shout of, 'Here comes a tiger!'. He always called the members of his term tigers and proceeded to slap me on the back with some vigour. He was a physical training specialist, and apt to be extremely hearty and vigorous. I hoped I looked tigerish, but in fact I was feeling rather small and nervous. The Admiralty was such a large and echoing building filled with hundreds of people all in a great hurry, none having time to stop and help a poor sub-lieutenant find his way.

The first question I was asked was had I had the 'flu. I knew Spanish 'Flu was raging, though I did not at that time realise how bad it was in the north. I was told to look after myself and not to catch it. I was to go to a brand-new destroyer, the *Tactician*, one of the new 'S' class of destroyers which were just coming forward. She was completing at Beardmore's Yard on the Clyde, and I should have to travel north that night, as she was due to commission the next day. With many good wishes for the future and the necessary railway warrants to get me to the Clyde, I left the Admiralty to re-join my Mother.

I had been looking forward to my next appointment but now that the moment of parting had come, I didn't want to go. We had already done some shopping but there were still a few more things my Mother thought I ought to have, so that afternoon we searched the shops for them and then went back to the hotel to add them to my luggage. Then we had to get through the three or four hours before it was time for me to go and catch my train. I shall always remember the uncomfortable, overcrowded, rather cold lounge of that depressing hotel full of soldiers at the end of their leave, about to go back to the front, together with their relatives perhaps for the last time.

Those few hours have always seemed to me to be the nadir of the First War. Curious that with the end so near the nation did not realise that its ordeal was nearly over. In the Second World War, we were gradually getting the upper hand throughout the whole of 1943 and 1944, so that one could forecast with fair certainty that the end would come in 1945; and, of course, once the Rhine had been crossed and the Russians were advancing from the east, only a pessimist could doubt that the end was in sight. But early October 1918 was a very different outlook. We seemed to have been completely stagnant since 1915, and anyone who forecast the end of the war before the end of the year was looked upon as being a silly nuisance. Anyway, as far as the Navy was concerned whatever the Army managed to do in France, we still had to win that naval battle in which the German fleet would be destroyed and that was not going to be any fun.

The next morning did nothing to cheer my spirits. Glasgow was cold with a gentle drizzle. I got to Beardmore's yard about eleven in the forenoon to find the *Tactician* looking very small, lying alongside the wall with her upper deck piled with packing cases and gear. On the wall was the final draft of the ship's company, looking cold and miserable in the charge of the coxswain, who himself had only just arrived. There was no officer in sight. I went onboard and eventually dug out the Gunner (T) who turned out to have only just been promoted from the lower deck and was very much at sea in his new responsibilities. He told me that both the first lieutenant and the engineer officer were in hospital with 'flu and not likely to return for some time – that we had a temporary engineer officer but no first lieutenant and that I should have to do the job. He further explained that the Captain and engineer officer had been doing a final inspection of the engine-room department with the inspecting Engineer Captain, and had gone up to the offices of the company to sign the necessary papers. I asked what was being done about the draft of sailors on the dock wall, at which he burst out that he didn't know, this was a something something of a ship, no organisation, nobody knew anything, and the Captain merely cursed anybody who asked him any questions. He would have gone on at some length about the Captain had I not shut him up pretty quick.

I came to the conclusion that someone had made a mistake in promoting the Gunner, and that he was pretty poor officer material. Looking back, I think my judgment was hasty. He was completely inexperienced as an officer, and thrown into an impossible position with a sick, neurotic captain. Later, under a good captain and a firm first lieutenant, he started to shape up as a useful officer.

HMS Tactician

In the meantime, I thought I ought to do something and the obvious thing seemed to be to get the sailors onboard and established and organised as a ship's company. I went up onto the dock wall and to my relief found that the coxswain was an experienced destroyer coxswain and had already done a lot towards getting the hands told off to their messes and in picking out men with some experience for special duties. The advance party had fortunately got the galley going and there was some sort of a dinner nearly ready for eating. We got the hands onboard with their gear, and soon after noon we had them stowed away in their messes with something to eat, which they wanted as they had been travelling all night.

Coming aft from making certain that the ship's company had at least got their dinner all right, I met the Captain returning on board. He didn't offer to shake hands. He wanted to know why I had not joined before. I explained that I had only been appointed at noon the day before, and I had come by the fastest possible train. This information was received without comment. He then went on to say that the First Lieutenant, who had served with him before on the same Grand Fleet destroyer, was sick in hospital with 'flu and I must take over as First Lieutenant. He went on to say that his First Lieutenant knew how he liked the ship organised, and he wished me to organise on the same lines, without giving me any idea what these lines might be. He then said he was going ashore to lunch and would not be back until late in the evening. The ship was due to go to sea at 7am the next morning for final trials, and I must have her ready for sea by then. He then turned to go down to his cabin and half tripped over a packing case of stores. Turning to me, he said with a snarl, 'For Christ's sake get the ship squared off!' and disappeared down the hatch.

Thinking that I should have quite a lot to do during the next twelve hours, I made my way down to the wardroom where I met our temporary engineer officer, with a glass of gin in his hand. In the next ten minutes, he told me how clever he had been to get four cases of gin for the ship (Plymouth gin was in very short supply at that time), how he intended to drink as much of it as possible during the time he was acting as locum for our pukka engineer officer, how he had been engineer officer of one of the block ships at Zeebrugge and had been given a D.S.C. for his share in that operation, how he had been celebrating the fact ever since and, as his proper appointment was to a ship being built on the Clyde which would not complete for another six months, he was anxious to get back to her as soon as possible in order that he could go on leave. In the meantime, the sooner he got out of the *Tactician* in which he had no interest, the better.

During our hurried lunch he gave me much advice on how I should carry out my duties as first lieutenant. Amongst these duties he suggested that I should employ the seamen on several duties which I thought were strictly the province of the engine-room department. I had had experience of engineer officers who tried to bounce me before so, as my informant had partaken of several gins in addition to the odd nip he had been given by the Company when he and the Captain signed the various papers during the forenoon, I listened, I hope politely, and said nothing.

During the afternoon I got the hands to work stowing away the gear on the upper deck and generally clearing up. Then the coxswain and I raided the first lieutenant's cabin for his draft of the watch bill. We couldn't find anything referring to the *Tactician* but there was a copy of the watch bill of his previous ship which showed that he had organised in three cruising watches which was the normal organisation for a three-gun ship. So, the coxswain and I got busy and made out a watch bill for the *Tactician* in three watches. Then we collected the hands together and told them off into their watches and gave them their special duties. I explained to them that we were going to sea for an acceptance trial at 7am the next morning and everything must be working by then. I and the senior upper deck petty officer went around the ship trying to think of everything that was required to be done Fortunately, he was a fairly experienced destroyer petty officer, though rather a gloomy disgruntled type. He was very good at telling me what was wrong, less active at getting things put right.

I was determined not to go to sea without a workable sea-boat. The whaler had been hoisted some weeks before and then used as a bin, into which stores for which the stowage was not yet ready had been dumped. When we had cleared the boat and mustered its proper gear, we tried to turn it out only to find that weeks of rainy weather and Clyde filth had seized up the equipment. It took half an hour's struggle to get the boat turned out, and then I found she had no boat rope and one had to be improvised. However, by 5pm when the yard packed up for the night and we got rid of the last of the dockyard men, at least the upper deck of the *Tactician* began to look a little more ship-shape.

I then remembered that while I was doing duty as first lieutenant, my primary duty as sub-lieutenant was to look after the navigational equipment. I went up to the chart house to find that all the charts, books etc. were still in their packing cases. Collecting one of the quartermasters off watch, we proceeded to unpack them and muster what we had received. This was not too easy as I could not find any supply notes, and nobody onboard seemed to have heard of them. Some days later I found them at the bottom of one of the drawers in the Captain's desk where he had stowed them away for safekeeping and forgotten all about them.

We were going to sea at 7am the next morning for the acceptance trial. The ship would still be the responsibility of the yard who would send a pilot who no doubt would have a chart, quite apart from the fact that he would know the whole of the Clyde better than he knew the back of his own hand. All the same I thought I should look pretty stupid if I had to admit to the Captain that we hadn't a ship's chart available and the moment the acceptance trial was completed, it seemed possible that we might be sent almost anywhere. It was therefore essential to get the charts unpacked and stowed away. It sounds a fairly simple job, but a destroyer's outfit contains quite a number of folios and of course none of the charts were marked off with their consecutive numbers so, having got the folios in their drawers, it still was not easy to pick out the right chart. Then I came upon the Notices to Mariners and realised that none of our new charts had been corrected for some time. But amongst the Notices to Mariners were none of the confidential series which were normally printed in red and which gave the position of the various net defences, where the gate vessels were situated and the signals indicating when the gates were open etc. I searched through every packing case and folio, backwards and forwards, but I could find no sign of these important documents.

While I was still wondering what I should do, I was interrupted by the coxswain who came to report 'Rounds' at 9pm. I went around all the mess decks, the ship's company seemed to have made themselves fairly comfortable after their own fashion, but it was clear that the messdecks were very small for the number of men who had to be accommodated. With the hammocks slung it was hardly possible to move. After rounds I had a few words with the coxswain who was a reasonably cheerful, optimistic sort of chap. He thought the ship's company were very young and inexperienced, but that they were a keen lot and that given a few weeks to settle down, they would be all right. Then what we wanted, he added, was a short brush with an enemy destroyer and the ship's company would get their tails up and be first class. I gathered that he had been in destroyers in the Harwich Force all the war, and thought it was a pity that the *Tactician* was not going to join up with that force.

About 10pm the Captain returned onboard. He complained of a headache and certainly looked unwell. I told him what I had done and about the missing confidential Notices to Mariners. He didn't seem much impressed by my efforts, but directed that I send a telegram to the Hydrographic Department first thing in the morning asking for a duplicate set of Notices to Mariners. He then went to bed and I felt free to see what sort of a fist the cabin hand had made of unpacking my gear and getting my cabin ship-shape. I did not think much of his efforts, but I was too tired to worry that night; I just rolled into my bunk and was immediately asleep. I had had little sleep in the train the night before and it had been a long day.

The next morning, we left the yard on time and made our slow way down the river to the Tail of the Bank, which is the anchorage off Greenock where the river Clyde debouches into the Firth of Clyde. Here we remained for an hour or more while we did a quick swing for compasses and embarked the inspecting staff, who would decide as a result of the trial we were about to carry out, whether the ship was ready for acceptance for service.

Anchored at the Tail of the Bank was the new cruiser *Hawkins*, still doing trials before joining the fleet. I was speaking about her to one of the inspecting staff who happened to mention that her captain was Captain Grace, who had come as commander of the *New Zealand* a few months before I left to join the *Asphodel*.

As soon as we had satisfied ourselves that the compasses were correct, we proceeded out of harbour. We were a bit optimistic about our compasses as in point of fact they subsequently gave us some trouble before they settled down. We were steaming quite fast by the time we reached the Cambraes, and then worked up to full power which we maintained for two hours. It was a fine bright day with a moderate westerly breeze which produced enough sea to cause the *Tactician* to wash down quite heartily while we were at full power, so that we got rid of a lot of the Glasgow grime. We had no trouble in getting the designed power from our engines and the inspecting staff declared themselves satisfied with the ship so that comparatively early in the afternoon we were back at the Tail of the Bank. I, of course, had to act as cable officer as there was no one else to do the duty. It was the first time that I had had anything to do with a destroyer's fo'c'sle, which is fitted with a very different type of equipment from the merchant service type of winch fitted in the *Asphodel*.

After anchoring we had one more trial to carry out, which was a test of the depth charge throwers with which the ship had been fitted but which had not previously been fired. We fired a dummy from each on the end of a line so that we could recover the dummy. The throwers were one of the Gunner's responsibilities, but he had not realised that in rainy weather the barrel of the thrower could collect a lot of water. When we fired the first thrower this water was thrown well up into the air and came down on the inspecting officers in the form of dirty rain. Neither they nor the Captain were pleased. The subsequent signing of a receipt for the ship by the Captain took place in the wardroom with very little of that joviality which is customary on these occasions.

All day the Captain had been on the bridge wrapped up in all the clothes he could find. I had been sent for at intervals during the day and asked why I had not done this, that or the other. I must admit that I had forgotten a great many things. I had never served in a destroyer before, which is a very much more sophisticated ship than a sloop. It would have helped a little if the Captain had given me a few suggestions as to what things required doing first. In all new ships there are number-less things to be done and, as the *Tactician* had had no first lieutenant for over a week, the list of things to be done had got out of hand. But that was not his way.

When we anchored, I had lowered the motorboat to land the inspecting team, but the stoker had never run the engine before and took half an hour to get it started. I could not get the accommodation ladder out until we had carried out the trial of the depth charge throwers. When we tried to get it out, none of the nuts and bolts seemed to fit. Then, when a shore boat came for the inspecting party, the jumping ladder which had been stowed away the night before could not be found. These maddening little things will happen in any organisation before it has settled down and everyone knows their particular duty.

All these little irritations were too much for my Captain's never very easy temper, and by now he was feeling very unwell and looking it. When he had cursed everybody in turn, driven the Gunner to hide himself in one of his storerooms and reduced the quartermaster on watch to a quivering jelly, he announced that he was not feeling well and was going to bed and that I must look after the ship. I suggested sending for the medical officer of the guard. I had noticed the medical guard pendant flying in the *Hawkins*. My suggestion was greeted with a snarl of rage; he 'didn't want any damn doctors'.

That evening was a gloomy one. The engineer officer was high with too much gin and would not stop talking about himself; the Gunman retired to his cabin and sulked, the wind got up and the barometer dropped. About 9pm I got worried about the weather, and thought we ought to set an anchor watch. I crept into the Captain's cabin but he had taken some dope and was right out looking pretty ghastly. I veered a little cable, I thought we had anchored at an unnecessarily short stay and set an anchor watch. The quartermaster of the first watch seemed to be moderately intelligent, so I gave him a couple of bearings to watch and told him to give me a shout if he observed any alteration while I got busy in the chart house, in an endeavour to produce some order out of the charts etc. But I was unnecessarily nervous as around midnight the wind eased and I felt I could go to bed with a clear conscience. But I left the quartermaster on the bridge, with instructions to keep his eye on those bearings and to call me at once if they altered.

Early the next morning the steward reported to me that he had taken a cup of tea into the Captain but he had only muttered incoherently and the steward further gave it as his opinion that the Captain was seriously ill. I went into his cabin and tried to talk to him. He was muttering to himself, but I could not make out what he said. I asked if I should send for the medical officer of the guard. He muttered something which might have been 'Do what you damn well please'. He was looking ghastly and was obviously very ill. I made up my mind I must get him into hospital and I must get some help; with no captain and no first lieutenant, the *Tactician* was clearly out of action.

I made a personal signal to the captain of the *Hawkins* hoping that my name would ring a bell, as having been a midshipman in the *New Zealand*. As far as I can remember I said: 'From Sub-Lieutenant Carne. My Captain was taken ill last night but refused to see medical officer of guard. This morning he is incoherent and appears to be seriously ill. Request medical officer of guard. First Lieutenant has been in hospital a week and is not likely to return in near future'.

The *Hawkins* reacted immediately. Her boat arrived alongside complete with her surgeon commander and a sick berth petty officer. I took them down to the Captain's cabin, but it didn't take them more than two minutes to decide that they must get the Captain to hospital immediately, so we made signals for a hospital boat and for an ambulance to meet the boat when it got inshore.

The Surgeon Commander wanted to know what the Captain had doped himself with during the night, but I was unable to help. He had not sent for the coxswain, who had the few medical stores which we carried, so he must have had something of his own in his cabin.

Within half an hour the Captain was out of the ship on his way to hospital. As he left with his patient the Surgeon Commander said that he would report direct to Captain Grace when he got back to the *Hawkins*, and in due course Captain Grace made the necessary signals to the various authorities reporting the condition in the *Tactician*, and saying that a relief captain and first lieutenant were required urgently. Further, he wrote me a friendly note saying that if I wanted any further assistance, I was to let him know; but he also warned me that he was due to go to sea for further trials in the course of the next day or so.

It must be admitted that as soon as the Captain had left the ship, the various tensions which had bedevilled her began to subside. In the three days which elapsed before the relief captain and first lieutenant arrived the ship began to settle down and to look and feel more like a destroyer. It was a busy period for me as I tried to carry out the duties of captain, first lieutenant and sub-lieutenant. I was worried by the amount of correspondence which came addressed to the commanding officer. A great deal of it was more or less formal stuff that could be stood over for a week or two, but I was inexperienced and did not know what I could ignore and what required action. The Gunner was even more ignorant than I, and anyway was frightened out of his life by the sight of a piece of paper. I don't think the Engineer could have helped but anyway ever since I had made it clear that I was not going to be bounced, he had made it equally clear that he was not going, as he expressed it, to do my job for me.

The papers that caused me most worry were the confidential books. In order to avoid mustering and returning his books when he left his Grand

Fleet destroyer, the Captain had brought his outfit with him, leaving the new captain of his previous ship to draw a complete new set of books. It may be asked why he did not elect to draw a new set of books for the *Tactician*. But in those days the Grand Fleet memos, i.e. the Grand Fleet Battle orders, manoeuvring orders, destroyer attack orders etc., were being corrected almost daily as new ships joined the Grand Fleet and others left. The orders were a mass of little corrections, frequently only a sentence or two on a slip of paper, but each with a confidential book number, and each had to be accounted for, mustered quarterly and a certificate of destruction forwarded when superseded. The Captain knew his way around his own books but to me they were an incomprehensible jumble. Twice during those three days at Greenock we received a signal to send an officer for confidential books. That meant me of course, the Gunner knew nothing about books and the Engineer was always too busy. But I couldn't do anything about the papers I drew which, in fact, were bundles of corrections to memos of whose existence I had little knowledge. The best I could do was to lock them in the safe and hope that in due course someone would be able to make head or tail of them.

I was busy by day and disturbed at night by the autumnal gales. I was not sure how firmly the *Tactician* would lie to her anchor. I was very conscious of her high fo'c'sle and was afraid that the strain on the cable when she veered across the wind would be too much for the anchor. So, when it blew hard, I let go an anchor underfoot which meant weighing it again when the tide turned, for which I required steam on the capstan. The engineer officer was a bit querulous about lighting up to provide steam each night, but when the new captain arrived, I could assure him that the ship had not dragged at all although one night the wind blew really hard.

The temporary captain was a senior commander much experienced in destroyers. He and his first lieutenant had been standing by a destroyer leader shortly completing a long refit. They arrived late one evening and as they stepped over the side, they seemed to breathe a breath of confidence and energy into the ship. Almost at once, one felt that at last the *Tactician* was a going concern and a ship to be proud of. We had dinner soon after he arrived onboard, at which he obviously summed us all up in turn. After dinner he sent for me in his cabin and I had to answer a number of very searching questions. He seemed to be satisfied with my answers, and added that he thought I had had a difficult time with a sick captain and no first lieutenant and that I had not done too badly.

Now I could turn over much of my worries to the new first lieutenant and get down to getting my charts up-to-date.

I then had a short session with the new first lieutenant and ran through the watch bill which I had made out. He seemed to think this was a reasonable organisation and when the coxswain reported 'Rounds' at 9pm, we carried them out together and I explained how I had organised the various messes. Although he had had considerable service in destroyers, this was the first time he had been onboard an 'S' class, which at that time were very new. He was a little astonished to see how crowded the messdecks were, and some of his remarks about the design of them were hardly polite.

The Captain went ashore immediately after breakfast the next day to report to the Senior Naval Officer and came back with the information that we should probably be ordered to sail the next day to escort a 'K' class submarine to Scapa. He then called me into his cabin and we went through the piles of letters and papers which had accumulated. Most of these he merely glanced at and put to one side for the proper captain when he returned, explaining that most of them would answer themselves if we let them lie doggo for a month or two. Then he unlocked the confidential book safe, sent for the petty officer telegraphist and gave him such code books as would be necessary for our passage to Scapa, and then hurriedly locked up the safe again saying that we would muster the books and try to get a hang of them when we had more time to spare. Then, calling the First Lieutenant, we all three went round the ship poking our noses into every hole and corner. I already thought I had been round the ship pretty thoroughly during the previous three days, but our new captain seemed to be able to find points of interest which had never struck me. He liked the high fo'c'sle and thought the bridge and gun and torpedo control positions were good, but he was a bit critical of most of the rest of the ship. This was 1918, and there was a grave shortage of almost all materials so that every effort had been made in the design to save material. The ships themselves were a material economy over the previous 'V' and 'W' classes, and further economies had been made by substituting galvanised steel for brass. The lack of the usual brass fittings gave the ship a dowdy appearance compared with the usual run of British destroyer, and the first lieutenant was complaining that he didn't think he could ever make the ship look really smart.

On his way the Captain spoke to every man we met, reminisced with the coxswain over destroyer life before the war, pulled the Chief Engine room artificer's leg, tasted the ship's company dinner in the galley, sat down in every mess, complained that most of them had not got room for his legs (he was a big man), and generally made touch with almost every man in the ship's company.

We had still not received our copy of the confidential notices to mariners. On the Captain's instructions I sent a further telegram to the Hydrographic Department but, in the meantime, it was essential that we should have the necessary information for entering Scapa and Rosyth. So that afternoon when the Captain went onboard the submarine to discuss our passage to Scapa, I went with him taking my charts of Scapa and Rosyth with me and persuaded the navigator of the submarine to let me take the relevant information directly off his chart. In passing, I might mention that we did not get our copy of the confidential notices to mariners until we arrived in Rosyth over a week later. It is true that they came with a polite note of apology from the Hydrographic Department, but I did not think that compensated for the anxiety and extra work their failure to arrive with the outfit of charts had given me.

We sailed the next morning in company with the submarine. I had the forenoon watch during which we were doing a zig-zag ahead of the submarine. All the afternoon we steamed north under the protection of the islands. When I came on watch again for the first watch i.e. at 8pm, we were entering the Minches and beginning to feel the sea which was being whipped up by a strong nor'west wind. We had stopped zig-zagging while navigating among the islands and the ships were now in line ahead with the *Tactician* leading. We made our way safely up the Minches until, in the early hours of the morning Cape Wrath light was switched on for an hour to allow us to fix our position before altering course to the eastward for Scapa.

When we arrived at Scapa Flow we were ordered to secure to buoys in Long Hope, the destroyer anchorage. I was surprised to see how few ships were present in the Flow and my first reaction was that the Grand Fleet was at sea either for an operation or an exercise. I had not realised that since I had left the battle cruisers, the whole of the Grand Fleet had been concentrated in the Forth. The only ships at Scapa were those carrying out their quarterly exercise periods. We had been sailed from the Clyde to join the 14th Flotilla but they were all in the Forth and nobody seemed to know what to do with us. Obviously, we were no use with the fleet until we had worked up, should we do this at Scapa or in the Forth?

In the meantime, we were secured in Long Hope, which is not an agreeable anchorage at the best of times – it was usually known by the sailors as Lost Hope; at the end of October, beginning of November it was definitely dreary. Having commissioned in a hurry, mostly with officers who were only in the ship temporarily, no action had been taken to order any mess papers or magazines. In fact, we seemed to be devoid of reading material. However, the coxswain unpacked a parcel of 'comforts' which had been issued to the ship on commissioning which comprised, besides the usual supply of mufflers and sea boot stockings, a few games. There were no takers on the lower deck for a set of chess men, so these were sent along to the wardroom and were soon in full use. As it turned out, the Captain was a bit of an expert. He was the sort of chap who could play two games at the same time without looking at either board. It is true that he had not played for some time and was a bit out of practice, but he was still much too good for the remainder of us. He used to take us on in turn handicapping himself by giving us a castle or a rook to start with. But he always seemed to win.

Eventually it was decided that we should work up in the Forth, so we sailed for Rosyth arriving there the next morning. The Forth was a remarkable sight with the whole of the Grand Fleet concentrated in it. When I had been there before in the *New Zealand*, all ships had been moored above the bridge, but by now the anti-submarine defences had been extended for many miles below the bridge and all this area was full of great ships. Above the bridge not only was the centre of the Forth full of ships, but all along the south shore interminable trots of buoys for destroyers extended away into the distance.

Our working up period started almost at once but for several days we remained at our buoy while various gunners' mates came onboard to drill the guns' crews and control parties. Soon after we arrived, our proper engineer officer re-joined from sick leave after being discharged from hospital. He had been away for well over a month, which made it fairly clear that neither the Captain nor the First Lieutenant would return for a week or two yet. Our temporary engineer officer left us, having made a big inroad into our supply of gin. Our temporary captain and our proper engineer officer had been flotilla mates in the Mediterranean early in the war, and had much the same idea how a destroyer should be run. The wardroom began to settle down into a more contented mess.

But we were soon to have another change round. Our temporary Captain's ship was due to complete very shortly at a southern port and he was anxious that both he and his first lieutenant should be on hand during the few days preceding commissioning. After the mess he had seen in the *Tactician*, due to so many of the experienced officers being absent during the critical few days before commissioning, one can appreciate his anxiety to be on hand to superintend the many details which require attention when a ship commissions. He pressed that both he and his first lieutenant might be relieved of their temporary duties in the *Tactician*. The Admiralty acceded to his request to the extent of relieving him with another senior commander whose destroyer was refitting but they were unable to provide a relief for the First Lieutenant.

The new temporary captain had served in Grand Fleet destroyers since the outbreak of war and was very experienced. He had been a divisional leader for the last year or more. His proper ship, which was now refitting, was one of the Admiralty 'V' class destroyers, the class immediately preceding the 'S' class to which the *Tactician* belonged. The 'V' class were considerably bigger and more powerfully armed than the 'S' class and had considerably improved accommodation particularly for the officers. The new captain had a very pleasant personality and we all liked him, but he didn't think much of the *Tactician*, and could hardly be expected to take much interest in her.

We pressed on with our work up as there was a general feeling throughout the fleet that the great naval battle to end the war must take place very shortly. It was now clear that the Germans were being heavily pressed on the western front. Turkey had surrendered and the Bulgarians were fairly clearly on the point of asking for an armistice. Surely the German fleet would make one last big effort to break the blockade and swing the war once more in her direction? To reinforce the Grand Fleet, additional destroyers had joined from the Dover command and from Harwich. The Forth was stiff with ships all itching to be at the enemy.

We had been exercising for two days below the bridge and had not received any newspapers. The wireless bulletins of those days were very brief, they recorded advances for the army in Flanders and on the Salonika front but there was no suggestion of a general collapse of the enemy. We returned to our buoys well above the bridge late in the evening and made no attempt to get a paper that night. The next morning came the extraordinary signal that the enemy were asking for an armistice. The first reaction in the *Tactician* was that this was some trick to keep us in harbour while the enemy fleet slipped out and before we knew where we were, the whole Atlantic would be full of cruisers gobbling up our convoys. But hardly had these ideas formed themselves in our minds than we received the signal that an armistice was being signed at 11am that day, the 11th of November.

What did it mean? What was an armistice? Did we just stop fighting while the enemy kept his fleet intact ready to have a go at us at a later date? It was not until later in the day that some of the terms of the armistice came through and we realised that the enemy was prepared to surrender the major portion of his fleet. Was this a great triumph or a very poor anti-climax? Had we struggled for over four years for the enemy to just scuttle away into a corner? It took time to sum up the new situation. In the meantime, a palpable feeling of doubt and uncertainty lay over the fleet. It was not until after dark that some of the wilder spirits took charge in some ships, starting by blowing the sirens, then letting off rockets and Very lights and flicking searchlight beams all around the horizon.

This Mafeking spirit did not penetrate to the wardroom of the *Tactician*, where our feelings were summed up by the Captain, who said that if we had sunk the German fleet he would be the first man up on the bridge to blow the siren, but as it was he thought the whole thing was a damp squib. However, the sailors were more easily aroused, and the Gunner who was officer of the day spent the evening chasing chaps who were doing most dangerous things with fireworks. One little game was to let off signal rockets in their hands at an almost horizontal angle directed at the nearest destroyer. Perhaps they thought that if they couldn't sink a German they might as well have a British instead. Fortunately, the Gunner caught up with them before anyone had burnt themselves severely.

In the next few days the feeling of anti-climax increased. News was received that our proper captain was out of hospital on sick leave and would be returning in the course of the next few days. Our second temporary captain immediately obtained permission to return to his own ship, turning over the *Tactician* to the temporary first lieutenant during the interregnum.

Our Captain returned a day or two later and while no doubt his spell in hospital had improved his health, it had done nothing to improve his temper. Everything that anyone had done during his absence was wrong, which was a little discouraging.

Wednesday 6/11/18

Dear Mother,
Very many thanks for your letter. The postal service seems to have fallen off greatly lately as your letter took four days to get here while it only took two days when I was in the New Zealand. Yes, I got the washing alright, thanks. The only method of getting them washed here is primitive and irregular. Do you think you could manage to rake up that sort of basket arrangement we used to use before as I don't think brown paper is a very good protection for one's clothes. I am beginning to settle down in the ship but still have a tremendous amount of work to do. An RNVR sub turned up today who will take some of the work off my shoulders, I hope. He has never been to sea before so he won't be much use in the practical working of the ship, but I hope he will be able to do some of the paperwork. This sort of job is very different from the Asphodel. There the only thing we had to worry about were stray submarines but here we are on the top line for anything at the moment. We have been very lucky with the weather so far; our last trip was like a mill pond but this packet is like a cork and I am quite certain I shall have a pretty thin time as soon as the bad weather starts. I have not been ashore since I joined the ship and see no chance of doing so for some time to come as we are much too busy and always on the move. I don't think there is any more news.
With love
Willie

This letter was sent just five days before the armistice – and clearly there was no sign of peace at that time.

During the next few days there was no break in the routine; we went on just as though the war was continuing. *Tactician* went to sea under her proper captain and completed her work up. I don't know that we were very efficient at the end of it, but at least we had fired our guns and run our torpedoes and could be described as a running destroyer ready to carry out an operation

Then came a spate of orders. His Majesty King George V would review the fleet on the 20th and the following day the whole fleet would go to sea to meet that portion of the German fleet which was due to be surrendered. I read these latter orders with astonishment. I could not believe that the German officers who had fought with such skill and bravery at Jutland would not only agree to the surrender of their ships but would actually themselves sail the ships to be delivered up to ignominious surrender.

The review of the fleet passed without incident, the *Tactician* was a small destroyer tucked away in a corner and nobody took any interest in her. Early the next morning, the fleet sailed to meet the Germans.

The plan was, very roughly, that two long lines of British cruisers and destroyers would meet the Germans and escort them to an anchorage on the south of the Forth. Here the German ships would be boarded by inspecting officers who would ensure that the terms of the armistice, as regards having no ammunition onboard, had been carried out. In the meantime, the battle fleet would hold off ready to interfere if the Germans did not carry out their instructions. The 14th Flotilla to which *Tactician* belonged formed part of the southern line. We were instructed to be at action stations when the two fleets met but all guns and torpedo tubes were to be fore and aft and no hostile action was to be taken if the Germans carried out their instructions correctly.

The 21st November 1918, broke with a fine November day, a calm sea but with a certain amount of fog around the coast and generally the visibility was low. The German fleet was reported dead on time and shortly afterwards they hove in sight from the *Tactician*. They consisted of all their battle cruisers, ten of their most powerful battleships, a number of cruisers and some fifty destroyers. Alternative arrangements had been made for the surrender of their submarine fleet. As their battle cruisers came past, I could hardly believe my eyes. Those enormous ships that had looked so menacing at Jutland came wandering into the Forth like cattle being driven into a farmyard. We let them pass us and then formed up on the southern flank of their destroyers who were following the big ships and escorted them to the anchorage. Here we remained for the rest of the day, not seeing much as the visibility near the coast was only half a mile or less in the low-lying fog.

Shortly before sunset, the 14th Flotilla got underway to escort a section of the German destroyers to Scapa. The visibility cleared as we left the land and we got a good fix off May Island before the light failed. We arrived at Scapa during the next forenoon, delivered our charges and sailed again for Rosyth. Shortly after leaving Scapa, we received a signal to cease to take precautions against submarines and to render all depth charges safe and at sunset we switched on navigation lights and did not darken ship. This was the first time since I came to sea, that I had steamed with navigation lights and the ship all lit up and it felt very strange.

Once we arrived again in the Forth, we were given a billet in the 'pens' at Port Edgar, which was an artificial harbour built on the south side of the Forth. Since the outbreak of war this harbour had been fitted with a number of timber piers, alongside which destroyers could lie in much greater comfort than if at buoys and billets in the pens were therefore much sought after.

Here our proper first lieutenant rejoined and our temporary first lieutenant left to rejoin his ship. I was sorry to see him go as he was a very efficient officer, and during the three weeks or a month he had been onboard, the *Tactician* had been a comparatively happy ship. This satisfactory state of affairs did not continue. The Captain and First Lieutenant may have served together for some time but that didn't mean that they liked one another, although they were prepared to drink together and, the war being over, were both inclined to celebrate the fact at frequent intervals. They found that there were a lot of loose ends to be tied up and were inclined to blame the Gunner and myself for not having dealt with these matters in their absence.

I was considered very inefficient in that the wardroom stock of wines and spirits was both small and lacked variety. Our temporary engineer officer had made big inroads into our supply of gin, and my applications to various wine merchants in Edinburgh had produced very disappointing replies. They were all very short of both gin and whisky. They let us have two or three bottles and made vague promises about supplying more next month. I was reduced to going round any ship where I had a friend and trying to borrow an odd bottle or two.

But it was the inexperienced Gunner who became the chief butt of the Captain's irritation and, in addition, was always falling foul of the First Lieutenant. Poor chap, he was very inexperienced and rather incoherent and was unable to explain that he had a very inexperienced staff and couldn't be holding all their hands all the time. One morning shortly after we got into Port Edgar, we were having breakfast in the wardroom when there was a gentle pop just overhead. The Gunner left rather hurriedly and returned ten minutes later looking very red and embarrassed. After breakfast he had to explain to the Captain that when we had been ordered, while on passage from Scapa, to cease taking hostile action against submarines, he had hoisted the depth charges, in the throwers out of their carriers but had forgotten to remove the cartridges that actually fired the thrower. An inexperienced sailor told off to clean the thrower had accidentally fired it. There being no depth charge on the carrier, the carrier itself had been thrown some fifty feet into the air and had sailed across the pens to land on the torpedo tubes of another destroyer, denting them sufficiently to make it impossible to discharge a torpedo from them. The Captain had to go and explain to the Captain of the 14th Flotilla, our immediate commanding officer who was known as Captain (D) 14, what had happened. He had to arrange that the destroyer with the dented tubes, who did not belong to the 14th Flotilla, should go to Rosyth dockyard, have the dented tubes hoisted out and a spare set supplied in lieu. In fact, the *Tactican*'s name was mud and the Captain did not forget to rub this fact in to the unfortunate Gunner.

But it was not possible to be depressed for long. If we were not at peace, at least the major portion of the German fleet were safely stowed away in Scapa and the German people seemed to be keeping to the terms of the armistice. Surely, therefore, we should get a little Christmas leave – the rumours on this subject were innumerable. While looking a little further into the future, someone started the idea that it was essential to have a flotilla of destroyers in China, and that the newest 'S' class were destined for this station, while of course all the reservists were attempting to calculate the date on which they would be demobilised.

In the congested area of the pens with thirty or forty destroyers living cheek-by-jowl, rumours were born, grew to fantastic heights and evaporated faster than they could be counted. But one came to fruition; everyone was to have eight days leave, a portion of the fleet at a time. And, the Heavens be praised, the 14th Flotilla was selected as the destroyer flotilla to give leave over the first period, i.e. the Christmas. The leave was to be given in two watches, that is to say half the ship's company at a time. It was decided that as regards the officers, the Captain and I would go with the first watch which actually included Christmas Day and return on 27th December when the First Lieutenant and Gunner would go on leave.

That first leave after the war was a good leave but like all leaves, too short. I had to start back from Cornwall on Boxing Day. But I got back to find a great surprise awaiting me. Someone's imagination at the Admiralty had been working at very high pressure, and had come to the conclusion that the chaps who went to sea from Dartmouth before they had completed their education should be given the opportunity to make good some of that academic education that they had missed. I got back onboard the *Tactician* to find that I had been appointed to the President additional for Caius College, Cambridge. I could not think what it meant, but I soon found that every sub-lieutenant in the flotilla of roughly the same seniority as myself had received similar appointments. With our minds full of every sort of conjecture, we gathered together to discuss these extraordinary appointments.

Our appointments were dated the 15th January so, early in the month, I was relieved and returned to Cornwall for a few days more leave. But in fact, the appointments were premature; the colleges at Cambridge to which we were appointed had been used during the war as hospitals and could not be made available at such short notice. So, our appointments were re-dated to the 30th January, and I got another fortnight's leave.

I left the *Tactician* with no regrets; the only ship throughout all my seagoing service that I can look back on without any feelings of nostalgia. The commission had started under very unfortunate circumstances, and although I had liked and admired the two temporary captains, they had not been in the ship long enough to have any lasting effect. On the other hand, I had learnt a lot about how new ships should not be commissioned. Some forty odd years afterwards, when I was appointed Commodore Superintendent Contract Built Ships, I was able to put those lessons into effect. But that is another story.

A few days before we joined our colleges at Cambridge, Kipling wrote a poem about us which was published in the Daily Telegraph. I still have a cutting from the paper. It was called 'The Scholars', not perhaps one of his better poems. I have never seen it chosen for an anthology, which perhaps is natural for it is quite out of keeping with the spirit of the present age. Nevertheless, for those of us who had survived, that wizard of words brought back very vivid memories; some almost too vivid. He started his poem with the words,

> *"Oh, show me how a rose can shut and be a bud again!*
> *Nay, watch my Lords of the Admiralty, for they have the*
> *work in train"*

I am not sure that we liked being compared to rose buds; we were inclined to think ourselves rather as chaps, pretty tough chaps at that, who had seen the world and thought we were too old to be treated as children. But as he went on with his poem, he brought back so many memories that we felt staggered that a civilian, and to us an old man, should have appreciated and realised so many of the experiences we had been through. How did he know what it felt like to

> *"guard the six knot convoys flank";*

or how it felt to have one's hands, when one made one's way to the bridge,

> *"scored where the life-lines cut or the dripping funnel-stays as the*
> *ship poked her nose into a green one and the resulting wave swept*
> *aft, fierce and relentless, to sweep one's legs from under one"*

How did he know what it felt like

> *"When they coaled in the foul December dawn and sailed in the*
> *forenoon watch; or measured the weight of a Pentland tide and the*
> *wind off Ronaldshay"*

Few people have ever heard of Ronaldshay; it is a rather insignificant island. But when he had astonished us with his knowledge of our trade and experiences, he went on to address a plea to Cambridge in words I shall always remember.

> *"Hallowed River, most gracious Trees, Chapel beyond compare,*
> *Here be gentlemen tired of the seas – take them into your care"*

I should like to record that for one waif from Dartmouth, Cambridge did her stuff, full measure and overflowing.

ÆGRAPH. WEDNESDAY, JANUARY 29, 1919.

THE SCHOLARS.

By RUDYARD KIPLING.

" Some hundreds of the younger Naval Officers whose education was interrupted by the War are now to be sent to various Colleges at Cambridge to continue their studies. The experiment will be watched with great interest."—DAILY PAPERS.

" Oh, show me how a rose can shut and be a bud again !"
Nay, watch my Lords of the Admiralty, for they have the work in train.
They have taken the men that were careless lads at Dartmouth in 'Fourteen.
And entered them in the landward schools as though no war had been.
They have piped the children off all the seas from the Falklands to the Bight,
And quartered them on the Colleges to learn to read and write !

Their books were rain and sleet and fog—the dry gale and the snow.
Their teachers were the hornèd mines and the hump-backed Death below.
Their schools were walled by the walking mists and roofed by the waiting skies
When they conned their task in a new-sown field with the Moonlight Sacrifice.
They were not rated too young to teach, nor reckoned unfit to guide
When they formed their class on Helle's beach at the bows of the "River Clyde."
Their eyes are sunk by endless watch, their faces roughed by the spray,
Their feet are drawn by the wet sea-boots they changed not night or day
When they guarded the six-knot convoy's flank on the road to Norroway.
Their ears are stuffed with the week-long roar of the West-Atlantic gale
When the sloops were watching the Irish Shore from Galway to Kinsale.
Their hands are scored where the life-lines cut or the dripping funnel-stays
When they followed their leader at thirty knots between The Skaw and The Naze.
Their mouths are filled with the magic words they learned at the collier's hatch
When they coaled in the foul December dawns and sailed in the forenoon-watch;
Or measured the weight of a Pentland tide and the wind off Ronaldshay,
Till the target mastered the breathless tug and the hawser carried away.
They know the price to be paid for a fault—for a gauge-clock wrongly read,
Or a picket-boat to the gangway brought bows-on and full-ahead,
Or the drowsy second's lack of thought that costs a dozen dead.

They have touched a knowledge outreaching speech—as when the cutters were sent
To harvest the dreadful mile of beach after the "Vanguard" went.
They have learned great faith and little fear and a high heart in distress,
And how to suffer each sodden year of heaped-up weariness.
They have borne the bridle upon their lips and the yoke upon their neck
Since they went down to the sea in ships to save a world from wreck,
Since the chests were slung down the College stair at Dartmouth in 'Fourteen,
And now they are quit of the sea-affair as though no war had been.
Far have they steamed and much have they known, and most would they fain forget,
But now they are come to their joyous own with all the world in their debt.

Hallowed River, most gracious Trees, Chapel beyond compare,
Here be gentlemen tired of the seas—take them into your care.
Far have they come, much have they braved. Give them their hour of play,
While the hidden things their hands have saved work for them day by day.
Till the grateful Past their youth redeemed return them their youth once more,
And the Soul of the Child at last lets fall the unjust load that it bore.

Certificate of recognition to Sub-Lieutenant W.P. Carne from the people of Falmouth at the end of the 1914–1918 Great War

PART TWO
BETWEEN THE WARS

CHAPTER 9
1919-1936

My grandfather's account of the First World War (Part 1) was written by him as a stand-alone entity. Sadly, we have few records of his life in the immediate years after the war. We know that he qualified as a torpedo officer which, in those days, meant torpedoes, mines and all electrics, at the torpedo school in Portsmouth, HMS *Vernon* in 1923, the year in which he married Valentine Tweedy. She was the daughter of Arthur Clement Tweedy, the town clerk in Monmouth. However, the Tweedy family had strong Cornish connections and it is probable that they met in Falmouth – Valentine's Aunt lived in Wood Lane, close to William's parents in Garras.

He then served on the junior staff of the torpedo school at Devonport, HMS *Defiance* and as the Torpedo Officer of the light cruiser HMS *Xerces* in the Mediterranean Fleet.

Following this he was in charge of trials and experiments on controlling mines from a shore base by means of electric controls underwater. These were done in the Forth and he and Valentine lived at the time in North Berwick. He then went back to the Mediterranean as Torpedo Officer of the 15" gun battleship, HMS *Revenge* and subsequently as First Lieutenant and Torpedo Officer of the heavy cruiser HMS *London*, again in the Mediterranean and was promoted Commander from there in 1933.

William and Valentine had four sons born at this time. Richard 1927, Oliver 1929, Gyles 1931 and Rodney 1933.

He served as the Training Commander at HMS *Vernon* from 1933 to early 1936 and then as Commander and 2nd-in-Command of the cruiser HMS *Danae* (Chapter 10).

Some of the letters that he wrote to Valentine through 1936 and 1937 have survived although, sadly, none of hers have. The 1936 letters reflect the journey to Australia and the diplomatic role of the Navy in hosting parties and building contacts with local people in the various ports at which they stopped. They are generally in the form of a travelogue. The voyage stopped at Columbo (from where he visited Kandy), Christmas Island, Shark's Bay,

Lieutenant William Carne and Valentine Tweedy on their wedding day,
May 23rd 1923

Freemantle, Adelaide, the Great Australian Bight, Melbourne, Brisbane and
Darwin.

In these letters, which seem rather self-centred, life on board was routine,
while time in port was spent on golf, a lot of tennis and seemingly endless
cocktail parties and dances. William was very good at sports in general, a
point made repeatedly in his Naval record which highlights his running,
shooting, golf, rugby and, particularly, tennis prowess. He did not comment
on the political situation in Europe – or really on any matter outside his
immediate experience. One exception is in his letter of 17th December 1936,
which ends with;

"The abdication of the King has cast a considerable gloom over both the Captain and myself. We feel that it is a very considerable disaster. But nobody else seems to worry very much, at least they don't talk about it. I fancy the Australians dislike it very much, but they didn't talk. The don't talk about anything that they don't like. When we first arrived, everybody talked cricket. But when England won the first test, they all shut up like oysters".

My own father told me that he saw very little of my grandfather while he was growing up, and I don't think they ever had the opportunity to form a strong bond. William's appointments took him away from the country and he only managed a few weeks leave occasionally. My remarkable grandmother naturally developed a strong-willed ability to cope; she had four boys to bring up alone. In the Second World War she became the first female Air Raid Protection (ARP) Warden in Falmouth and had American soldiers, preparing for D-Day, billeted in her house. In later life she became a Justice of the Peace. She was a warm, affectionate, but very forthright and self-determined person.

CHAPTER 10
THE EVACUATION FROM SHANGHAI - 1937

Editor's note. In July 1937 the war between Japan and China escalated considerably following an incident at Lugou Bridge near Beijing. By 13th August the conflict had reached Shanghai.[5] Accordingly, the Secretary of State for the Colonies (William Ormsby-Gore MP) ordered the evacuation of some 4,000 British men, women and children. The Royal Navy requisitioned the *Express of Asia* in Hong Kong and on the 16th August the ship sailed for Shanghai, arriving there on the 18th where she anchored at Blockhead Buoy some 20 miles from Shanghai.

HMS *Danae* was heavily involved in trying to evacuate people from Shanghai in conditions of great confusion and danger. During the next two months, William wrote several letters to Valentine and the following narrative is based on these letters.

---

[5] This was an extraordinarily bloody war. The death toll in Shanghai is contested – but was in the hundreds of thousands.

19th August 1937

On the 17th August we got off our first batch of evacuees in the Rajputana, 1000 of them. At the last minute it was decided that it was too dangerous to send them down river in tugs, so we transferred them mid-stream to the Duncan and Falmouth and stowed them all between decks, 500 in each ship, a tight fit and all women and children. While I was loading up a tug and had a couple of hundred or so on the pontoon, the Chinese carried out an air raid. The Japs fired anti-aircraft in every direction and their flagship loosed off with a pom-pom in fuses set to burst close over our heads. All the children screamed and there was pretty average pandemonium.
PTO

Luckily part of the pontoon was roofed with light galvanised iron and I got them under that, which made them think they were protected. Fortunately, nobody was hit, although there were lots of fragments falling in the water round us. We got 1,400 away on the 19th August, going down river in the Duncan, Delight and Duchess. Luckily by then it had stopped blowing which made the boat work eaiser, but if remained challenging in a river with 3 Kn current and the tail of a typhoon blowing. But finer weather also meant more aeroplanes. The plan is to ensure 450 more tomorrow, 600 on Saturday and the remainder of the residue on Tuesday. There was heavy firing again last night, ships firing heavy stuff just around Garden bend.

Photo from The Times *showing the women and children being evacuated from Shanghai. William's letter of 29th September suggests that the Naval commander, standing on the right, must have been himself.*

24th August 1937

We are not sure when we will evacuate the next crowd as the Japs landed yesterday near the mouth of the river and the whole place is in rather an uproar at the moment. However, it means that things have quietened down a little this end but that didn't prevent an aeroplane, nationality unknown, crossing over the International Settlement yesterday and dropping two bombs from a very great height. One bomb went through four floors but didn't explode and did practically no damage but the other fell outside a very large shop during the busy time of the day and killed over a hundred people.

The worst of the fires are burning out now, but four days ago the whole horizon to the north seemed to be nothing but flames. The Captain has been running the evacuation scheme, having turned the Shanghai Club into a large office and has hardly been onboard at all, so a good deal has been left to me. We are acting practically as a depot ship for the destroyers and sloops. As they come up-river to evacuate people or bring soldiers we supply them with oil, meat, potatoes, bread and anything else they want. I have a small fleet of tugs acting under my orders, but I always seem to be short of a boat.

All stores, provisions etc. have to be brought from the Pooting side, to which coolies have to be transported under armed guard and brought back at night as they all deserted the place and will only go back during the daytime if we send lots of chaps with rifles and tin hats to look fierce. No ship can come up-river so all stores arriving from Hong Kong have to be transhipped into tugs at Woosung, which is one of the worst anchorages in all the world. The army arrived and were bought up-river as quickly as possible in destroyers as the situation was a bit tense, leaving their baggage, described as hand baggage only, in the transport. When we came to bring it up-river we found that a list of gear a yard long was headed by seven field kitchens and twenty water carts!

MAP OF WAR ZONE
IN SHANGHAI AND NEIGHBOURHOOD
圖　地　爭　戰　近　附　及　海　上

30th August 1937

We had a front row seat view of the Japanese aeroplanes when they
bombed Nantao on Friday. They were trying to hit the railway station
which is only about half a mile from us and one could clearly see the
bombs as they went down. The whole episode was of course shear
murder as it is quite impossible to pretend that the railway station
has any military value.

    The stores question seems to be a never ending one. Shanghai is
very short of food as the railway service is almost completely blocked
by troop movements and everything in the immediate surrounding
country is being consumed by the rival armies. The Commander-in-
Chief is keeping a destroyer and two sloops in the vicinity, one is
always at Woosung as the guard ship and the other two anchored at
intervals in the river. Our major commitment is the provisioning of a
guard of two platoons that are looking after the waterworks and who
are completely cut off except from the river.

7th September 1937

We have had a comparatively quiet time of it recently except for a
little battle that flared up alongside us. The Japanese bombarded
Pooting at point blank range, starting a huge fire and driving out
Chinese parties. As soon as the fire died down the Japs landed but
found that the Chinese had also returned and were in force. A fierce,
bloody business and very close to Danae.

    The Dorsetshire arrives in Hong Kong on October 18th but whether
the Commander-in-Chief will let us leave or not is entirely another
matter. At present the Captain is completely bottled up the river
at Nanking by a boom which the Chinese have built across the river.
Until she is free again it seems to one impossible that we should be
allowed to go.

PTO

We are all suffering from bad tummies caused I think, by the plague of flies. Mine has been very disturbed for several days and shows no signs of settling down. Shanghai is running short of food and the shortness is likely to become worse if the Japs manage to push the Chinese back. So far none of the Japanese attacks seem to have had much effect but it is very difficult to say how much effort they have put into them. Their much-heralded big push has not yet commenced and every day the Chinese are digging themselves in more firmly.

12th September 1937

We have now got into a more or less steady routine. The Chinese planes come over every night usually two or three times. All the Japanese ships open up on them but as they never pick the plane up in their searchlights, they must be shooting absolutely blind but it looks rather attractive as all their pom-poms are fitted with tracers. The Chinese always come down the river so they always open fire in our direction and their shells burst more or less vertically over us. Any duds go into the Settlement. Last night I was coming off in a sampan when they started off with a proper fusillade. One felt very unprotected in an open boat with thirty or forty shells bursting just overhead and knowing that every burst meant that several pounds of metal were starting to fall vertically downwards.

On Friday I went ashore with the Admiral to play tennis. After we left the Sandwich, who had been alongside Danae for provisions, the Chinese guns in Pooting opened up on the OSK wharf in Hungke, where there was a Jap transport (armed) and two destroyers all of which promptly replied. The Admiral was naturally anxious about the Sandwich so we ran into the Shanghai Club to watch from the roof. Chinese shells were falling around the Sandwich but it would obviously have been stupid to have turned where she was in the line of fire, so she went full speed ahead and got safely out of the way. We stopped and watched the battle for about three quarters of an hour.

PTO

The Chinese hit the transport and started a fire behind the Jap Consulate but as they only have small field guns they didn't do much damage. The Japs got some planes up very quickly and as soon as they arrived the Chinese guns ceased fire as is their custom. The Japs went on pouring broadsides into Pooting aiming, as far as I could see, at nothing in particular. They knocked a lot of bricks about but otherwise did no harm.

It is astonishing how much noise even a broadside of destroyer's guns makes when they are firing more or less straight at you and they are surrounded by high buildings. From where we were standing the noise of the guns and the crash of the shells bursting was almost simultaneous. Anyway, they spoilt our tennis. The Japs are reported to have started the big push that they talk so much about. They have certainly landed a lot of men, I think about 80,000. So far they haven't done much. The Chinese have dug themselves in very scientifically and are taking a lot of turning out. They seem to have learnt a lot from their German advisors.

16th September 1937

In one of the "Times" we have just received is a very good photograph of harvesting in Cornwall near the Nare Head. Made me feel quite homesick. It is also interesting to read in the "Times" about the curious things which have been happening at that place Shanghai. Our local papers are very poor and hardly tell us anything. Not that there is much going on at the present. The Chinese chose this time to go back to their first defensive line which has taken the war further away from the river. The low clouds have prevented any flying at night, so we have not had a Chinese raid for three nights. The Chinese snipers are still busy on Pooting point. At intervals the destroyer at the NVK wharf opens fire at them with a pom-pom. The snag about this is that if they aim a little high, and they are very erratic, their shots fall all around us and the Frenchman.

29th September 1937

After a period of comparative peace, we were all woken up this morning about 5.00 am by a very heavy explosion either on Pooting Point or just beyond it. I don't know what it was, but it seemed to thoroughly alarm the Japs who started a bombardment from every ship in the river and made a tremendous noise for about half an hour.

Glad to hear that you have bought another wireless set and hope it is a success. When I read the first part of your letter, I was going to say get another one and going to suggest either a Murphy or a Ferranti. Very good of your Aunt to give us one, I hope that she can afford it. I haven't seen the photograph in the "Times" but I think that it must have been of me. I was the only commander who had anything to do with the evacuation. A lot of press men came down and took photographs but those published in the local papers have all been very poor.

I discovered a pair of bowls in a curio shop and took the Captain to see them. After a bit of haggling we bought the pair for thirty dollars, reduced from fifty! He has taken one and I the other. I don't know what they are, some sort of earthenware or rough china but they are an intriguing shape and good colour, design of dragons on the outside and horses on the inside.

I think that the Commander-in-Chief is leaving on Monday next in the Falmouth and going to re-join the Cumberland at Woosung, preparative to a trip down the coast to Hong Kong. He has not yet made his mind up whether we are to be allowed to go at the end of October or not. The fact that the Capetown has got herself shut up the Yangtse with no fuel and no chance of getting out makes him very loath to let his only other 6-inch gun cruiser leave the station. But I think he is now being brought round to the view that the conditions at Shanghai are such that he might as well let an 8-inch cruiser come here. Up to date he has taken the views that the 8-inch ships are too vulnerable to run the risk of a chance bomb and also, of course, he has been very loath to bottle up one of his best ships just when relations with Japan may tend to depreciate very rapidly at any moment.

PTO

Mrs Maund is going home leaving Hong Kong on the 1st October. She has apparently been very bored with HK which is flooded out with refugees with nothing to do but talk over their misfortunes.

The Captain and I have decided that we are fed up with wandering and our one idea now is to get our nose pointed for home and go full speed by the shortest route.

I shall be very glad to get home again. I am fed up with China and loathe the sight of Shanghai. And I want to see my home and my wife again.

All my love
William.

The Captain of the Danae during this episode was Captain Loben E.H. Maund, who went on to command the Ark Royal during the operation to sink the Bismark. He sailed in a number of Malta convoys. He was made a Rear Admiral in 1946 and died in 1957.

Admiralty, S.W.1.

22nd March, 1938

M.01374/38.

Sir,

    I am commanded by My Lords Commissioners
of the Admiralty to inform you that they have
had under consideration a report from the
Commander-in-Chief, China, dated the 15th December, 1937
concerning the services rendered by certain
officers at Shanghai between August and December,
1937, and My Lords desire that you will convey
to Commander W.P. Carne, R.N., H.M.S. DANAE, and
Lieutenant M.G. Haworth, R.N., H.M.S. VERITY,
an expression of their high appreciation of the
meritorious services rendered by them in the
difficult conditions resulting from the Sino-
Japanese conflict.

             I am, Sir,

             Your obedient Servant,

             (Sd). S. H. PHILLIPS.

The Commander-in-Chief,
  H.M. Ships and Vessels,
     Portsmouth.

Signal from the Admiralty following the successful evacuation of British subjects from Shanghai in 1937

PART THREE

THE SECOND WORLD WAR

CHAPTER 11
THE FORMATION OF THE MEDITERRANEAN FLEET

The following notes are a few recollections of my service on the staff of the Commander-in-Chief, Mediterranean, Admiral Cunningham, from the outbreak of war with Italy until the end of March 1941. I kept no diary, nor have I any notes with me, so that I make no claim as to the accuracy of the details. Nor do I claim that these notes are in any way comprehensive; they are merely an attempt to show some of the work of the junior members of the staff during this period – some of their hopes and ambitions, and to give some idea of the extent to which we were able to fulfil those hopes and ambitions.[6]

After the Munich crisis it was clear that the war, if and when it came, would be an axis war. In preparation for this menace, a homogeneous fleet was built up in the Mediterranean and preparations were made to base this fleet in Alexandria.

Alexandria being in Egypt, a foreign country, certain difficulties arose, but by the summer of 1939 a floating dock capable of accommodating fleet ships had been towed from Portsmouth to Alexandria, a quantity of stores have been collected and stored in Egyptian warehouses, and, in conjunction with the Egyptian government, the defences of Alexandra have been improved. With this fleet we felt confident that we could deal with the Italian fleet in the Eastern Mediterranean; the Western Mediterranean was the responsibility of the French fleet.

However, when war actually broke out, Italy remained neutral for the first nine months and naval activity in the Mediterranean was reduced to

---

[6] The account given in this chapter of the activities of the Mediterranean Fleet is less specific than that given by Admiral Cunningham in his autobiography, *A Sailor's Odyssey*, published in 1951. It is likely, therefore, that these memoirs were written before this date.

Commander William Carne when he was a Fleet Torpedo
Officer in the Mediterranean fleet circa 1940

contraband patrols to implement the economic war which was being waged against Germany. The Mediterranean Fleet was scattered to carry out other duties, the destroyers were sent home to assist with the anti-submarine campaign, while the larger ships proceeded to the outer trade routes to deal with possible commerce raiders. The Commander-in-Chief went to shore in Malta from where he directed the patrols enforcing the contraband control. Although the fleet was reduced to a few old cruisers and destroyers, he retained his complete staff as it was realised that the Mediterranean Fleet had to be built up again at very short notice.[7]

In May 1940 as the Germans swept forward in France, the attitude of Italy became more and more doubtful and it appeared that war with the latter country might commence at almost any time. The Commander-in-Chief hurried to Alexandria where a fleet was being collected as rapidly as possible. But the British ships were all very widely scattered over the ocean trade routes, and some time must elapse before a reasonable force could be concentrated. To cover this period the Admiralty asked the French government for help and they responded generously, sending four battleships – true, they were old battleships, but they were of some value as the nucleus of a battlefleet – and a squadron of modern 8-inch cruisers. Gradually the British ships started to arrive; cruisers from the South Atlantic and Indian oceans, the battleships *Malaya* and *Royal Sovereign* from escort duty in the North Atlantic and finally the *Warspite* direct from the Battle of Narvic. The arrival of the *Warspite* represented an important addition to our strength as although she was a veteran of 25 years, she had been completely reconditioned; she now had reasonable speed and her guns had been given additional elevation which enabled them to compete with modern weapons. The Commander-in-Chief, Admiral Cunningham, hoisted his flag in the *Warspite*.

The resulting fleet was not however well balanced, as it was strong in battleships but very weak in destroyers and other light craft. In fact, when all ships had assembled, we only had twenty-three destroyers, which was all that the Admiralty could spare. Out of these, no less than five were veterans of the last war and consequently were slow and low in endurance compared with modern destroyers. This lack of small craft has been a problem which

---

[7] This account omits an event recorded in Admiral Cunningham's autobiography, probably around March or April 1940; "In writing to the First Sea Lord …. I pointed out that in my opinion insufficient emphasis had been laid on the necessity for holding the Gallipoli Peninsula and the European side of the Bosphorous if the Turks had to fall back in Thrace. I suggested that unless we held both sides of the Dardanelles and the Bosphorous, U-boats and possibly other enemy units would certainly be able to pass in and out of the Black Sea ….. considerable progress was made, particularly as regards the defences of the Dardanelles, the Bosphorous and Smyrna. The plans for the defences of these areas, drawn up after a month's sojourn in Turkey by Commanders WP Carne and Geoffrey Barnard, the Fleet torpedo and gunnery officers on my staff, were accepted with little alteration by the Turkish General Staff."

admirals of all generations have had to face; no matter how eloquently they have pleaded for more vessels they have never persuaded the government power at the time to meet their requirements with a generous hand. Drake and Hawkins pleaded with Elizabeth for shallops and shore boats. Blake wanted fire ships and small craft; Hawke, and all the various admirals who blockaded Breste at different times, wanted more frigates for inshore work; Kempenfelt stressed the necessity for frigates for repeating signals; Nelson said that lack of frigates would be written on his heart, and Jellicoe has recorded that the operations of the Grand Fleet were hindered by lack of destroyers. Nevertheless, at the outbreak of this war it was found that no precedence had been broken, the best traditions had been followed and we were woefully short of destroyers, trawlers and the host of other small craft which are so necessary for the successful waging of sea warfare. Also, the additional stresses and strains which war brings on all classes of ship had, during the first nine months of this war, fallen unduly heavily on our destroyer force, which had then to face the evacuation of Dunkirk where heavy losses to invaluable destroyers were incurred.

The Commander-in-Chief commenced the training of this international collection of ships to bind them together until he could operate them as one fleet. Thanks to the willing cooperation of the French officers, particularly of Vice-Admiral Godfroy commanding the French ships, considerable progress had been made when, with the situation vis-à-vis Italy becoming still more menacing, the French government asked that three of their battleships should return to the Western Mediterranean. This left at Alexandria the French battleship *Lorraine*, three 8-inch cruisers and one 6-inch cruiser.

This was the situation when one afternoon we heard on the wireless the report of Mussolini's speech in Rome in which he declared his intention of attacking France.[8] At that time the French officers did not consider that their standard of training was sufficiently high for them to operate in company with the British fleet, but within an hour all our ships were raising steam and the British Eastern Mediterranean Fleet proceeded to sea soon after dusk that evening.

That first war cruise of the Mediterranean Fleet was disappointing. We

---

[8] This occurred on the 10th June 1940.

had hoped to cut off a few Italian merchant ships before they could escape to their own ports. But we were too late; they had all been warned in good time and were already safe in their own harbours. The cruisers, covered by the battlefleet, carried out a sweep of the Libyan coast. Those who approached the coast near Benghazi saw nothing.

The *Gloucester* and *Liverpool* found some minesweepers at work off Tobruk, but received a hot fire from these shore defences when they attempted to interfere with the sweeping operations. However, during the sweep both *Gloucester* and *Liverpool* cut mines with their paravanes which gave us the approximate position of one of the Italian minefields.

A less satisfactory incident occurred during the night when the old cruiser *Calypso*, who was stationed with *Caledon* ahead of the battlefleet, was torpedoed and sunk in a little over half an hour. The night was very dark and the submarine which fired the torpedo must have penetrated the destroyer screen. It was a good piece of work on the part of the submarine and showed that at least some of the Italian submarine commanders were bold and skilful officers.

To our surprise throughout the sweep into the Central Mediterranean we did not encounter any enemy air attacks, not a single hostile aircraft being sighted throughout the whole time.

While we were at sea the enemy submarines had been active off Alexandria sinking a merchant ship and laying mines off the port. They sprang a surprise on us by laying their mines in deeper water than we had thought possible for submarine mines to be laid. By the time the fleet returned, the sweepers had cleared the channel and the old Australian destroyers who had been left behind had chivvied the submarines to good purpose and there was strong reason to believe that the *Voyager* had sunk one of them.

On return to harbour, the Commander-in-Chief sent the old cruisers of the 3rd Cruiser Squadron and the French battleship *Lorraine* to bombard Bardia. They could not achieve very much but it served to keep the Italians guessing. This, alas, was the first and last combined operation with the French ships. We planned another one, which was to have been on an ambitious scale, consisting as it did of a bombardment of Augusta by the *Warspite*, and a sweep towards Tripoli by the French 8-inch cruisers. We actually got underway for this operation and were in the Great Pass leading out of

Alexandria when we were directed by the Admiralty to return to harbour. The breakup of the French nation had commenced, and the Admiralty were anxious to keep the French ships in Alexandria as we were uncertain of the attitude they would adopt. If they were once allowed to go to sea, they might make a dash for a French port and then we should lose control of them.

In the next few days, the French attitude could be summarised as a wish to fight on with their British allies. However, as the terms of the French armistice were published and the attitude of the French government became better known, and in particular the instructions of Admiral Darlan from the French Admiralty were received, a very rapid cooling in the French war like spirit was observed. In particular, the French began to ask what would happen to their families; would their relatives be persecuted if they threw in their hand with the British, and who would pay them and how would they get money to their families?

At first Admiral Cunningham had hoped to get an appreciable number of the Frenchman to join the Free French, but as the propaganda from France increased, this hope died fairly rapidly. Then came the press reports of the takeover of the French ships at Portsmouth followed by the reports of the unfortunate action at Oran[9]. Admiral Cunningham was still hoping to get a reasonable agreement with Godefroy, with whom he had struck up a mutual understanding and friendship in the previous weeks; he was careful not to show too openly the steel hand inside his velvet glove. But his hand was forced by events and by peremptory signals from the Admiralty instructing him that the French ships were not, on any account to be allowed to return to France or to any port where they might be taken over by the Germans.

Faced with this order from London, the Commander-in-Chief took a firm line with the French requiring them to surrender their ships. The French pretended to be astonished at this change of attitude and were indignant they should be treated in such a manner by their allies.

As no constructive suggestions as to how they should surrender the ships were forthcoming from the French, the Commander-in-Chief said he would sink the cruisers at the moorings by gunfire from the battleships. Once the

---

[9] This refers to the sinking of the French Fleet at Mers-el-Kebir in Algeria on the 3rd July 1940 after they refused to scuttle their ships or hand them over to the British.

Admiral came to this decision, a forenoon of great activity on board the *Warspite* developed. Godefroy and his chief of staff were sent for and the ultimatum delivered on the quarterdeck. The captains of all British ships were sent for and given their orders; all ships were to be cleared for action by noon. I am not sure that he actually said he would sink the French ships at 4pm if they had not surrendered, but he certainly gave that impression.

In the meantime, some members of the Commander-in-Chief's staff were a bit worried that Godefroy might call his bluff. It was all very well to say he would sink the cruisers by gunfire, but it was something one could hardly contemplate calmly. Loosing of broadsides of 15-inch in the open ocean is quite a thing, to fire at unarmoured cruisers at a range of three or four cables in a restricted harbour is not a practical job. Quite apart from the appalling mess we should make at the time, we should be left with three wrecks taking up valuable space in Alexandria's already very crowded harbour.

An additional rather longer-term problem, which was causing me, as FTO, some worry, was the problem of setting up efficient minesweeping organisations for Alexandria, Port Said, the Canal and at Haifa. The Italians had already been active in laying mines from submarines off Alexandria and it seemed probable that it would not be long before we were faced with magnetic and acoustic mines, of which, up to that point, we had had no experience. Such organisation as existed at that time was largely centralised on the Commander-in-Chief in *Warspite*. With the war becoming active in the Mediterranean, it was clear that the minesweeping organisation must be decentralised onto each individual port as *Warspite* might be engaged on operations over periods of several days and therefore out of contact. Further, the sweeping problem in each port was likely to vary and should be dealt with locally.

I had therefore prepared a memorandum on this subject detailing the responsibilities of the senior officers of each port and allocating such sweeping forces as we possessed. The memorandum encouraged all Officers to seek any local craft which might be used against the unpleasant menaces of magnetic and acoustic mines.

The draft of this memorandum had been passed by the Captain of the Fleet, albeit rather glumly, as he remarked that as we had already squeezed the Egyptian Ports and Lights Administration for every form of craft until they had screamed, he saw little hope of our being able to get any more. Further, he added, that we had absolutely no reserves of Officers or men and I should not dare to ask for any. From him I had gone to the Chief of Staff, who had in general approved what I had written, amending it slightly to make it rather more forceful, but adding that he had talked it over with the Commander-in-Chief who wished to see me in person before the memorandum went out.

All very well to say 'see the Admiral', but I could not get near him; he was furiously busy all the forenoon arranging to deal with the French ships and to get him to deal with any paperwork was out of the question. Eventually, when the *Warspite* cleared for action, he returned to his sea cabin in the bridge structure taking with him Admiral Tovey. Tovey was the only other Admiral in the fleet at that time; he was known as Flag Officer Light Forces as he combined the duties of Rear Admiral destroyers with that of Flag Officer of our only cruiser squadron.

Tovey was a lovely man, quite belied by his rather grim appearance and the rat trap mouth. When I first went to Osborne, he was lieutenant of one of the senior terms, I was glad he was not the officer of my term as he seemed to be a very fierce looking person. But during the 'phoney war' in the previous year I had got to know him well. I had been made the staff officer responsible for contraband control duties and in the latter months of that period Admiral Cunningham had bought Tovey into the Commander-in-Chief's office to help out with the contraband control affairs, which were rapidly multiplying. So, I became responsible to Tovey and, as I had become familiar with dealing with the long and involved signals that came addressed to the Commander-in-Chief regarding bills of lading, manifests etc, I think I was useful to him. I had learnt that he was a calm person with a nice sense of humour and a delightful smile that used to start at the back of his eyes and slowly spread across his face until it eventually got to his lips.

I made my way up to the bridge with the draft of my memorandum. This was not as easy as it sounds, as most of the hatches had been closed when the ship cleared for action. As I made my way along the upper deck, the time was about 1.30pm, I noticed that there was a boat alongside each of the French ships and that they were evidently going to land a few libertymen.

Normally, we gave leave in the afternoon to men who could be spared until dusk, which was about 6.30pm. However, in the British ships, all leave had been cancelled that day as, in accordance with the Commander-in-Chief's orders, ships were cleared for action.

Having arrived out outside the Admiral's sea cabin I ascertained that the Admirals had reached the coffee stage, so I thought I might intrude on them. They were both sitting around the table looking pretty gloomy. They had evidently talked themselves to a standstill and were now awaiting whatever the afternoon might bring forth. Admiral Cunningham demanded to know what I wanted. I told him that I had the memorandum of the organisation of the minesweeping forces ready for his approval, and that I understood that he wished to see me about it. He immediately attacked all my suggestions, wanting to know this, that and the other. But I had not been one of his staff officers for more than a year for nothing. I knew the drill, and was ready with answers to all his arguments. He was very searching with his questions; he had obviously read the original draft very carefully and had given the whole question considerable thought. Eventually he said, 'Alright, give me the file and let me read it through'. He then started to read and became completely absorbed; once he concentrated on a single subject, he had the capacity to shut himself off completely from all extraneous matters.

Tovey, who had remained silent during my interview with Admiral Cunningham, and seeing that he was now completely absorbed, asked me in a soft voice what was happening on the upper deck. I told him that I had seen the French landing the libertymen and, as far as outward appearances went, they seemed to be treating the afternoon in a perfectly normal manner, in no way interested in the fact that the British ships had gone to action stations. Then, as Tovey seem to want to talk, I went on to say that I thought that if I collected thirty or forty likely-looking chaps from the *Warspite* and went ashore about 6pm, we could grab the French libertymen as they returned to their boats, lock them temporarily in the police barracks, pinch their caps and jumpers and man their boats. Keeping near to the south side of the harbour we should approach the French ships screened by the British ships and, in the rapidly fading light, we could be alongside the French ships before anyone woke up to the trick. It would of course be necessary to synchronise the arrival of the boats so that they all arrived alongside at the same time. It would then be a simple matter to rush the gangways, seize the Captain of the ship and demand that he surrender his ship to Admiral Cunningham.

As I outlined my ideas Tovey became interested, and a smile started at the back of his eyes which gradually spread right across his face. As I finished, he lent forward and grasping my arm he said, 'What awful fun you would have. I have always longed to take a ship by boarding. I would almost volunteer to come with you'.

Just at that moment we were interrupted by a great roar of laughter from the other end of the table where Admiral Cunningham, having finished reading the minesweeping file, had been listening to the latter part of our conversation. 'You two silly schoolboys', he said, 'I can just see you clambering up the gangway with knives gripped between your teeth', and his laughter reverberated off the bulkheads of his sea cabin. Tovey looked a bit ashamed for a moment at being caught out playing with such silly fancies, then he too laughed, and we all laughed as if my ideas had been of no practical use. At least they had done something to dispel the gloom in the sea cabin.

Then the Commander-in-Chief became serious and said, 'No, no Carne, I can't have you playing your nasty Cornish piratical tricks. I am sure that they have armed sentries on their gangways and somebody would get hurt – and there would be bitterness and a bad business would be made worse. I am sure Godefroy is going to be sensible if we give him the chance to do it with dignity'. And of course, he was quite right. Godefoy surrendered during the course of the afternoon and they voluntarily disarmed their ships and pumped out most of their oil fuel. But afterwards, if I ever managed to do anything the Admiral approved of, which was very seldom, he would call me a Cornish pirate.[10]

The compromise that was reached was largely due to the exertions

---

[10] Tovey was appointed Admiral of the Home fleet in 1940 and his best known achievement was the pursuit and destruction of the Bismark, for which he was awarded the KBE. He insisted on being a "sea-going" admiral, believing that this was a key element in maintaining morale in the fleet. He retired from the Navy in 1946 and was ennobled as Baron Tovey. He died in January 1971, six months after his wife of 55 years, on the island of Maderia.

of the French liaison officer in the fleet flagship. This officer who was wholeheartedly devoted to the Allied cause (he subsequently joined the Free French) was a man of considerable personality and a good negotiator. He did his best to obtain our requirements, while at the same time, he understood the outlook of the French officers and was able to put their point of view to the Commander-in-Chief.

The compromise eventually agreed upon was as follows: The French ships were to be emptied of their oil fuel so that they could not go to sea. They were to land the pistols of the warheads of their torpedoes, making their torpedoes useless, and were to land the obturators of all their guns except the AA guns. We still hoped that they would use their AA guns against any hostile aircraft which came over the harbour. The obturators are essential portions of the breach mechanism of the guns without which the guns cannot be fired. In return we agreed that three fifths of the ships' companies should be repatriated to Syria and that the remainder, who were left behind to look after the ships, were to be paid and fed by the British and were to be supplied with such stores as might be necessary to maintain their ships.

As a sop to the pride of the French officers, it was agreed that the warhead pistols and obturators should be landed and locked up in a room in the French consulate, the door to be sealed in the presence of the French Consul and the British Consul General. The situation was a difficult one for the French officers, but they did their best to assist us and behaved with a certain natural dignity. The French Consul, on the other hand, made no bones about showing how much he disliked his task. He was without exception the rudest man I have ever met.

During the period of negotiation with the French, it was necessary to retain the bulk of the fleet in Alexandria to ensure having an overwhelming preponderance of force over the French. Active operations did not, however, cease altogether. The forward RAF aerodromes in the Western desert were sufficiently close to Tobruk to enable a Swordfish aircraft to reach that harbour even when carrying a torpedo. The RAF had obtained a number of good photographs of Tobruk which clearly showed the positions in which Italian ships were anchored. The Commander-in-Chief therefore directed the Captain of the *Eagle*, at that time our only aircraft carrier, to plan an attack on the shipping in Tobruk. As the *Eagle's* aircraft had spent a lot of time doing practice dive-bombing attacks, they were anxious to carry out this method of attack, but I persuaded the Commander-in-Chief that torpedoes would be far more effective, and he eventually ordered that the attack should be a torpedo attack. The torpedoes were therefore landed already prepared and fully charged and transported to Dekheila aerodrome.

The aircraft took off from Dekheila in the afternoon and proceeded to one of the forward aerodromes where they refuelled and took off again, adjusting their time so that they arrived at Tobruk at the latter end of the afterglow. They steered a course well out to sea so that they should not be reported by the Italian forces on the frontier. Tobruk harbour lies nearly east and west with its entrance to the east so that the aircrafts approaching from the east were coming out of a dark sky, with the Italian shipping silhouetted against the last of the afterglow. The attack was an almost complete surprise. The aircraft came in low over the boom and no anti-aircraft fire was encountered until the first aircraft was actually over the boom. Thanks to the good photographs received from the RAF and the careful planning of the attack, each aircraft knew exactly where to drop its torpedo and therefore had no need to spend more than an absolute minimum of time over the harbour. There were no casualties in this attack and all the aircraft returned safely to the forward aerodrome and proceeded to Dekheila the next day. RAF photographs the next day showed a scene of considerable confusion in Tobruk harbour and it is fairly certain that of the eight torpedoes dropped in this attack, six obtained hits.

We were pleased with this attack. Much time and money had been spent before the war in developing the torpedo aircraft but attempts to use the weapon against the Germans had been disappointing. The results of the first attack on Tobruk did much to reassure us as to the potency of this weapon and encouraged us to use it again in the future.

CHAPTER 12

THE ACTION OFF CALABRIA – JULY 1940

With the defection of the French, the strategic situation in the Mediterranean altered considerably. There was now no longer a strong Naval force in the Western Mediterranean. The best that could be provided was the force to hold the Straits of Gibraltar and possibly to make a raid occasionally into the Western Mediterranean. As a result, the Italians were able to concentrate the whole of their fleet against the British Eastern Mediterranean Fleet.

We possessed two bases in the Eastern Mediterranean; Malta and Alexandria. Malta has a good harbour and a well-equipped dockyard but its proximity to the Sicilian aerodromes made it certain that it would be subjected to very heavy air attack and therefore was not suitable as a fleet base. On the other hand, Malta's geographical situation made it of the greatest value to us, firstly as a base from which Italian convoys to Libya could be harried by surface, submarine and air attack, and secondly as a port of call halfway along the length of the Mediterranean. It was therefore essential that Malta should be held. Which in turn meant that frequent convoys must be run to Malta with military supplies for the garrison, fuel for the ships operating from Malta and also large quantities of food, as the island produces only a small percentage of its requirements.

Alexandria, on the other hand, suffered from the considerable disadvantage that it was situated in the territory of a foreign power, a power which – although it was bound by treaties to Great Britain – had distinct links towards the Italians. In peacetime there was not much ship repair work done in Alexandra and no shipbuilding; therefore, a dockyard had to be improvised out of most unpromising materials. Although the harbour is in many respects a good one, it has the serious disadvantage that it is approached by a narrow channel through a reef known as the Great Pass, in which there is so little water that a damaged battleship with a list of ten degrees would be unable to enter the harbour. And a ship sunk across the great pass would effectively bottle up the whole battlefleet in the port.

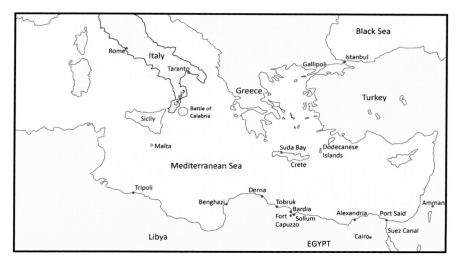

The Eastern Mediterranean 1940

The distance from Alexandria to Malta is 860 miles. There was no destroyer built which could do the round trip from Alexandria to Malta and back again in war conditions without refuelling. Therefore, all destroyers escorting convoys to Malta had to fuel at Malta, which necessitated sending tankers in the convoys to maintain a fuel store in Malta. This was a considerable disadvantage, as it reduced the speed of the convoys. There were a number of modern merchant vessels which could make good 13 or 14 kn, but very few tankers could exceed 10 kn. It is therefore easy to understand that one of the first objects of the Commander-in-Chief, was to obtain a fuel base roughly halfway between Alexandria and Malta and from the outbreak of the war with Italy, we cast covetous eyes upon Suda Bay in Crete, which was very suitable for our purposes.

Thus it will be seen that from an operational point of view, the position of the Eastern Mediterranean Fleet was at least as precarious as Nelson's fleet during the blockade of Toulon and from a maintenance point of view, taking into consideration the far greater requirements of modern ships, the situation was even more difficult.

Greece produced many materials which were valuable to our war effort, for which reason it was necessary to organise a system of Aegean convoys as soon as possible. It was clear that these convoys would have to run considerable risks as they would have to pass either to the east of Crete through the Kasso Strait, where they would only be a few miles from the Italian Dodecanese Islands, or they must go west of Crete through the Kithara Channel where they would be subjected to raids by cruisers operating from Taranto and other Italian ports. Whichever way they went, they would be in danger of air attack throughout their voyage.

The first operation which the Commander-in-Chief undertook after the defection of the French had the following objects in view; to cover convoys both to and from the Aegean; to cover the passage of a convoy from Malta to Egypt (this convoy consisted of ships which had been trapped in Malta on the outbreak of war with Italy) and thirdly to demonstrate to the Italians that we intended to contest the command of the Central Mediterranean. The forces available for this operation were: the battleships *Warspite*, wearing the Commander-in-Chief's flag, *Malaya*, and *Royal Sovereign*, aircraft carrier *Eagle*, cruisers *Orion* wearing the flag of Admiral Tovey, *Neptune*, *Sydney*, *Liverpool* and *Gloucester*, and about fifteen destroyers.

Up to this time the fleet had been subjected to very little air attack. There had been a night raid on Alexandra and some light forces had been bombed at sea, but the scale of attack had on each occasion been small. For this operation the Commander-in-Chief decided to shape a course to pass close to the south coast of Crete with the object of keeping as far away as possible from the aerodromes in Libya and it was hoped that the high mountains in Crete would be some deterrent to aircraft operating from the Dodecanese. These hopes proved to be based on a false promise. The mountains proved to be no hindrance to the enemy aircraft which flew very high, but the fact that the fleet was close to the coast of Crete assisted the enemy so that they had no difficulty in finding us.

The first attack occurred during the forenoon of the second day at sea when we were close to the island of Gavdos, south of Crete. It was a lovely Mediterranean summers' day, little if any breeze, practically no clouds, and rather hot. The cruisers were out of sight carrying out a reconnaissance; the destroyers were forming an anti-submarine screen around the battlefleet. One of the Swordfish aircraft from the *Eagle* was doing an anti-submarine patrol across the line of advance of the battlefleet. On the Admiral's bridge in the fleet flagship, all was quiet and peaceful. The Mediterranean fleet might have been carrying out a summer cruise in peace time.

Without warning, a stick of bombs fell right across one of the destroyers forming the starboard wing of the screen; luckily without doing any damage, but it gave us a nasty shock. The destroyer completely disappeared in the splashes which were high and narrow and black, the result of the Italian bombs being fitted with an instantaneous fuse which exploded on contact with the water. The aircraft had come straight out of the sun at great height and got away without a single gun being fired at it. There was immediately considerable activity on the Admiral's bridge; all the staff arrived to discuss the new development. Admiral Cunningham expressed his opinion on the failure of the lookouts to see the enemy and of the guns to open fire, in a few pungent and forcible phrases. The fleet was informed of his opinion by signal. The general opinion was that we were lucky to have got off without damage and that was that, and we could now get on with our nice pleasant cruise. These reflections were interrupted by the FWO who reported that there was someone, probably a hostile aircraft, making 'longs' in the immediate neighbourhood of the fleet. The precise implications of this curious signal did not sink in at once, but it was clear that there was an aircraft hanging about and the possibility of another attack could not be discounted.

We had not long to wait. In the early afternoon an attack developed. No single machine this time, but a formation which came over very high and carried out a 'pattern bombing' attack, with disconcerting accuracy. They were very difficult to see, but on this occasion, they were picked up by our lookouts and the guns opened fire before the bombs were released, but with insufficient accuracy to cause any of the bombers to break formation. From thence onward we had an attack about every half hour until sunset. For about a quarter of an hour or twenty minutes before each attack we heard our friend overhead making 'longs' which, by this time, we had decided were a method of 'homing' the attacking aircraft on to the target. It was fairly clear that if we could shoot down the shadower, we should have peace until another search had again located us. But the shadower remained straight up sun and at a range of 10 miles or more, well out of reach of our guns.

In each attack our inexperienced guns crews became a little quicker at opening fire and more accurate until, by the evening, the enemy found it necessary to fly through quite a heavy barrage before he could release his bombs. But he continued to press home his attacks with determination and skill, and it appeared to be only a matter of time before he scored a considerable success.

Warspite, as leader of the battleships line, was a favourite target and had a number of near misses. A number of splinters came in board, making holes in the superstructure. Amongst the guns crews two men suffered minor casualties. The black spray thrown up by the exploding bombs marked all the paintwork with a pattern of black dots. Some of the spray even fell on the Admiral's bridge, and several of us had our white uniforms marked as though dyed with a pattern of very small black dots – very difficult to wash out.

At the first alarm, the whole staff had assembled on the Admiral's bridge and stood in more or less respectful attitudes around the Admiral, endeavouring not to look as frightened as we felt. Except for the duty commander there was nothing for most of us to do and it was nervous work standing still.

During the afternoon, *Warspite* was straddled by a stick of bombs, one of which fell very close to the starboard side abreast the bridge. A large sprinter from this bomb weighing two or three pounds came through the side of the Admiral's bridge, which was made of bullet-proof steel, and did various bits of damage which made it clear that it still retained sufficient velocity to have made a very nasty mess of anyone it had hit. After this convincing demonstration of the risks which we were running, the Admiral gave orders that the staff was to disperse as far as possible during attack; only himself and the duty commander would remain on the Admiral's bridge and everyone was to wear a tin hat. We persuaded Admiral Cunningham to stand inboard of the 6-inch control huts, where he was protected by two thicknesses of bullet-proof steel and had some headcover, but nothing would persuade him to wear a steel helmet, although he was apt to be very rude to anyone else who neglected to put one on.

The attacks continued until dusk with equal skill and determination. Most of the attacks were made at a height of over 14,000 feet and in the Mediterranean summer sky conditions, we found it very difficult to see the enemy. We subsequently learnt that all these aircraft were members of the famous 'Green Mice' squadron which Ciano had trained and which had made its name in Spain. The most satisfactory thing I can say about the squadron is that nearly all its original members became casualties, and they did not appear to have passed on either their skill or their determination to any of their successors.

Italian bombs dropping in the sea close to Warspite
– Photo William Carne

By the evening all ships in the battlefleet and had had near misses and had suffered one or two minor casualties similar to those suffered by the *Warspite*. However, no ship in the battlefleet had received a direct hit nor had any ship suffered damage which in any way affected her fighting or seagoing efficiency. The cruisers who had also been attacked had not been so lucky and the *Gloucester* received a direct hit on the fore director tower. The bomb exploded on the upper bridge level where it killed the Captain and six other officers, besides a number of ratings[11]. The fore-control, compass platform and TCP were all out of action. In the flagship we assessed the *Gloucester* as still being 80% efficient but I think we were rather optimistic. A ship which is seriously short of officers and has to be fought from aft is at a very serious disadvantage.

---

[11] Admiral Cunningham's account says that Captain F.R. Garside and seventeen others were killed.

The next morning found us steaming a nor'-westerly course across the Central Mediterranean towards the coast of Calabria. Reconnaissance aircraft had been flown off at dawn from the *Eagle* and in due course located the enemy. They were still steaming a nor' nor' easterly course as though towards Taranto and it appeared that they would cross our bows before we could bring them to action. Throughout the forenoon the two fleets approached each other on converging courses. No air attack developed on the British fleet and it appeared fairly certain that the Italians did not know where we had got to. Perhaps they thought they had sunk us all the day before.

From the air reports, it was fairly clear that the majority of the Italian destroyers had broken off and gone into Messina. It appeared that whatever operation the Italian fleet had been engaged upon, was now finished and the main portion of the fleet was returning to Taranto, having left the majority of the destroyers at Messina. This appreciation, however, proved to be incorrect.

Throughout the forenoon we received a steady stream of reports from the reconnaissance aircraft which enabled us to plot the enemy with accuracy. Everything was going just like a peacetime tactical exercise. Just before noon, the Commander-in-Chief decided to fly off the striking force of torpedo bombers from the *Eagle*. It appeared that the enemy were escaping from us and our only hope was to catch them with the aircraft and slow them down sufficiently for us to overtake them. Owing to the small number of aircraft carried by the *Eagle*, we could only muster nine in the striking force. Further, there were insufficient additional aircraft to maintain one in constant touch with the enemy, and at about 12.30pm, for half an hour, the enemy was not shadowed. Unfortunately, during this time, he reversed his course with the result that the striking force missed the enemy battlefleet and returned without expending their torpedoes. Just about the time that the striking force returned, the shadowing aircraft once more obtained touch with the enemy and we received the news that the two fleets were rapidly closing one another, and further, that there was a detachment of the enemy also approaching from Messina. It appeared that the enemy destroyers had gone to Messina to refuel and were now once more re-joining their Admiral. The situation was such that the two Italian forces were bound to meet before we could get a touch with either.

Before the war at the Tactical School, we used to play a tactical game which was located in just the same part of the Mediterranean. Each of the two fleets were in two separate sections and, each 'Admiral' knew where the sections of his own fleet were located; he only knew of the existence of one section of the enemy. Thus each 'Admiral' had a nasty surprise, just as action was about to be joined. The result was a very good game. On this occasion the Italians had brought off a surprise on us but unfortunately there was no second section of the British fleet to give the Italian Admiral an equally nasty jar.

The Admiral proceeded to dispose the fleet for action. The battleships were stationed on the line of bearing at right angles to the bearing of the enemy, the *Eagle* took station on the disengaged side protected by the damaged *Gloucester*, while the remainder of the cruisers were sent ahead to reconnoitre. The speed of the fleet was seriously hampered by the old *Royal Sovereign* who could only do about 16 ½ kn. The cruisers proceeding at nearly twice this speed were soon over the horizon and, shortly after they disappeared, we began to receive signals from them reporting a large number of enemy cruisers and destroyers.

After this, things began to move very fast. Hardly had the cruisers disappeared than they were in sight again on our port bow in the line ahead and steering from port to starboard, i.e. across our bow. They were firing hard at some target which was still out of sight from us and were obviously heavily engaged as we could see the splashes of the enemy shells all around them.

The Admiral decided that we must use the superior speed of the *Warspite* to support the cruisers, accordingly he went on at the *Warspite's* maximum speed of about 23 kn, instructing the two other battleships to follow at their best speed. *Malaya* could do about 20 kn so she drew away from *Royal Sovereign* and *Warspite* went away from both of them. This resulted in the British fleet becoming very strung out. At the commencement, the Admiral had kept about half the destroyers with the *Warspite*, leaving the remainder to screen the other two battleships but it soon became clear that *Royal Sovereign* was going to be left far behind so he ordered all destroyers to take station ahead of *Warspite*, but this took some time as by now *Warspite* had drawn ahead.

In the flagship we rearranged ourselves in preparation for the battle.

During the approach the centre of interest is in the plot where all the signals are received, but very shortly it was possible for us to see the situation for ourselves from the bridge. The Admiral and COS went into the compass platform, where they ensconced themselves with the flag captain. The Fleet Gunnery Officer (FGO) and I were just abaft the compass platform where we endeavoured to recognise the various enemy ships as they appeared, and kept the plot informed of the bearing of the enemy and of our own ships as the situation altered. On this occasion both the Master of the Fleet and SOO were in the plot, but in subsequent engagements, as a result of our experience on this occasion, SOO came up on the upper bridge with me. I kept telling myself that we were about to take part in a battle in which we should almost certainly be considerably outnumbered, but I found it very difficult to make myself realise the situation. Everything up to that moment had been so similar to an ordinary peace-time exercise that it was extremely difficult to realise that something more dramatic was about to happen. At this time, I had been serving at sea for about twenty-six years, during which time all my energies had been directed towards perfecting myself for this one great crucial test; battle at sea. But somehow the preliminaries appeared to be singularly unimpressive.

As soon as *Warspite* was within extreme range of the enemy cruisers she opened fire at a large ship in the van, apparently an Italian 8-inch cruiser. Although we did not score a hit, the effect of *Warspite's* 15-inch shells was immediate, as the enemy sheered off. The flagship had been preparing to fly off one of her aircraft, as she had a Swordfish on the catapult. Owing to the rapidity with which the battle had developed the aircraft was still on the catapult when the first salvo was fired. This, and the subsequent salvos fired at the enemy cruiser in the van, wrecked the aircraft and it had to be catapulted over the side. In the lull which ensued after the enemy cruisers sheered off, we were able to get the second aircraft into the catapult and successfully launch it before we again opened fire. It was to play an important part in the subsequent battle.

As the *Warspite* crossed the wake of our cruisers, she turned to approximately the same course. The two other battleships followed the Admiral's motions, cutting the corner as much as possible in an endeavour to catch up. The formation of the British fleet was therefore as follows: In the van the four

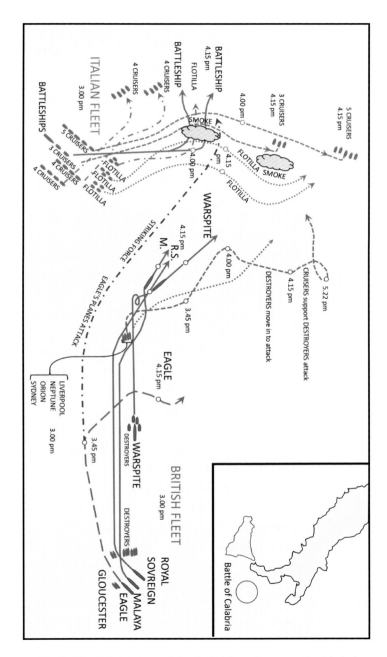

The Battle of Calabria – Map adapted from the account in Admiral
Cunningham's autobiography 'A Sailor's Odyssey', 1951

undamaged cruisers still engaged in a long-range duel with the cruisers in the enemy van, followed about three miles astern by the *Warspite*. About half the destroyers were close head of the *Warspite*, the other half was passing up the starboard side in an endeavour to get ahead. *Malaya* was about two miles astern of *Warspite* and *Royal Sovereign* another 2 miles astern of *Malaya*. *Eagle* was well clear of the fleet roughly on *Warspite's* starboard beam covered by *Gloucester*. From here she was able to operate aircraft freely, at the same time keeping visual touch with the flagship. Luckily, such breeze as there was, was from the northward.

About this time the remaining enemy vessels hove into site. They were steaming almost directly towards us and were therefore difficult to identify. However, almost at once, they altered course to the north in the wake of their cruisers so that now both fleets were steaming to the north on slightly converging courses. Even so, it was difficult to identify the enemy ships owing to the fact that their 'Conti de Cavour' class of battleship had a silhouette very similar to some of their cruisers. However, we eventually came to the conclusion that there were two battleships present and about fourteen cruisers, but they were never all in sight at the same time.

Warspite chose as her target the leading enemy battleship, which subsequently proved to be the 'Conti de Cavour' wearing the Italian Commander-in-Chief's flag. At the same time both enemy battleships opened fire at *Warspite* as well as several of the cruisers in the centre of the enemy line. Several of our destroyers were still passing up the starboard side of *Warspite* and these received the benefit of the overs.

The Admiral ordered *Warspite* to reduce speed to 15 kn to give *Malaya* a chance to catch up as we were obviously up against more than we could take on single-handed. For a few minutes *Warspite* was surrounded on all sides by the splashes of enemy shells. Many passed ahead, the enemy evidently not expecting a battleship to be steaming at only 15 kn when heavily engaged. The range was still very long as the Italians made no attempt to press their advantage by closing the range. The result was that the danger space from their projectiles was very small, particularly from the 8-inch cruisers, and although *Warspite* was straddled on several occasions, she was not actually hit.

It was a period of considerable nervous tension. Despite one's best resolutions, it wasn't possible not to duck when a real 'whistler' came singing close over the bridge. I endeavoured to distract my attention from the unpleasant noises around me by taking bearings of the enemy and by arguing with the FGO as to the identity of various enemy vessels. During this period, I lunged up against one of the staff signalmen not looking at all happy. I sang out to him to write down the bearings on the pad as I took them, so that in the lulls, I could pass them to the plot. There was so much noise that at times it was impossible to make oneself heard down the short voicepipe of the plot. The signalman came and did his simple job efficiently, evidently pleased he'd been given something definite to do amidst the terrifying clamour that was going on all around him.

Somewhere about this time, I allowed myself to be knocked over by the blast of our own guns. Normally the guns of a battleship are fired as a 'double' salvo, i.e. four guns are fired together, followed about 10 seconds later by a second salvo of four guns. Then comes a lull of 30 to 50 seconds, depending on the range, before a second double is fired. One reckons on this quiet interval to pass any messages by voicepipe or telephone, or to carry out any other business one may have to perform. I was taking a bearing off the Italian cruiser which was on our port quarter; this necessitated leaning well over the port side of the bridge – the engaged side – while adjusting the azimuth mirror. Owing to the smoke, I had some difficulty in seeing my object and delayed too long before getting back into safety, with the result that I was caught by the blast from 'B' turret and blown over backwards. I put out my right hand to grasp the bridge rail but only got it with the tips of my fingers. As I picked myself up, I felt a considerable wrench in my right hand but thought nothing much of it at the time; there were too many other things to think about. Later, I was to find that I had a broken bone in my right hand.

In the meantime, *Warspite* had been firing steadily and, aided by some useful spotting signals from her aircraft, which by this time was over the Italian fleet, she obtained a hit on the leading enemy battleship. This hit was clearly seen from the flagship's bridge and we subsequently heard that one 15-inch shell had penetrated the forward boiler room of the *Conte di Cavour*. This put six boilers out of action, reducing the ship speed to 20 kn and caused 60 casualties.

It was during this engagement that the air striking force from the *Eagle* got in their attack. After their first abortive attempt, they had been flown on and refuelled. As soon as it was clear that some sort of engagement was inevitable, the Commander-in-Chief made a request to the *Eagle* to fly off everything that could carry a torpedo. Their attack coincided with the engagement with the *Warspite* and there is no doubt but that the confusion into which the enemy line was thrown, does much to explain the immunity of the *Warspite*. They obtained a hit with one torpedo on a cruiser.

At about this time, we observed that the enemy destroyers were coming out from the enemy lines and steaming towards our van as though to make a torpedo attack. The Admiral ordered our destroyers to counterattack. Accordingly, they went ahead at full speed and soon were engaged in a long-range gun duel with their opponents. As *Warspite* had reduced to 15 kn, they rapidly left the flagship behind. Our surmise, that the enemy destroyers were making a torpedo attack was, however, incorrect, and we soon saw that they had come out between the lines to make smoke, and in fact the whole enemy lines started to make smoke, cruisers and destroyers included, with the result that the enemy ships were soon obscured. *Warspite* fired a few more salvos, assisted by her spotting aircraft but soon had to ceasefire.

As it seemed probable that the enemy was using smoke to close the range and that he would shortly launch a destroyer attack on our van through the smoke, using his very superior number of destroyers, the Admiral decided to concentrate his scattered fleet. For this purpose, *Warspite* turned through 32 points to allow *Malaya* to catch up, while the destroyers, which were rapidly disappearing in full cry of the enemy smoke layers, were ordered to return and once more take station ahead of *Warspite*.

An Italian cruiser in the rear showed up intermittently in the smoke. *Warspite* fired a few salvos at the ship and *Malaya*, as she came into station, also opened fire, but the enemy was outside the range of her guns, which had not been modified to give increased elevation.

Warspite's aircraft, as well as a reconnaissance machine from *Eagle,* was still in touch with the enemy and we were getting a number of good reports from which we were able to plot the enemy's movements with considerable accuracy. To our surprise, all these reports indicated that the enemy, instead of pressing his advantage, had turned away first to the westward and subsequently to the southwest and was opening the range as fast as possible[12].

The Admiral immediately turned the whole fleet to the west to follow up the enemy. *Eagle* was unable to obey at once as she was landing the striking force; consequently, she became rather separated from the rest of the fleet and was the source of some anxiety. Our cruisers, after the enemy cruisers had disappeared in the smoke, had reversed their course and joined up with the battlefleet again about this time.

All day we had been steaming across the Central Mediterranean towards the coast of Calabria, and by this time we were only some 40 miles from the coast. We had been expecting a heavy air attack all the afternoon after we had been located by the enemy fleet. This air attack now developed and was on the heavy scale, which we had anticipated.

For two hours we were subjected to high-level bombing attacks by formations of three, five and even more aircraft, all of which carried out the same 'pattern bombing' form of attack, which our experience of the previous day had begun to make us accustomed. *Eagle* was a favourite target for the attackers, and again and again she disappeared in a cloud of enormous splashes only to emerge again with all her guns firing and apparently unhurt. Each individual captain was taking avoiding action on his own, putting the wheel over just before the bombs were released. This resulted in the fleet losing formation, but by now we had realised the importance of all ships keeping close together and giving mutual support with their AA fire. Without instructions, therefore, the three battleships and

---

[12] Admiral Cunningham describes these moments somewhat differently in his account of the "action off Calabria". "At 3.30 the enemy turned away under a smoke-screen and fire was checked. The *Warspite*, steaming at 24½ kn, turned a complete circle to allow the Malaya to catch up. A few minute later, we fired a few salvoes at two cruisers, which were trying to work around to the east to get at the Eagle; but the great moment came when at 3.53 the *Warspite* opened fire on the leading enemy battleship at a range of 26,000 yards. Both the Italian battleships replied. They shot well and straddled us at this great range: but the culminating point of the engagement soon came. The *Warspite's* shooting was consistently good. I had been watching the great splashes of our 15-inch salvoes straddling the target, when at 4.00 pm, I saw a great orange-coloured flash of a heavy explosion at the base of the enemy flagship's funnels. It was followed by an upheaval of smoke, and I knew that she had been heavily hit at the prodigious range of 13 miles. This was too much for the Italian Admiral…. His ships turned away."

Eagle took up a rough diamond formation with one ship at each corner and with the cruisers and destroyers outside them. Thus, the ships gave each other support but left room for the individual ships to manoeuvre separately to take avoiding action. So successful was this formation, that the Admiral's first action after the battle was to devise a signal to bring into force this formation for future use. We called it 'loose formation'.

Warspite's aircraft and the reconnaissance machine from *Eagle*, were still maintaining touch with the enemy. We were considerably cheered to receive a signal from the *Warspite* machine reporting that at least one formation of enemy aircraft bombed the Italian fleet, obviously having lost their bearings, and mistaking the Italians for ourselves.

It was a lovely summer evening with a clear sky and calm sea when we sighted the coast of Calabria and altered course to the southward, roughly parallel to the coastline. Shortly before sunset we sighted a lighthouse and were able to fix our position accurately. This was just as well as our first experience of action had proved that our blast proof arrangement for the plot was sadly lacking in efficiency. Racks and shelves for boxes had come tumbling down and the blast had blown open the door and entered the plot, tearing the chart to ribbons – even though three people had been leaning on it to reinforce the drawing pins that were holding it down on the automatic plotter.

Just before sunset, *Warspite's* aircraft gave us a final report of the enemy and then proceeded to Malta to land, thus avoiding the necessity of *Warspite* stopping to pick her up. This machine was of course a floatplane and therefore could not land on the *Eagle*. This last report made it clear that the enemy was retiring in the direction of Messina and at a speed which made it quite impossible for us, with our slow fleet, ever to catch him. But the report also gave us the encouraging news that one of their cruisers had stopped and was being taken into tow by another ship. This was the cruiser that had been hit by an aircraft torpedo. We immediately started to plan a night operation for the destroyers and cruisers to try and catch this ship, before she reached the safety of her own harbour. But she was already well into the Gulf of Messina. The enemy was certain to cover her retreat with strong forces and we were up against our old trouble, the lack of endurance of the destroyers. The older ones, after the hard steaming they had indulged in that day, had only enough fuel to just reach Malta and as the newer ones would have to remain at sea until the afternoon of the next day, to form an anti-submarine screen for the battlefleet while the older ones were fuelling, had no fuel to spare either. There was also the possibility that our fuelling programme the next day might be delayed by enemy air attack, so the Admiral decided with considerable regret, to make no attempt on the damaged Italian cruiser.

The fleet was therefore formed up for the night and we proceeded to the south of Malta, detaching the first section of destroyers before dawn to go into Malta and fuel. Thus ended this astonishing engagement; one can hardly call it a battle, in which a fleet vastly superior in cruisers and destroyers, and backed by an overwhelming air force operating in sight of its own coast line, retired before an inferior and older fleet which was almost out of fuel.

As soon as it was dark, I managed to get down below to show my hand, which by this time was becoming very painful, to the Surgeon Commander. I found him in the wardroom, where several hungry officers were hurriedly wolfing hard-boiled eggs and corned beef sandwiches while the FAO, Dryson, eyeglass in eye, gin glass in hand and smoking a cigarette, greeted each entrant with one of the gentle witticisms which had so endeared him to the rest of his messmates. I did not escape a certain amount of raillery at what was termed my 'self-inflicted wound'. The Surgeon Commander confirmed that a bone was probably broken and, after strapping up my hand and extracting a promise that I would visit the sickbay next morning to have it X-rayed, I returned to the bridge, first arranging for my marine to bring me something to eat.

When I arrived on the bridge, I was greeted by a string of remarks from Admiral Cunningham addressed to myself in particular and the staff in general, on the uselessness of staff officers who wasted their time scribbling nonsense on pieces of paper, and who didn't know enough about ships to keep themselves out of harm when the guns were fired. However, when we were alone together and there was no third person to see his human side, he became most solicitous for my welfare and I shall always remember how, in the next few days, when he was beset by every form of anxiety and trouble, he always found time to enquire after my welfare.

The next day was spent by the fleet patrolling up and down south of Malta, while the destroyers and the old battleship *Royal Sovereign*, who was also short of oil, went to Malta to fuel. The operation took longer than had been expected. In peacetime, ships usually fuelled from the fleet boilers, but these had all been sent to Alexandria and the operational fuelling direct from the tanks had not, at this time, been worked out to the state of efficiency which it afterwards attained. There were also complications about the convoys. Vice-Admiral, Malta, (VAM) had organised the ships in Malta into two convoys, a fast and a slow. The fast convoy was a comparative term only, as it was limited to 10 kn. When the first news of the battle had reached Malta, VAM decided that the enemy would be kept too busy by us to worry about hunting for convoys, so he had sailed off the fast convoy the previous evening for Alexandria. This was therefore well on its way eastward but quite unsupported.

The last reports received the previous evening, had appeared to indicate that some of the enemy cruisers were making for Port Augusta. This was confirmed in the morning by the RAF, who reported that there were three cruisers in the harbour. It was clear that if the ships got wind of our fast convoy they could get out and attack it while the fleet was still tied to the south of Malta, fuelling the destroyers. *Eagle* was ordered to be prepared to carry out a torpedo aircraft attack on the ships at dusk; after the attack, the aircraft to land at Halfar in Malta and to return to the *Eagle* next morning, thus avoiding landing on the carrier at night, which necessitates burning a number of lights. About 4pm, a reconnaissance plane reported that the ships had sailed from Port Augusta and were last seen steaming to the north as though for Messina. It appeared that we had lost our chance, but the Admiral decided to send the torpedo aircraft to Port Augusta on the chance that they might pick up something. From the aircraft signals it was not clear whether all the ships in Port Augusta had sailed or not. Accordingly, the striking force took off from *Eagle* about an hour before dusk and proceeded to make a landfall near Cape Passero with a view to working up the coast and then steering straight in when opposite Port Augusta. The attack was as much of a surprise as the first attack on Tobruk, but unfortunately the harbour was empty. However, they found a Navigatory class destroyer in a bay to the north of Port Augusta, which was torpedoed and sunk, so the night was not completely blank. All the aircraft returned successfully to Malta and landed on *Eagle* at dawn the next morning.

In the meantime we had sailed the slow convoy, with an escort of destroyers, on the same evening as the attack on Port Augusta and all ships requiring oil had been fuelled, so that as soon as the aircraft had landed on *Eagle,* the fleet proceeded to the eastward to cover the convoys.

The slow convoy was only making good about 8 kn and was obviously going to take a long time to reach Alexandria. In the meantime, the fast convoy, having had a good start, was steadily drawing away from any protection that the fleet might be able to give it. Also, the Admiral was anxious to get back to Alexandria as there were many things which required his personal attention. He therefore turned over the command of the bulk of the fleet to the second-in-command and proceeded in *Warspite,* with two cruisers and a small screen of destroyers, at *Warspite's* best speed in order to get back to Alexandria as soon as possible and to be in a better position to protect the fast convoy if it was attacked.

During the day which the fleet had spent south of Malta, to our surprise, we had been free from air attack. However, as soon as we approached the Libyan coast on our passage eastwards our little friend could once more be heard making 'longs' on his wireless set and heralding the approach of the enemy bombers. As we had suffered a heavy attack on our westward passage, when we kept close to the coast of Crete, on the return journey we kept to the south near the coast of Libya. This choice was no happier than our previous one. Libya was apparently full of large Italian bombers, all of whom were itching to unload their bombs on the fleet. All units were heavily attacked on both days of the eastward passage, except the fast convoy which was apparently missed by the Italian reconnaissance and got through without any attack.

In the *Warspite,* the second day of that passage was, I think, the worst day of all. The attack started before 9am and continued at intervals of 20 to 30 minutes until 4pm. By this time, *Warspite* was well clear of the rest of the fleet and with only two cruisers in company, there were not many guns available to put up an effective barrage. There was nothing much that the Admiral or staff could do. It was up to *Warspite* and her consorts to beat off the attacks. Few ships turn more rapidly than the *Warspite* and these qualities were used with effect by the Flag Captain who, judging the moment of release of the bombs, put his wheel over sufficiently early for the ship to be well into her turn before the bombs arrived without making the turn so early that it was observed by the enemy. The screen did their best to keep station on us, frequently receiving the benefit of salvos of bombs which were obviously intended for the *Warspite*. On this day we noticed, for the first time, a tendency on the part of the Italians, when the fire became reasonably accurate, to alter course and release their bombs over a ship of the screen; a more difficult target, but a safer operation then forcing their way into position to bomb the battlefleet.

Following our new principles, the staff were dispersed throughout the fore superstructure. I spent the forenoon trying to make a few notes on what must be done on arrival at Alexandria. *Eagle* would require a number of aircraft torpedoes to replace those expended. We were very short of aircraft torpedoes and if we were going to expend them at this rate we must endeavour, once again, to persuade the Admiralty to send us an adequate supply. *Gloucester* was obviously severely damaged and the whole of such dockyard resources as existed must be put into the job of getting her to sea again, other ships assisting if necessary. My thoughts were being continually interrupted as attack succeeded attack.

At 12.30pm I went up to the Admiral's bridge to take over the afternoon watch as duty commander. Almost at once, one of the cruisers hoisted the signal for aircraft in sight and I ran forward to the chart house to inform the Admiral, only to be badly bitten for not wearing my tin hat. As the attack developed, I remained close to the Admiral in case he had any orders. At that time, the orders were that all exposed personnel were to fall on their faces when they heard the sound of bombs. In due course down came bombs and the Admiral, in deference to the order, bent slightly at the knees. I, being a dutiful officer, followed the Admiral's motions only to be badly bitten for not having fallen on my face. By this time my nerve was so shaken that I could almost wish that a bomb would arrive. However, the Admiral stalked away, fell into his chair which was on the bridge, and promptly fell asleep. Thereafter, everything went wrong with me. My hand was throbbing considerably and the hot sun beating down on my tin hat was more that I could stand, so I kept taking it off. The nerves of the young signalman I had on watch with me were not in too good a state, and he kept making mistakes with the signals. As each attack developed, I called the Admiral, forgetting in my hurry to put on my tin hat and received the benefit of his irritation in return.

One hundred and seventy-one bombs were dropped on the *Warspite* during the afternoon watch. I know, because I counted them all. The Admiral slept in his chair between each attack; at least, he sat still with his eyes closed and if he did not sleep, he was a very good actor. When other men were frankly frightened as they heard the whistle of the bombs, the Admiral's reaction was to become quite furious at his inability to hit back. These attacks only lasted a few seconds but at the time it was just as well to keep clear of him.

Just before 4pm we were attacked by twelve planes in the formation of three groups of four planes from the port quarter. We saw them a long way off and put up a good barrage, but they came steadily on. I obediently fell on my face as the first twelve bombs fell close to the port quarter. As I was getting up, the Admiral turned to me and said in a furious voice, 'that was a very determined attack'. This seemed to me to be a very obvious remark not calling for a reply and, as I once more heard the whistle of bombs, I again fell on my face. These straddled the ship, two or three on the port quarter, the remainder on the starboard side. As I again got to my feet a red face was thrust into mine and a voice, sick with rage, said, 'I said, that was a very determined attack!'. Thinking that there was enough war going on outside the ship without starting a new one on the Admiral's bridge, I hastily gave a soft answer, saying, 'yes, it was a determined attack'. Just then I heard the third lot of bombs arriving and once more took up a recumbent position. These fell close alongside the starboard side of the fo'c'sle and the resulting noise, smoke, spray and chaos was such as to make it difficult to believe that I was still alive. As I got up, I found a clenched fist being shaken in my face, and from a face purple with rage and through clenched teeth, came the strangled words, 'why the hell didn't you say so the first time!'

The letter on the following page is the way in which the Action off Calabria was described to Valentine.

Office of C-in-C
Med Station
c/o/ GPO
London
13/7/40

Darling

We have just returned from the so called battle of Calabria. Please excuse bad writing in pencil. I got blown over by one of our own 15-inch salvoes and have broken a bone in my right hand. Nothing at all serious but a damned nuisance. Understand I am not to have the use of it for three weeks. All my own fault, I ought to have known better than to have been snooping around where I was. We have had some very unpleasant bombing but this ship has been very lucky and we have had only three minor casualties. No news of you. We are pressing for the introduction of some form of letter telegram. If introduced must use it even if it is a bit expensive. I wish I knew how you were getting on. I regard the BBC announcement of raids on South Western towns with suspicion. Will try to write a description of unsatisfactory action when my hand is better.

All my love
William

CHAPTER 13
TORPEDO ATTACK ON TOBRUK

On our arrival back at Alexandria, we were immediately plunged into the mass of administrative detail which always collected while the Commander-in-Chief was at sea. At the same time, it was urgently necessary to consider the events of the last five days and to produce an appreciation of risks which must be run if the fleet was to be taken into the Central Mediterranean in the future, and to decide what steps should be taken to minimise these risks.

We started by collecting information of the number of bombs which had been dropped on the fleet as a whole and of the account of damage which had been done. Nearly all ships had good 'bomb' stories. In some cases, more than one ship was claiming to be the target of a particular attack, but by analysing the returns from all ships, it became clear that in the five days the fleet had been at sea, a total of about one thousand six hundred bombs had been aimed at various units of the fleet. As regards the damage, only one ship, the *Gloucester*, had received a direct hit. Several ships had splinter holes in the superstructure which were of little importance. The *Liverpool* had a large number of small splinter holes in her fo'c'sle which had to be patched before she could go to sea again, but it was all simple straightforward work which the dockyard could do very rapidly. There had been a number of casualties, a few of which besides those in the *Gloucester* had proved fatal. But the fact remains that out of one thousand six hundred bombs, only one direct hit had been obtained.

Before the war, very high percentages of hits had been claimed by the protagonists of high-level 'pattern bombing', of the type which the Italians had used against us. Some had stated that the percentage of hits would be as high as 5%. But I think the general opinion in the fleet had been that the results from high-level bombing would become comparable with the results obtained by long-range gunfire, i.e. 2% hits under easy conditions dropping to about 1% hits under difficult conditions. Allowing that the conditions on the first day, when our gunfire was inexperienced and inaccurate, were easy for the Italians, and that conditions gradually became more difficult for them, they should have scored between 1–2% hits, i.e. somewhere between 16-32 hits. Had we received anything approaching this number of hits, the fleet would have been in a very poor way. We had been phenomenally lucky. But it was now necessary, in fact imperative, to find a method of countering this form of attack, otherwise we should have to surrender the Central Mediterranean to the Italians and Malta would rapidly be starved into submission. Although we did not immediately realise it, this problem had already been largely solved for us.

Up to that time the *Eagle* had carried nothing but Swordfish aircraft. The accommodation for aircraft was strictly limited and it had not been considered advisable to sacrifice offensive and reconnaissance aircraft in order to carry fighters. It happened, however, that the commander flying at that time (Keighly-Peach[13]) was an ex-fighter pilot. Looking round the stores at Alexandria, he had found two Gladiator aircraft; an obsolete type of fighter, but still effective. He persuaded his captain to embark them; there was no room for them in the hanger, so they were stowed on the flight deck above the island.

On the last two days of the passage back to Alexandria, Keighly-Peach persuaded his Captain to let him have a shot at shooting down an Italian shadowing aircraft. Accordingly, he went up shortly before dawn and took up a position up sun and about 10 miles from the fleet. From there he had a good view of the fleet, and therefore, he argued, it was the position which the enemy machine would take up. That his argument was sound was very shortly proved, as an Italian Cant sea plane arrived, obviously looking for the fleet. Keighly-Peach dived onto it and shot it down before it had even realised that it hadn't got the sky to itself. Unfortunately, the Gladiator had a very short endurance, so Keighly-Peach had very soon after to return to the *Eagle*. But one of the other pilots, although not trained as a fighter pilot, took up the other Gladiator and he and Keighly-Peach between them kept up a nearly constant patrol over the fleet during those two days. Keighly-Peach shot down three Italians for certain and his opposite number got one

---

[13] Commander Charles Lindsey Keighly-Peach (KP) became a fighter ace. He was awarded the DSO in 1940. He became Naval Assistant (Air) to the Second Sea Lord, 1941–43, being promoted captain in December 1943. He retired in 1953 and died in 1995.

certainly and possibly another. As a result of their efforts the fleet suffered a very much less severe attack than had developed on the *Warspite*. The lesson was obvious, during daylight hours the fleet must always have a patrol of fighters overhead. We learnt our lesson then and we never forgot it. Many times afterwards we had to go to sea without fighters, or with an inadequate number, but we always did so reluctantly.

While we were digesting the experience of the Calabria engagement, naval operations developed into a series of sweeps against enemy submarines. One of these was particularly successful. A division of destroyers of which *Dainty* was senior officer, accounted for no less than three Italian submarines in twenty-four hours. This success did much towards keeping enemy submarines out of the Eastern Mediterranean for several months.

A similar sweep by four destroyers of the 2nd Flotilla was carried out around the western end of Crete. As it was thought that they might be interfered with by enemy surface vessels, the cruiser *Sydney* was sent to give them support. The enemy did in fact attempt to frustrate the sweep. Soon after dawn the destroyers sighted two Italian 6-inch cruisers and were forced to fall back on the *Sydney* being engaged all the time by the cruisers. The initial enemy report was intercepted in Alexandria, and as it appeared that the Italian fleet might be out in strength, the Commander-in-Chief ordered the whole fleet to raise steam with all dispatch. The fleet left harbour shortly before noon, but before leaving we knew that the *Sydney* had severely damaged one cruiser which had subsequently been sunk by the destroyers and was then engaged in chasing the remaining cruiser, who was retiring in a southerly direction. The cruiser that had been sunk subsequently proved to be the *Bartolomeo Colleoni*, one of the Italian 6-inch cruisers. We shaped a course to meet the returning destroyers. From signals which we had intercepted, we knew that the destroyers had been subjected to an air attack while they were picking up survivors from the Italian cruiser, and that one of them, the *Havoc*, had been damaged in one of her boiler rooms. We therefore felt a certain amount of anxiety for her safety, but we met her just before the light failed and were assured that she could make Alexandria safely under her own steam.

As it appeared probable that the escaping cruiser was making for Tobruk, the Admiral ordered the *Eagle* to carry out another torpedo aircraft attack on the harbour that night.

After the attack, the aircraft were the land at one of the RAF forward aerodromes in Egypt in order to avoid having to land on the carrier in the dark. It was presumed that the attack would be made at dusk as on the previous occasion, but the final arrangements were left to the Captain of the *Eagle* who, although the ship was at sea, was not actually in company with the *Warspite*. The aircraft, however, elected to attack after the moon had arisen later in the night. The attack did not achieve so great a surprise as on the previous occasion and was met with considerable AA fire. Nevertheless, all the machines got into the harbour and released their torpedoes. The Italian cruiser, unfortunately, was not at Tobruk, but considerable damage was done to various merchant vessels so that after this attack, for all practical purposes, Tobruk was no longer used by the enemy for supplying his army. Several of the aircraft were hit by the AA fire and some casualties were incurred, but all machines returned to the forward aerodrome, although one crashed on landing and became a write-off.

Shortly before sunset *Warspite* had flown off her aircraft with instructions to be over Tobruk at dusk and to drop a few bombs from a good height with the intention of causing a diversion at about the time that the torpedo aircraft were expected to make their attack. This was not a success as *Eagle's* planes did not attack until later, as has already been explained. It is not clear what happened to *Warspite's* plane, but at about 9pm a signal was received stating that she was making a forced landing and giving a position about 15 miles to the north and east of Tobruk. The Admiral sent the *Jervis* back to find the aircraft, but she was unsuccessful. It was a rather hopeless task as it was a dark night and she had to leave the area well before daylight as it was unpleasantly close to Tobruk. The loss of this aircraft was a considerable blow to the *Warspite*; both the pilot and observer being popular members of the wardroom. We were therefore very relieved when about three months later we heard that the whole crew had been captured and were safe.

The next few weeks were comparatively quiet ones for the fleet as it was necessary to dock battleships. This was rather a long process as the floating dock as Alexandria could only take a Queen Elizabeth class battleship if she was empty of oil fuel and had disembarked all her ammunition. However, we were able to use this period to run a convoy to and from the Aegean, escorted by cruisers and destroyers. And we were considerably cheered by the fact that the East Indies squadron succeeded in running a convoy both up and down the Red Sea without it being attacked. We had felt some anxiety about our supply route as it was so susceptible to attack by the Italian Navy and Air Force based in Eritrea.

After the successful torpedo aircraft attacks on Tobruk using the forward RAF aerodromes, the Air Officer Commanding in the Western Desert, Group Captain Collishaw, suggested to the Commander-in-Chief that it would be a good idea to have some Swordfish aircraft equipped with torpedoes stationed in the desert, ready to attack any shipping which might be sighted by the RAF reconnaissance machines. We had no spare aircraft, but as the fleet was committed to remaining in the harbour for at least a week, the Admiral sent three of *Eagle's* Swordfish, each with a torpedo, and put them under the operational control of Group Captain Collishaw, commanding 202 Group. We were a bit nervous as to how the torpedoes would stand up to conditions in the desert, but we made large canvas covers to try to keep the sand out of the after bodies, arranged to change them around as often as possible and hoped for the best, and our optimism was justified.

A few days later an RAF reconnaissance machine reported two ships in a small bay off the Gulf of Bomba, which appeared to be a submarine and a merchant ship. The Swordfish set off to attack keeping well to seaward to avoid being seen. They made good landfall and went into attack keeping low down. The Italians were completely surprised, the leader attacked the submarine and hit her full amidships with his torpedo. The other two planes went on to attack the merchant vessel spraying the leaders target with machine-gun fire as they passed. They attacked the merchant ship from either side observing as they did so that she was apparently a depot ship with a destroyer alongside one side and a submarine the other. Both torpedoes hit, and as the Swordfish were retiring to seaward, they saw a very large explosion in the destroyer as though a magazine had exploded and all three ships sank. So, in that operation, for an expenditure of three torpedoes, no less than four ships were sunk. We called this operation the 'Sandwich'.

But all our operations were not so successful. We started the war with Italy with ten submarines in the Mediterranean fleet and in six weeks no less than five of these had been lost. The Italians claimed to have sunk one of them by ramming it with a destroyer, but we had no idea how the others were lost. We could only presume that they ventured too close to Italian ports and had been sunk by hitting mines. It was a heavy blow. Looking back on those weeks, one remembers them as a time of great strain and anxiety. However carefully an organisation is worked out, one can never be sure it will work smoothly when it is put to the enormous strain that modern war brings in its train. I think it may be said that the fleet as a whole, and the staff in particular, adjusted themselves to the new conditions quickly and efficiently. The staff, led by the Admiral, who was always optimistic, was certainly cheerful. One officer at a later date told me he used to visit the staff and always came away feeling better. Personally, I found it very difficult to be optimistic. I have always thought that the months of June and July 1940 were the worst in this war.

Many months later, when I had left the staff and had a command of my own, I was having lunch with the Admiral and he asked me which period of the war I had thought was the worst. I replied, 'just after France surrendered'. But he disagreed with me, saying that he had always been certain that we could beat the Italians at sea, and that his worst period was after Crete. But he went on to say that he was then in the mood to say 'I told you so', and, he added, that helps no one, neither oneself nor anyone else.

But it was not until the middle of August that we produced what we might call a staff laugh. We called this the 'Pooh trap'. Those who have read the classic works of Mr A. A. Milne will remember that when Christopher Robin wished to catch a heffalump, the way they set about it was to build a heffalump trap. This trap consisted of a pit dug in the ground and covered with branches, leaves etc. Well, without going into technical details of heffalump traps, the principle was that it was something into which one placed one's foot. And we thought that if we could provide a sufficiently tempting bait, we might persuade the Italian air force to walk into a trap.

At that time Graziani was assembling an Italian army on the frontier of Egypt in the vicinity of Sollum, Fort Capuzzo and Bardia, with the intention of invading Egypt. The army were very anxious that this Italian force should be harried as much as possible in order to delay the date of the invasion to allow our reinforcements to arrive, and the RAF fighters were very anxious to have a crack at the Italian bombers.

It was therefore arranged that the fleet should appear off the coast at dawn one morning, bombard the various concentration positions of the Italian army and retire on Alexandria, keeping as close to the Egyptian coast as possible in order that the RAF fighters, operating from the RAF forward aerodromes, might maintain a patrol of fighters over the fleet to beat off the inevitable attack.

For this bombardment the fleet was divided into two forces; the *Warspite* with her long-range guns, and the *Kent,* an 8-inch cruiser that had recently joined the fleet, went close in to Sollum to bombard Fort Capuzzo and various concentration points in that area. Meanwhile the two other battleships bombarded Bardia and the wadis opening off the Gulf of Bardia where RAF reconnaissance machines had reported concentrations of the enemy. The whole area was suitable for mining operations, so it was necessary to have a minesweeping force with each detachment.

The fleet made the coast at dawn, and soon after the sun had risen, both detachments opened fire. The battleship's spotting planes had been landed at Alexandria and were operating from the RAF forward aerodromes. They were ready in position to spot by the time we arrived.

Warspite, at a range of about 13 miles, put her first salvo slap into Fort Capuzzo. This much impressed the army officers who were watching from the advanced British positions. During the next few days the Fleet Gunnery Officer spent much time in explaining that it was quite usual for battleships to hit an unseen target at 13 miles. Some of the army officers were polite enough to pretend to believe him, but the other members of the staff were more sceptical and made pointed remarks to the effect that any gentleman would consider such a gift of good luck an occasion for opening several bottles of the best champagne.

It was a lovely calm summer morning in which nothing came to disturb the *Warspite* as we lobbed our shells over the hills at an unseen target. The only incident in the bombardment occurred when a driving band from one projectile came loose so that the round could be heard setting up an unearthly screech as it tore on its journey through the blue sky. A small gun at Bardia fired a few rounds at the other two battleships, but it was quite ineffective. We completed the bombardment, both detachments joined up together again and we returned, leaving an enormous pall of smoke and dust over Bardia. It was clear that the Italian air force are not early risers so that the destroyers had time to recover their mine-sweeps before the next phase occurred and we had breakfast in peace.

The air attack arrived about 9.30am. It was the familiar high-level bombing attack which developed from abaft our port beam. The first wave pressed home their attack with some determination, and bombs fell close to the battleships. The aircraft had to make their way through a considerable barrage as everyone was on the alert and fire was opened early. An RAF Group Captain, who had come to sea in the *Warspite* to witness the operation, was an interested spectator from the Admiral's bridge. In the *Warspite* the AA guns were on the fo'c'sle deck, almost abreast the bridge, so that when the target is near the zenith the engaged side of the bridge is almost vertically over the guns and the resulting shock and blast is considerable. One therefore watches from the disengaged side. This was where the Group Captain was standing and was leaning back using the disengaged bridge rail as a support for his back, as the enemy aircraft came over the battle fleet. What he did not appreciate was that as the aircraft crossed the zenith, the guns on the disengaged side would open fire. This is what happened, with the result that he was thrown forward on his face under the impression that he had been struck by a particularly unpleasant Italian bomb, to such an extent that we thought this incident was a cause for some merriment.

Some more bombs were dropped rather wide, then a single aircraft was seen. Somebody thought they saw a fighter very high up. The Admiral, always optimistic, thought he heard machine-gun fire. The remainder of the forenoon passed without attacks or news. It was not until we were nearly abreast Mersa Matruh that we received a signal from the RAF saying that the RAF and FAA fighters had got amongst the enemy bombers and had shot down twelve for certain and possibly another. This, of course, was before the days of the Battle of Britain and at that time to shoot down ten aircraft in a single day was a big achievement. On arrival at Alexandria we received reports of the results of the bombardment which appeared to be satisfactory. It therefore seemed obvious that this operation, in which all three forces had cooperated together, had produced satisfactory results without loss to ourselves.

This may be said to have completed the first phase of the war in the Mediterranean.

19/8/40

Darling,

There is a chance that I might be able to get a letter to you by a quick route so I am hurriedly writing to you. We had a good crack at the wops on Saturday at Bardia and Capuzzo. We were firing at the latter and as it is someway inland we were unable to see our shell bursts but we think we did good shooting. I managed to keep out of the way of the blast this time and came to no harm. We evidently surprised the enemy as their air force did not get on to us for about three hours and as we were well prepared for them, they did us no harm and lost ten of their bombers. We actually saw two come down from the ship.

I have no other news. I hope you are keeping well and the boys are getting a little fun out of their summer holidays but from the reports we get from the BBC of almost continuous air raids, I imagine that conditions are very unpleasant for you. You have all my sympathy, I can get no amusement out of an air raid either at the time or in retrospect.

All my love
William

CHAPTER 14
HANDS ACROSS THE SEA

Towards the end of August, the Admiralty decided that they were strong enough at home to reinforce the Mediterranean fleet and at the same time the war office came to the conclusion that despite the threat of invasion to England, they could spare some much-needed material for the army of the Nile. Some additional troops had already arrived in Egypt from India and Australia via the Red Sea and others were slowly making their way from England via the Cape, but if the threatened Italian invasion of Egypt from Libya was to be countered, additional mechanised equipment was urgently required. To get this equipment to Egypt as quickly as possible, the Admiralty decided to send a convoy through the Mediterranean escorted by the reinforcements for the Mediterranean Fleet. This convoy was to be covered in the Western Mediterranean by Force 'H' from Gibraltar, make the passage of the Sicilian channel during dark hours, and be met west of Malta by the Mediterranean Fleet, who would cover it on its passage from Malta to Alexandria. The convoy consisted of four modern merchant ships all capable of 14 kn and each of 9,000 to 10,000 tons capacity. They were all fitted with paravanes as it was realised that the Sicilian channel was certain to be mined.

The reinforcements for the fleet consisted of the battleship *Valiant*, a modernised battleship like the *Warspite*, but with an even more up-to-date AA armament; the new aircraft carrier *Illustrious* and the two AA cruisers *Coventry* and *Calcutta*. These were also full of munitions, mostly AA guns, anti-tank guns and ammunition. Most of that in the *Valiant* was for Malta.

Before the war the possibility of passing a convoy through the Mediterranean had often been considered. Estimates of the losses which might be expected varied between those produced by the optimist who thought 50% of the convoy might get through successfully, to those of the pessimists who were convinced that the whole convoy would be sunk before it had completed half the passage. The Commander-in-Chief, Mediterranean, was responsible for drafting the orders for this difficult operation. As this was the first occasion since the outbreak of war with Italy that we should have had any contact with Force 'H' at the other end of the Mediterranean, the operation orders were given the title Operation HATS, being the initial letters of the phrase Hands Across The Sea; a piece of sentimentality for which I think we were afterwards rather ashamed.

Editor's note.

Regrettably, we do not have the next chapters of this narrative. However, Operation HATS was a success, despite the considerable risks. The Mediterranean fleet was strengthened by the arrival of the *Valiant*, *Illustrious*, *Coventry* and *Calcutta*. The latter two ships are the principle players in Chapter 17.

The following extracts from letters to Valentine Carne give an insight in the action that took place in these months.

30/9/1940

Not too good a day yesterday as the enemy aircraft got on to our tail early in the day and carried out two bombing attacks. In the second they got a stick of about thirty bombs from five aircraft in formation all around the Warspite. Several near misses which have honeycombed several portions of the superstructure but with the ship's proverbial good luck, we only had three minor casualties. As we are at sea my cabin is shut down and I am living on the bridge so I am unable to get any writing paper hence the reason why I am writing in pencil on a signal pad.

17/10/40

I was glad to hear that the aircraft have been giving you a little peace.
We have had a good many visitations from them but we have also
been getting a little of our own back. We had quite a good view of
the sinking of the Artigliere, the destroyer which was damaged by the
Ajax. She was sunk by a torpedo which exploded one of her magazines.
The result was a fearsome sight. The column of flame, yellow green in
colour shot with vivid crimson took about ten seconds to grow to its
maximum height and die away again and the resultant column of smoke
was tremendous. We were bombed pretty heartily afterwards but the
enemy had no success. The unsatisfactory part of our trip to sea was
the fact that someone pinched my razor. It was my old Gillette which
I have had for twenty-five years. It was given to me by my father
during my first leave in the last war in 1915. That leave is one of the
most vivid memories I have of that period and I am annoyed at having
lost a connection with it. I seem to be more busy than ever, we were
short-handed in torpedo officers from the word go and since then we
have had three torpedo officers and two gunners (T) killed. I don't
know which way to turn to find anyone who knows one end of a torpedo
from the other.

The Artigliere exploding after being torpedoed by HMS York *12th October 1940 – photo from W.P. Carne's album*

CHAPTER 15
THE BATTLES OF TARANTO AND MATAPAN

In 1942–43, Captain William Carne was assigned to Washington on a British Supply Mission and on the Combined Munitions Assignment Board. During this time, he visited the factory of the Bullard Company in Bridgeport, Connecticut. While there, he gave a speech on the important work that the factory was doing making torpedoes for the British. The following narrative is taken from this speech and describes a number of actions that he was directly involved in, including the Battle of Taranto (November 1940) and Matapan (March 1941). In fact, the Battle of Matapan took place after the events in the following Chapter, concerning the capture of Tobruk (January 1941). His letters concerning Matapan are therefore found at the end of Chapter 16 to retain the chronological narrative.

You are engaged in making a torpedo which is very complicated and difficult to manufacture. This torpedo is going to be used by another Nation; many of you must have fathers or sons, friends or cousins who are part of the American forces and you must often wonder why you should be manufacturing an article for another Nation instead of directly helping your own relations and friends. I know very little about the inside of these torpedoes and I do not propose to talk about it, but I do know something of the uses to which this torpedo can be put and the great assistance it can be towards bringing that final victory for which we are all looking. I propose to tell you how this torpedo has been used and perhaps when you have heard what I have to say, you will agree that the production of this weapon in large numbers is one of the most telling things you can do towards bringing about the defeat of our common enemies.

For the first two years of this war, I was a Staff Officer on the staff of the Commander-in-Chief of the Mediterranean, where my particular duties dealt with all forms of torpedoes. After France collapsed, we found ourselves in a very critical position, cut off at the eastern end of the Mediterranean with a superior fleet between us and Gibraltar. Under these circumstances the Commander-in-Chief decided that, though we were the weaker fleet, we must take every possible form of offensive action. This was not easy to do as the enemy showed a tendency to remain in his harbour and harass us by long-range air attack.

In the autumn of 1940, when we had been reinforced by the modern aircraft carrier *Illustrious*, the Commander-in-Chief decided to carry out an operation which he had had in mind for a long time. This was the attack on the Italian battlefleet in Taranto harbour itself. We had considered this attack on many occasions, but the difficulties had always appeared to be very great. Several considerations were essential. Firstly, the Italian fleet must think either that the British fleet were in harbour or were returning to harbour without any particular offensive object in view. Secondly, the weather must be fine and the moon in the right quarter, and thirdly arrangements must be made to distract the enemy's attention from the main object. Our plan was to escort a convoy with the battle fleet to the south of Malta and then double back with the battle fleet at high speed as if making for Alexandria. We knew that we should be sighted by an Italian reconnaissance aircraft while south of Malta and we thought that if they saw us leave the convoy at Malta, they would reckon that we had completed our operation and that we were returning to Alexandria. The first part of the plan worked well. We took a convoy to Malta (11th November 1940) and the battle fleet turned back, being duly sighted by the Italian aircraft. After dark we turned northwards and steamed at high speed into the centre of the Mediterranean.

All the next day we were steaming north-east until shortly after dark we had attained a position off the Island of Cephalonia, off the Greek coast. As soon as it was dark the cruisers were dispatched into the Adriatic to shoot up the Italian convoys running from Italy to Albania. The battle fleet took up a position between the aircraft carrier and Taranto to cover it during the flying operations. At this time, we were less than 100 miles from the Italian main base at Taranto. As soon as the moon rose the aircraft were flown off, divided into two groups, one of which was to remain at good height and drop flares and bomb the Italian cruisers in the harbour. The second group were to attack the Italian battleships in the outer harbour with torpedoes. As the Italians had barrage balloons flying from the breakwater it was decided that the aircraft should make a circuit round the harbour and attack from the landward side. Thus, if any aircraft were lost, on the barrage balloon cables, they would be lost after they had released their torpedoes. The attack was a great success.

The Italians were distracted by the high-flying aircraft and the flares and as a result the torpedo aircraft were not detected until they had got right in amongst the battle fleet. The result of this attack was to put the Italian battle fleet out of action for several months, and, in fact, one battleship which was sunk has never yet been repaired sufficiently to be able to steam.

While this was going on, the cruisers had found a convoy in the Adriatic and, of the four ships comprising it, they sank three and left the fourth burning. The aircraft that survived the attack all landed in the early hours of the morning and before dawn the whole fleet was steaming at high speed to the southward. We expected a heavy air attack shortly after dawn, but the distraction put up by the cruisers appears to have completely confused the Italians. They put their main effort into searching for us in the Adriatic. It was not until noon that their reconnaissance planes located us and then our fighters shot down three of them in quick succession before they had time to report our position. The Italian counterattack did not, therefore, develop before dark and by the next morning we were so far away that they had no chance to attack us.

Early in 1941, when the campaign in Greece started, an opportunity came to attack Italian transports in Valona. For this purpose, we flew aircraft with their torpedoes from Egypt to Crete and from Crete to Salamis, near Athens. Here we used a rather decrepit Greek torpedo depot to charge up the torpedoes, and from there they went in long hops to an advanced airfield near the Grecian front line. There the aircraft were parked with their torpedoes for weeks at a time, among the early spring flowers on the Grecian hills, until a suitable target appeared and then attacked either at dusk or at dawn, swooping down on Valona and taking a heavy toll of the Italian transports.

When the Italian fleet came out to interfere with our convoys to Greece, and we met them at the Battle of Matapan (28th March 1941), the action was brought about by torpedo aircraft who, attacking in relays throughout

116/11/40

Darling,

Very many thanks for your air mail letters which all arrived together. I got them on our return to harbour after a particularly strenuous but satisfactory eight days at sea. You will have heard about the FAA attack on Taranto and the raid on the Straits of Otranto, we also covered the movements of some very important convoys and incidentally shot down eight enemy aircraft. Not too bad for one week. The Taranto attack was of course the high spot. We have had this in mind ever since the Munich affair just after I came out here, but it required the complete co-ordination of a number of forces and perfect weather and torpedoes that will do their stuff. I think it can be said that we produced all the requirements.

Your three air mail letters were mostly concerned with taking the boys to school and your visit to Prestwich. The school doesn't sound too bad from your description. Pity it is such a shocking journey from Falmouth. I can't think why Jim should think it was a good idea to send some of the boys to Canada. As regards safety, it is still safer to spend six months in London than to make a single crossing of the Atlantic and think of the upset it would be to their education to start in a new country at this stage. Also, I am against this wholesale evacuation in principle. It may be a good thing to get rid of children from heavily bombed areas but for the rest of the country, we have got to dig our toes in and tell everybody to go to hell. This evacuation business is an army mania, they will evacuate anywhere if they are given a ship. Luckily there are no ships around this part of the world to spare.

the day, slowed down one of the enemy battleships and torpedoed and stopped an Italian 8-inch cruiser. It was the fact that this cruiser had stopped that brought about the night action which followed. We in the battleships had been chasing the enemy all day, but at dusk we were still fifty miles away. We knew one of the cruisers was stopped and we thought that the enemy would send back some ships to cover her retreat. This proved to be the case and in the early hours of that night we detected an enemy ship and the Commander-in-Chief moved the whole of the battle fleet with intent to attack. Then came a dramatic moment when we first sighted the enemy and we altered course, bringing all guns of the battlefleet to bear. At the crucial moment, just as we steadied on our new course, one of our destroyers, *Greyhound*, switched on a searchlight and there, picked out in silver against the black night, was a lovely Italian 8-inch cruiser. We were all ready for her. The Commander-in-Chief's flagship, *Warspite*, fired her complete broadside of eight 15-inch guns. We believe no less than five of these eight shells struck the ship in that first salvo. She was stunned, dumb and numbed and never fired a round in reply. She had ceased in that short interval of time to be a warship but as a spectacle she became the centre of a raging fire from which shot up large explosions to illuminate the night and to show up a second 8-inch cruiser which suffered the same fate from our consorts. It is true that these two ships were not sunk by aircraft torpedoes, but had it not been for the action of the aircraft earlier in the day, in damaging that Italian ship, that night action would never have been bought about.[14]

In these few instances I think that I have shown that aircraft equipped with torpedoes can be a very powerful weapon if used with skill, determination, and confidence. I would like to stress the last word, 'confidence'. No pilot could make an attack unless he was confident that he had a good aircraft and that his torpedoes would run accurately on the course upon which he had directed them. In all these actions which I have described, we never had one of these torpedoes fail to do its duty. Not one signal torpedo failed, although we left them, as I have said, exposed to sun and dust in the Western Desert, although we took them to Greece and exposed them to the elements for weeks on end without any care or attention.

Can there be any more effective way of helping our friends than by sinking the enemy laden troopships and supply ships before they ever reach the enemy's bases? This is what the aircraft torpedo is doing each day and each night, and it is only limited by the fact that the torpedo is in short supply. These torpedoes are being assembled in two factories in England.

---

[14] At the battle of Matapan the Italians lost three 8-inch cruisers Zara, Pola and Fiume, together with two destroyers, *Alfieri* and *Corducci*. It was a resounding victory for the British forces, which only lost one aircraft.

Although these factories are in easy bombing range, thank God, the enemy has been able to do them very little damage, but at any moment he may have a lucky break and put one of these factories out of action.

The only other place in the world where these torpedoes are being manufactured is at the firm called Bullard Company at Bridgeport. You will therefore understand with what anxiety those who are controlling the British war effort are watching the progress of this firm.

To sum up, the Bullard Company has very great strategic value as being the only factory of 18" torpedoes that is not within range of enemy bombers, and secondly its output is very urgently needed to supplement the English factories in order that the full weight of our heavily increased air force may be brought to bear upon the lines of communication at sea of the enemy.

Christmas card from William Carne 'to all at Garras', 1940

8/1/41

Our last trip at sea was in order to have a last crack at Bardia, our efforts appear to have been successful. The Wops had a Battery mounted high up on the cliffs which gave us a certain amount of trouble. It was in an impossible place to get a direct hit on it with a naval gun and whenever we fired at it, they packed up and ran into their dugouts. They eventually nearly got a hit on us and one shell which burst close to the port quarter has taken several large chips off the quarterdeck enamel. We are now endeavouring to keep them on the run before the Germans can come to their help.

PTO

I cannot pretend that the last lot of promotions was not a great disappointment. I thought I had a good chance and I understood that the C-in-C thought the same and had my relief booked. I understand that I am now to stay on here for a little while at least so that I can get another recommend for my last chance in June. I can't pretend that I am overjoyed at the prospect but it would be hopeless to change one's horses at the last moment.
Three days later.
The Germans have arrived with their dive bombers and given us a most unpleasant surprise. This ship has had two attacks, our luck has just held out. One enormous bomb released from over the mainmast, just missed the foremast and either hit the starboard lower anchor or just missed and burst alongside. The starboard hawse pipe which is a very large casting, is cracked and the PV chains carried away but otherwise only superficial damage and no one hurt. Other ships were not so lucky. I see that Portsmouth has had another raid. If the house has survived do you think it worthwhile trying to get Mrs Carpenter to pack up one or two of the pictures and send them to a safer place. I should hate to lose the Pocock prints or the Chinese woman.

CHAPTER 16
THE CAPTURE OF TOBRUK - 1941

16/1/41

Darling
I think it probable that I may not have the opportunity to write for
some time. I have volunteered for a job for which I thought I was well
fitted to carry out and to my surprise the C⁻in⁻C agreed, on certain
conditions. The first was that I did not get bombed to which I agreed,
but beyond writing a polite note to Musso, I am not quite certain how I
am to carry out this condition.

Editor's note. This Chapter is compiled from details contained in a letter
to 'Roger Dick' and the 'Fleet Torpedo Officer's Diary of Proceedings at
Tobruk and Derna, 21st January – 8th February 1941'

When it looked as though Tobruk might fall in the not-too-distant future,
Admiral Lyster[15] in *Illustrious*, during one of our sweeps, proposed to drop a
few of our new magnetic mines, which we called 'cucumbers', in the entrance
to Tobruk and Benghazi. I said I thought this was unwise as we might want
to use Tobruk ourselves in the near future and we had no effective magnetic
sweep. The Commander-in-Chief sent me to argue the pros and cons with
Lyster and Boyd.

---

[15] From 1940 Lumley Lyster served as rear-admiral in charge of the Aircraft Carriers in
the Mediterranean Fleet. He developed the plan of attack for Taranto, beginning in 1935
and put it into execution in November 1940. In 1941 he was appointed as Fifth Sea Lord
and Chief of Naval Air Services and Commander of the Aircraft Carriers in the Home
Fleet, with his flag in HMS *Illustrious*. His last appointment was as Flag Officer, Carrier
Training, in 1943 before he retired in 1945. He died in 1957.

Boyd was very keen to use the new weapons as we had no experience with them and did not really know if they would go off. I quoted the case of using the first tanks in penny numbers at the Battle of the Somme and so losing the advantage of surprise which a new weapon can give if used in reasonable numbers. Lyster retorted that if one mine went off, its effect would be to make the Italians organise a magnetic sweeping force at every one of their ports and the effort required would do much to prevent them taking effective action against us elsewhere.

The Commander-in-Chief's decision was to let the Air boys go ahead, and they laid six mines in the approaches to Tobruk.

When it appeared probable that Tobruk would be captured in a few days, I produced a paper saying what would be required, if we wished to use the port. This included sweeping our own and the enemy minefields, charting the wrecks in the harbour after *Eagle's* torpedo attacks and getting the net defences into working order, if they had been sabotaged by the enemy. Algy[16], the Chief of Staff, sent for me and asked me who would be a suitable officer to go in charge of such an operation. I replied that I thought I was the only officer with the knowledge of the minefields and of such resources as we had to sweep them. To my surprise he said, 'By Jove, that is a good idea, I will think it over'. I didn't think much more of it, as I knew that the Commander-in-Chief did not like sending his staff off on odd jaunts at a time when the fleet was so busy and had so many problems to solve. I was therefore pleasantly surprised when an hour later I was sent for and told that I could go. Later, I had to explain my plans for entering the harbour to the Commander-in-Chief who said, 'Carne must have everything he wants', and then proceeded to veto just about every suggestion I made. What he really meant was that I could have anything that the Commander-in-Chief had to spare, which was not a great deal.

A day or so later, Captain Hickling SNOIS, Senior Naval Officer Inshore Squadron, came to Alexandria to talk over the bombardment which was to be carried out by HMS *Terror* and the gunboats in support of the Army during the assault on Tobruk. My part of the scheme was explained to him and we agreed, very roughly, on our plan.

---

[16] Admiral of the Fleet Sir Algernon Usborne Willis KCB DSO (17 May 1889 – 12 April 1976)

I was given *Fiona*, one of the so-called boarding vessels to act as HQ ship, together with a party of a hundred officers and men, known as the temporary party, to clear up the harbour. *Fiona* was commanded by a lieutenant commander called Griffiths[17], a nice chap, had been a P&O officer, but hardly a strong enough character for the rather piratical life we lived up the coast. For sweeping the 'cucumbers'" I had two trawlers, *Arthur Cavanagh* and *Milford Countess*, commanded by a lieutenant RNR called Maltby. These were fitted with a double 'A' sweep, the only magnetic sweep we possessed. They could only operate on a smooth sandy bottom, quite useless at Alex, but I thought they might sweep the immediate approaches to Tobruk. Finally, I had the old target towing trawler *Moy* for the reconnaissance of the approach and to sweep inside the harbour. The Commander-in-Chief was very insistent on this; if he had been the Italian SNO he would have filled the harbour with mines before he left. I did not think this was likely; no intelligence report had been received of a mine depot at Tobruk nor any minelayers. It is not easy to lay mines from improvised vessels effectively without blowing yourself up.

I was known as COT, Clearance Officer Tobruk, and I assembled my 'squadron' at Sollum on the 22nd January, where I immediately went ashore to see SNOIS. There were vague rumours that Tobruk had fallen that day and I was keen to sail the same night, but SNOIS refused to let me go until we had confirmation that the *San Grigio* and coast defence batteries were out of action. The result was that we wasted a valuable twenty-four hours. However, we used the time to talk over my instructions for the entry of the harbour. I called this operation order, 'Enter Tobruk Harbour', ETH.

The next morning, I persuaded the SNOIS to let me sail in the evening. Tobruk was definitely reported to have fallen and the *San Grigio* to be in flames. I sailed in the *Moy* to arrive at dawn and *Fiona* to follow to be in the offing at noon.

From a captured Italian coaster, we had an idea of the swept channel, so I

---

[17] Arthur Griffiths RNR was killed on 18 Apr 1941 when the Fiona was lost in action. A letter from William Carne to his wife of 24th April 1941 said "The ship in which I went to Tobruk, the Fiona, has been sunk with a very large number of casualties. This has depressed me a lot, she was a first-class little ship. The Captain, navigator and engineer, all excellent RNR Officers, have been killed".

followed that until near the entrance. I then I crept down to the south shore, which is very steep with the cliffs almost vertical below the surface, so that I was able to creep along at 2 or 3 kn within about 20 yards of the cliffs. The First Lieutenant was hanging over the rails to look out for rocks and we had two chaps with lead lines going either side. By doing so I hoped to avoid the area in which the 'cucumbers' had been dropped.

I could see quite a lot of the boom buoys as I approached, but no sign of the gate. When I got to the boom, I turned along it and followed it to the centre where, on the bottom, I could see the two drifters which had been used as the gate working vessels. With the gate working vessels they had of course sunk the gate, so I turned through it and entered the harbour. I should add that I had been buoying my route with dan buoys all the way.

Once inside the harbour I streamed the Oropesa, a type of mine sweep, and swept all the harbour clear of the area of the wrecks which, in fact, was only a small part of the total area, but I felt confident that there were no mines.

The harbour had a very desolate appearance. *San Grigio* was half submerged, there had evidently been a big explosion amidships where she was still burning while the funnels and masts leant over towards the seat of the fire. *Liguria* was gently smouldering; a fierce fire was burning at the oil fuel depots and there were several minor fires in the town. Besides *Liguria*, the *Seventias* was ashore on the south coast, a large merchant ship was on her side in the middle of the harbour, the wrecks of three destroyers could be seen beyond this ship and a merchant was lying upright but with her upper deck awash at the head of the harbour. It was clear that the Fleet Air Arm had done their work only too well.

I then went to sea again, reversing my inward route and lead the *Fiona* into the harbour. Griffiths caused my heart to go into my mouth once or twice as he had difficulty in manoeuvering the *Fiona* around the tight turns of my swept channel. However, we got in safely and I called up Maltby who arrived with the double 'A' trawlers the next morning and almost immediately swept one of the 'cucumbers'. One of the few occasions when a double 'A' sweep has worked! But we were unable to sweep any more. The sandy bottom only extended for about half a mile beyond the boom; as soon as the sweepers got off the sand, they were in trouble carrying out their sweep. But the bottom shelves very rapidly and I reckoned that, if the 'cucumbers' were outside the sandy area, they were too deep to be effective and I therefore reported the port open to receive merchant ships.

The San Grigio in flames in Tobruk after being scuttled by the Italians

We never knew what happened to the other 'cucumbers' but during the evacuation of Greece one of the Irish Channel packet boats was mined almost in the entrance to Tobruk, and I have always thought her fate may have been to pass over one of the 'cucumbers', but I had ceased to be FTO by then and never saw the report of the enquiry if, indeed, one was held.

As soon as *Fiona* had anchored, I landed with Captain Smith RNR and his maintenance party. His job was to run the port and he was first class at it, taking a firm line with some of the Australian soldiers. In fact, the scene ashore was a bit chaotic the oil fuel tanks were still burning so that everything was covered in a cloud of smoke, and Australian soldiers were looting right, left and centre. Their principle was to walk into a house and throw everything into the street. They did not find much except some raw Italian red wine and a dump of small automatic pistols abandoned by the

Italian Officers when they surrendered. Of course, they had to try out the pistols and any glass windows made a good target, but after several glasses of red wine their aim was rather erratic.

Townsend went off to examine the remains of the boom and came back to say that the company of Australians who had marched along the coast and were encamped on the southern side of the entrance, were using the buoys of the boom for target practice and already several had been sunk. I sent him back to request the CO to stop this practice and to add, if he was not cooperative, that I would come in the morning and carry out some target practice myself with my 12-pounder gun using the hut he had as an HQ as the target. Apparently, the CO's reaction to the first part of the message was to the effect, 'The boys are only having a little fun, leave them alone'. Townsend then delivered the second part of the message. He was a man with cold china-blue eyes, had originally been a signalman, was made a mate during the First War (one of the first promotions from the lower deck), subsequently commanded an ML on the Danube. When he retired, he became a demonstrator at Oxford and to his naval training as a chief Yeoman, he had added a pedagogy mode of speech. The result was quite effective, the CO said, 'Aw, I didn't know the commander was serious, I will tell the boys to lay off'. I have often wondered what I should have done if my bluff had been called!

That afternoon I set Fyson, a young lieutenant assigned to me from the *Warspite*, to work with his team rounding up all the available craft in the harbour. We found some half dozen motor fishing craft, some of which were in good order. That night we moved them close to the Naval HQ, we called it Admiralty House, using a new coil of rope we had bought from Alex. During the night the Australians cut it and stole most of it. I protested mildly to the Australian Brigadier who thought it was rather a joke. He said, 'Aren't my boys bloody awful! Never mind, Commander, we are marching at dawn tomorrow'. The Army did continue its advance at dawn, but the Australians were so drunk that they could not be rounded up until 4pm. However, they marched all night and were up with the rest of the army by dawn the next morning.

On first landing I was worried about booby-traps. We found a torpedo in the submarine depot with its warhead on, complete with its pistol and a lot of electric wires hanging round it. As the only 'T' officer present I decided to take out the pistol, using as my helper Gubb, the Commissioned Gunner (T) ex-*Southampton*, who I had brought as an assistant to Fyson. HMS *Southampton* had been lost shortly before – set on fire by bombs and burnt like a torch with lots of men lost. The poor chap had lost his nerve in the *Southampton* and was all in a dither. I had to do the job entirely myself; there was nothing in it, a very amateurish attempt at a booby-trap which would never have gone off anyway. I kept the pistol as a memento and still have it.

The first merchant ship to arrive was one of the Prince line, *Cingalese Prince*. Smith had the port well organised by then and unloading was proceeding quickly. The army asked how many prisoners they could send back in her. I said none, I could not have her hanging about the port, we were having intermittent air raids and I was afraid of her being sunk so planned to sail her the minute she was empty. I asked why there was such a hurry about

The pistol from the Italian booby trapped torpedo

the prisoners, surely they could wait on more important matters. To which they replied that there were about 20,000 in the cages south of Tobruk and they were dying at the rate of twenty a day. I thought, 'Oh God, I must do something about this'. So, on the Army promising to send a really strong guard, I agreed to fill the holds of the Prince line with prisoners. The Captain of the ship was a grand chap who took everything in his stride quite calmly, and in fact by careful organisation the sailing of the ship was only delayed by a very short time. I went on board the ship when it was half full of prisoners for a final conference with the Captain. The gangway was engaged so I went alongside the jumping ladder leading up to the after-hold deck. Immediately, half a dozen young Italians came forward to help me over the bulwark and brush down my clothes, which had got pretty grubby. They were all smiling and cheerful and I could not help wondering why we were fighting against such nice people.

About the third day Harold Hickling, SNOIS, arrived with the *Terror* and took up his residence in *Fiona*. He wanted to run the whole port, his idea was to hold meetings and write voluminous orders which were out of date before they could be reproduced. His rather sarcastic, very impertinent questioning of Smith drove that rather incoherent officer to a state of subdued fury. He, Hickling, spent his time writing long reports to the Commander-in-Chief taking credit for everything that had happened.

I went for a short trip around the outskirts of Tobruk where we visited the coast defence batteries, one of the AA batteries, port war signal station and the coal dump and water installation. At first sight the town did not appear to be too much damaged as most of the bomb craters had been filled in, but on closer inspection it was clear that conditions must have been pretty unpleasant. The large number of air raid shelters were a feature, many of which were very deep with elaborate concrete structures over the top. The town had been badly pillaged by the first troops to enter and the streets were covered with gear thrown out of the houses. One of the most pathetic sights was the large number of masterless dogs that were certain to die shortly from starvation.

I think it was the fourth or fifth day that the Commander-in-Chief and COS arrived by air. After Hickling had blown his trumpet at them for some time, I took them round the harbour in one of the captured fishing vessels that Fyson had got running efficiently and had turned into a useful tender.

We stood on the foredeck while I acted as a guide. Admiral Cunningham as pleased as Punch, stood there with his walking stick and a self-satisfied grin on his face, loving every moment of his triumphant passage. A rather curious conversation took place between Algy and me, in the intervals of me pointing out the beauties of Tobruk. We talked together but we were both directing our remarks at the Commander-in-Chief, who absolutely refused to be drawn and to give a decision about anything. Algy was saying that the sweeping organisation at Alex was not building up satisfactorily, the enemy was starting to mine the canal, SBNOC, Senior British Naval Officer Canal Area, was screaming for help and he, Algy, had no one on the staff to help him. When was I returning? Could I not turn over Tobruk to Smith and return to my proper job? I was saying that the Army was pressing on, soon they would be in Derna and Benghazi was a possibility, but only if they had supplies. It was essential that someone should go ahead and open up Derna and get it going as a supply base. The Commander-in-Chief stood there like a grinning sphinx and said nothing, but I had a feeling that he had at least a sympathetic ear for my wish to push on.

Shortly I had to take them back; the RAF were giving them fighter cover and they were running to a very tight schedule. That evening I heard that the Army had got a company of Australians across the Derna wadi, which had been holding them up, and that they expected to be in Derna next day. The following morning, I had a nasty shock in the form of a signal from the Commander-in-Chief saying that Commander Carne was to return as soon as possible. I spoke firmly to Hickling, saying that we definitely ought to do something about Derna and he eventually agreed that I should go that evening in *Moy* taking Lambe with me who would take over duties of Naval Officer in Charge as soon as I opened the port. We sent off a signal to this effect giving it an early time of origin hoping that the Commander-in-Chief would think that it was made before his signal arrived.

Later that day we heard that *Huntley* was due at 6pm, and it was decided that I should go in her as her higher speed and shallower draught made her a much more satisfactory vessel for the attempt. However, by 6pm there was no sign of *Huntley* and by then it was too late to change the plan back again to use *Moy*. About thirty minutes later, there was a sudden alarm of aircraft and three machines flew up the harbour at only 300 feet and dropped five or six bombs. None of the shore guns opened fired at all and we were frankly taken by surprise with only a few rounds of small stuff being fired.

The next morning reports began to come in and it was clear that enemy aircraft had been pretty active during the night. This was the first effort that they had made since the fall of Tobruk. Sollum had had a heavy raid and something, suspected as being a magnetic mine, had been dropped in the harbour. One of these went off almost at once. Further east an Egyptian Government vessel carrying prisoners from Sollum to Alexandria had been attacked and driven ashore with some casualties to prisoners. Later in the day reports came in that the *Huntley* had been sunk near Sidi Barrani, and that most of her ship's company had been lost.

In view of the loss of the *Huntley*, I decided to go to Derna in *Moy*. Our plan was as follows: – I was to sail that night and sweep a passage the next morning. Two schooners would sail the next morning with a party of stevedores to work the port. The SNOIS to follow in Voyager after he had got my signal that all was well, picking up the schooners en route and escorting them to Derna. We had some difficulty in persuading the Army to send the stevedores – they had no orders from Middle East and did not like to act on their own authority. But we threw all our weight about and quoted General O'Connor's statement that supplies were vital to the campaign, and eventually they agreed.

The passage to Derna was uneventful and we arrived in Derna having swept a channel, at about 10am on the 2nd February, two days after it had been captured. I found Green, the Naval Liaison Officer with the 13th Corps, waiting for me and in his usual efficient manner he had bagged an excellent building for the Navy Office. This was a shipping agency on the ground floor with two well-furnished flats above, a nice garden with two fountains, a roof garden and other quarters at the end of the garden for the ratings.

I at once went with Green to call on Brigadier Robertson commanding the Australian Brigade operating on the coast. He was moving his Headquarters fifteen miles up the coast as his troops were already twenty miles ahead and advancing rapidly. As I walked back to Navy House, a general passed in a car and on seeing me stopped to speak. He turned out to be General Wilson[18],

[18] Field Marshal Henry Maitland Wilson, 1st Baron Wilson, GCB, GBE, DSO (5 September 1881 – 31 December 1964)

Military Governor Designate Libya, who was taking a look round. He was very pleasant in a typically bluff military manner, but I formed the opinion that I knew more about the requirements for stores for the immediate future of the campaign against Benghazi than he knew himself.

At 5pm SNOIS arrived in Voyager with the stevedores. The wind had got up so the schooners were unable to make the passage. The stevedores were transferred to Voyager and brought on to Derna while the schooners returned to Tobruk. Most of the rest of the day was spent in collecting a little food and arranging our quarters. Luckily the Australians had taken pity on us and gave us some of their rations, but we could only muster two or three knives and spoons and no forks at all, and one or two plates. However, we spent a reasonably comfortable night.

On Wednesday 5th I received instructions to turn over to Cox in the *Aphis* and to return in *Moy*, so I sailed that evening taking Lambe with me. I was very disappointed at going back as I had hoped to go on to Benghazi but the town had not yet fallen so I had no excuse. We had a bad trip back, a gale from the south veering to west with severe dust storms. We were lost by the time we struck the coast west of Tobruk, and the visibility was frequently down to less than a cable but we crept on sounding all the time and eventually made a good landfall east of the harbour entrance and crept up to the boom. Here we were rather bluffed as only one buoy could be seen at a time and the one with the flag marking the gate had sunk. However, after going twice up and down the boom we took a risk, hit off the gate and crept up harbour to anchor close to *Fiona*.

Upon going aboard, I found both Captain Hickling and Captain Polard, who was taking over from him, and received instructions to return in *Fiona* the next day. I talked about Benghazi but could not raise any enthusiasm. Everybody was worried by the mines which had been laid by aircraft in Tobruk and Sollum, and which had damaged *Rodi* and sunk a schooner in which Cochrane lost his life. I was tired out after the bad trip in *Moy* and felt that I had to acquiesce but when, soon after we left Tobruk in the *Fiona* the next morning, we heard that Benghazi had fallen, I was very annoyed with myself for not having been more insistent that I should be allowed to go on and try my luck.

✂

Editor's note. Admiral Cunningham, in his autobiography, also describes an event in around April 1941 which involved Commander Carne.

'After we had been a day at sea the Vice-Admiral, Malta, reported that his harbours were completely mined in, and that the destroyer flotilla there could not sail to join the convoy. All the sweepers that dealt with magnetic mines had also been lost or damaged. This was a sorry business; but having started I was certainly not going to order our convoys for Malta back to Alexandria. So I sent for the Fleet Torpedo Officer, the rather silent, imperturbable and never defeated Commander WP Carne, and told him to do something about it. Incidentally, we had a corvette fitted with magnetic minesweeping, the *Gloxinia*, with one of the convoys, though she could never be expected to deal with all the mines. However, in about an hour's time Commander Carne reappeared with a long signal in which the Vice-Admiral, Malta, was directed to blast a channel into Malta with depth-charges, of which, fortunately, there were plenty in store. I do not know if the procedure was strictly orthodox: but the basis of the idea was that a depth-charge dropped every so many yards would countermine or upset the firing mechanism of any magnetic mine in the vicinity of the explosion. The scheme was a triumphant success. Various mines were destroyed in the approaches and a swept channel buoyed. It has to be recorded, however, that when *Gloxinia*, towing her magnetic sweep, or 'fluffing the tail', as they called it, led the convoy into harbour next day, nearly a dozen more mines went up as she steamed through the breakwater entrance'.

9/2/41

Darling,

I got back from my adventures yesterday evening to find your letter of 10th Dec and two telegrams. For some time I have had a feeling that your nice house (*) was doomed but I must admit that it was a bit of a shock when I actually got the telegram. I suppose we should be thankful that you were able to salvage some of the contents.

I have written a full account of my trip a copy of which I hope to send you but as it is somewhat bulky it must go by ordinary mail. All I will say now is that I had the job of opening up Tobruk after it had fallen and as Derna fell while I was still at Tobruk I went on there. I actually commanded myself the first of HM ships which went into both ports. I collected a Wop rifle as a trophy which I thought might amuse the boys but I am doubtful if I shall be able to lug so much old iron around with me. It was a most interesting trip and I enjoyed every minute of it and came back feeling twice as well as I have felt for the last two years but I am furious at being recalled before I had a chance of getting into Benghazi. Now I am faced with absolute mountains of paper which have accumulated while I was away.

Although things are going well just at present there is a terrific strain on the naval side and everyone on the staff is living on the edge of their nerves. I wish I could get away from it. I was in my element at Tobruk when I had my own little boat to paddle, it is all the harder to come back here and drive a pen again.

All my love

William

* This letter refers to their house, 96 St Thomas Street, Portsmouth, that they bought together in around 1939.

19/3/41

Darling,

Very many thanks for your letter of the 4th Feb. Sorry I didn't answer your telegrams but as you will now know I did not get them for at least a fortnight and, in fact, did not get them until after you wrote this last letter. Afraid you have had a very trying time with the furniture in Portsmouth, hope you have squared it off now and found the various things that were lost. I enclose a chit for you to give the Bank authorising then to transfer £50 to your account. I shall in any case pay for the carriage of the furniture to Falmouth. I hope you will be able to get Jocelyn to take on our claim for the house, I am sure he will make a much more satisfactory job of it than someone we don't know in Portsmouth. Glad to hear that Gyles is settling down more happily.

COS is going home, I was very pleased to hear that his relief is Edelston who I shall be very pleased to see again. I fancy he will be good at this job, not too many nerves. COS is more cheerful now that he knows that he is being relieved but he is obviously very tired. I forgot whether I told you that we now have a small aeroplane, a Vega Gull, attached for use of the staff. One sits beside the pilot and the machine is fitted with dual control. Once in the air I have flown it two or three times. On my last trip it was blowing hard and bumpy, the pilot insisted that I should fly it and somehow we arrived at our destination.

All my love

William

The following letters refer to the Battle of Matapan, which is described in Chapter 15, in the speech that he gave in the United States to staff at the Bullard Company making torpedoes for the Allies.

31/3/41

Darling,

We have got back to harbour feeling rather pleased with ourselves after our battle with the Italian fleet when I found a signal saying that my relief had been appointed so I reckon that it is quite a good day. My relief, Watson, is appointed to date 4th April which I think means the date he leaves England so I shall have to soldier on for some time yet, but it is encouraging to know that I am not to continue in this job forever. No letters from you for some time but we know that a mail was lost early in February, so I am afraid one of your letters disappeared at that time.

The battle was rather an extraordinary affair. We chased the enemy all day from before 9.00 am until nearly 11.00 pm, the old battleships doing their best to pretend that they were not 25 years old but not succeeding very well. Eventually we surprised two eight inch cruisers at close range and about literally blew them out of the water. It was a dark night but we sighted them at about 4,000 yards, Warspite fired a broadside of all eight fifteen inch guns within a couple of seconds of the searchlight going on and it seemed if almost every shell hit the enemy. She was hit right amidships and was well on fire at once and exploding like a cracker. She was out of action from the word "go" and never fired a round. The other cruiser appeared to get off a few ill directed rounds but she was hit very early and was also soon on fire.. During the engagement two and probably more Italian destroyers attacked us with torpedoes but thanks, at least in part, to the good lookout kept by the FTO, we altered course away and avoided them. The battleships part in the action was very short but it was so overwhelmingly effective that it completely decided the result.

PTO

To write it down sounds as though it was all very simple but I don't think there is any Admiral except ABC who would have had the courage to risk the battleships in that melee at night. The amazing thing was that none of our ships were hit although the air seemed to be full of objects moving at high speed with that unpleasant whining sound which it is so difficult to ignore. Edelson joined before we went to sea and came to sea as COS although he had not completed taking over. Willis remained ashore to look after the paperwork.

We have a new padre whose hobby is the collection of engraved jewels but he also knows quite a lot about china. He has leant me a most interesting British Museum book on oriental ceramics which I have been studying. It helps to keep one's mind off dive bombers and other daily irritations, but I shall never learn to sort out the various dynasties and certainly not the various emperors. Have you heard anything more of my luggage from Malta? I shall be seriously annoyed if my celadon dish is lost or broken.

All my love

William

The following letter was written to Oliver, his son and my father, who at the time was just eleven years old.

5/4/41

Dear Oliver,

This is to wish you very many happy returns of your birthday. I hope it will arrive somewhere near the right date but it is impossible from here to judge how far ahead to write. However, I hope I shall not suffer under this disadvantage much longer as my relief has been appointed. He will of course take some time to get here and I shall take a long time to get home but I hope to be back in the summer.

I enclose a small cheque as a present for you to buy something for yourself. You will have to get Mummy to cash it for you.

PTO

We have had an exciting time with our battle with the Italian fleet. They made for home as soon as they heard that our battlefleet was at sea so that we had to chase them all day from nine o'clock in the morning until nearly midnight when we came up with one of their squadrons of big eight inch cruisers.

We saw them first and opened fire at a range of only 4,000 yards (2 miles). At that range the trajectory of a fifteen inch shell is nearly flat so provided the deflection has been calculated correctly, one is almost bound to hit. Warspite made no mistakes and our first salvo produced several hits, probably five out of eight rounds. At night we fire broadsides, that is all eight guns together. The other two battleships opened fire at about the same time and the effect on the enemy was completely devastating. They were out of action almost at once, in fact the ship at which Warspite first fired never fired a round in reply. Some of their destroyers attempted to save the cruisers by making a torpedo attack but we illuminated them in our searchlights and opened fire on them with the six-inch guns and they turned away to avoid any torpedoes which they might have fired. By that time the cruisers were blazing wrecks and were shortly afterwards finally sunk by torpedoes from our destroyers. The enemy attempted an air attack on us next day but they obtained no hits, we shot down one aircraft and badly damaged another.

Please give my love to the other boys.

Love from

Daddy.

4/5/41

Darling,

I have just heard that Watson is well on his way so I am hoping to get out of this job fairly soon. I hope I shall be able to get away altogether but I am a bit suspicious of the C-in-C. I am doing a particular job at the moment and I went last night to report progress to date. He said, "that's alright. By the way, I have just turned you down for the command of ———— (one of the Danae class cruisers) as I can't spare you yet". I could have screamed, there is nothing I should like better than one of these ships for a first command. However, the old man did have the grace to say that I shouldn't lose by it in the long run

CHAPTER 17

THE FIRST 10 DAYS AS CAPTAIN HMS COVENTRY

10 DAYS

22/5/41

Darling,

I have got my command at last. Signal arrived yesterday morning for me to join forthwith with acting rank of Captain. I have relieved David Gilmour who has been invalided home. The ship, which was originally similar to the Ceres, has been modernised and now has few points in common. But the Captain's quarters are the same as when she was originally built and I hardly know myself after my dogs hole of a cabin in the Warspite. I finally turned over to Watson on Sunday and since then I have had forty-eight hours unofficial leave while I waited for my appointment to come through. I feel much better for my rest, most of which I spent at the Sporting Club either bathing of knocking a golf ball about. I appear to have got a first-class ship's company but the ship herself is a bit knocked about and will probably require considerable repair shortly. That is if she can be spared but the situation is not easy at present. It is almost impossible to lay up a ship for more than a day or two at a time. I had a very good dinner with the Peel's on Monday night and played a little bridge but the standard of play was a bit high class for me. I have no more news to tell you, I am a bit busy settling into my new job which is completely different to the last one.

All my love
William

Note on Envelope. WP Carne Capt RN! But I am not using the rank yet, having waited all these years for the chicken to hatch I can wait six more days!

In May 1941, I had been nearly 3 years in the Mediterranean Fleet serving as a Fleet Torpedo Officer (FTO) on the Commander-in-Chief's staff. My relief had just arrived when I was sent for by the Admiral, I thought, to say goodbye. But after I reported to him that I had turned over my duties as FTO to my relief, he turned to me and told me that the captain of the *Coventry* was being invalided home to England. He went on to say that he didn't know whether the Admiralty were going to promote me in June but if, in the meantime, I liked to remain on the station, he would appoint me to the *Coventry* with the rank of acting captain.

He went on to add that he realised that I had been away from England for a long time; that I had a young family growing up, and that if I preferred to go home, he would quite understand. However, I didn't hesitate; my last chance to be promoted would be in the following June, and I knew that I would stand a much better chance if I was already an acting captain in command of a ship. So, I immediately accepted his offer and he told me to join my new ship the next morning; he would make the necessary signals at once.

When I joined the *Coventry* the next morning, she was tucked in alongside the dockyard wall surrounded by other ships. During the forenoon my predecessor was introducing me to my new officers, mustering confidential books, writing up reports and generally finishing off in a hurry all the things which have to be done when one gives up command. Before noon we were interrupted by a signal directing *Coventry* and two frigates to escort one of the Glen ships to Crete sailing at 11pm hours that night.

I spent the rest of the day finding out the particulars of this operation; the Glen ship was loaded with stores for the army in Crete, on the assumption that the battle for the island was to continue, and arranging to get the assistance of a tug to get me clear of the dockyard. I saw the tugmaster to explain to him that this was my first command and he promised to give me a good tow stern first out into the centre of the harbour, from where I could get a clear run.

When I went up on the bridge at 11pm to take the ship to sea for the first time, the night was very dark and I was filled with trepidation. However, in the event, everything went very well; the tug towed us gently out into the harbour, the *Coventry* behaved perfectly, and we slid out through the boom and then the Great Pass with no difficulty at all. Soon after 1am, we were clear of the swept channel, formed up in our cruising formation, and had set course for Crete. I was free to get a little rest, feeling rather pleased with myself but rather weary after a long day. Had I realised how strenuous the next ten days were going to be, I should not have been so complacent.

HMS Coventry

After dawn action stations, half the ship's company fell out. Compared to the bugle calls and pipes repeated on the loudspeakers of the *Warspite*, there appeared to be rather an air of casualness about the *Coventry*. However, I need not have worried. During the forenoon many aircraft were reported by our radar, our radio direction finding (RDF) as we called it in those days. If any aircraft came within twenty miles of us a whisper went down the improvised loudspeaker system to 'stand to', which brought every man to his action station at once. It was clear that the Coventrys had learnt their lesson and were not to be caught napping.

I don't think any of the aircraft reported by our radar that forenoon were hostile, but it was clear from intercepted signals that there was a great deal of enemy activity in the vicinity of Crete, and of course one assumed that all

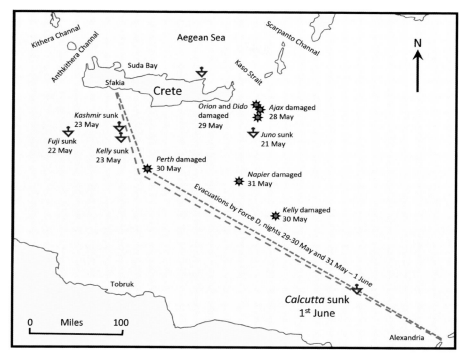

Movements of HMS Coventry *and HMS* Calcutta *28th May – 1st June 1941*

aircraft were hostile until they had been definitively recognised as friendly.

During the afternoon we intercepted a high-priority signal from the Admiralty to the Commander-in-Chief (I feel sure the signal should have been made in Commander-in-Chief's cypher and that we were not intended to read it). It caused me much worry as it started by agreeing to some proposal of the Commander-in-Chief's, which was not in our possession, and then went on to say that all forces should be withdrawn to Alexandria except *Coventry* who should continue to the northward.

No further signal came from the Commander-in-Chief and as dusk approached, I had to make up my mind what to do during the night. I felt certain that the Commander-in-Chief would not allow me to go on to Crete entirely unsupported. From intercepted signals I knew that our forces had received considerable damage and we were retiring on Alexandria. If I went straight back, I should arrive before dawn and have to hang about in the way of the other forces returning from Crete.

One thing I had learnt from Cunningham during my service in the *Warspite* was never to make a manoeuvring signal at night, except in an emergency. Before dusk he always made a night policy signal detailing exactly what was to be done during the night and, if an alternative course was involved, ships were directed to alter to the new course at a definite time without signal.

Before dusk closed down on us, therefore, I made a night policy signal to my little force directing them to alter course without further signal at midnight onto a course which would bring us back close to Alexandria during the following forenoon.

At a quarter to midnight, I was on the bridge for the alteration of course. Up to that time no signal had been received from the Commander-in-Chief and I was considerably worried in my mind as to whether I had anticipated the Admiral's intentions correctly. However, at five minutes to midnight the wireless office rang up to say that there was a high priority signal for *Coventry* from the Commander-in-Chief just received that they were deciphering. When a few minutes later it arrived on the bridge it was to the effect that I was to bring my convoy back to Alexandria. So, it appeared that I had read my Admiral's mind correctly.

During 'stand to' the next morning, before it was properly light, the radar picked up an aircraft approaching from the direction of Crete and apparently quite low. It appeared to be going to pass about 5 miles clear of us when it suddenly altered course directly towards the convoy. I was about to order 'open fire' when it fired a recognition signal and it turned out to be an RAF bomber. It circled close around the *Coventry* asking by Aldis lamp for its position. We gave it a position and it disappeared in the direction of the east of Egypt, which was then only some 30 miles distant.

To my surprise, it appeared again after about 10 minutes, and without making any further signal ditched close alongside the *Coventry* and sank rapidly, but not before the crew escaped in a rubber dinghy.

The two frigates were on either bow of the convoy operating their Asdics with *Coventry* zigzagging astern. I did not wish to remove a frigate from the screen, so I decided to pick up the survivors with the *Coventry*. Before we could get the way off the ship, we had considerably overshot the position of the rubber dinghy and had to turn and come back to it.

When we had got the survivors out of the rubber dinghy, the gunnery officer asked if he could exercise one of the four-barrelled half inch machine guns by sinking it. As I had never seen one of these weapons in use, I was interested to see how effective it could be, so I told him to get on with it but to be quick; I was not anxious to remain stopped. I had a feeling that there might be a submarine about.

Actually, the demonstration by the half-inch machine gun was very disappointing; it took several bursts at a range of little more than a cable to sink the rubber dinghy. They were disappointing guns, much too unhandy for close range work and too limited in range to be effective at more distant targets.

The pilot of the aircraft informed me that they had been sent to bomb Maleme airfield, which by this time was being used by the Germans. They had got lost and didn't know where they had dropped their bombs. After we had given them their position, they had gone on for about 10 miles but not having sight of the coast of Egypt and being down to the last few pints of fuel, decided that they had better return to us and ditch alongside rather than risk running out of fuel completely before they were over Egypt.

No further incidents occurred during our return to Alexandria. We were ordered to berth astern of the *Calcutta* alongside a small breakwater close inside the boom where the two AA cruisers were in a good position to use their guns in the event of an aerial attack on Alexandria. To get alongside this breakwater one had to turn the ship 180° and approach it from the landward side with the sea breeze blowing one off. Not an easy place to get alongside; fortunately, the *Coventry* had been there several times before, knew the drill with the boats and I had an experienced navigating officer to assist me in manoeuvring the ship. But I gave a sigh of relief when we were safely alongside.

As soon as we were alongside, I went along the breakwater to call on the captain of the *Calcutta*, Captain 'Bunny' Lees, who gave me a number of helpful tips as to the best way of approaching our berth on the breakwater and also told me of his recent experiences at sea. He had been with the forces to the north of Crete and had been engaged with enemy aircraft on several occasions.

I could have done with a good night's rest that night, but before I could go to bed an air raid developed and kept us up for a long time. *Coventry* opened fire on several occasions to reinforce the barrage. But standing on the bridge it was difficult to appreciate what was going on. A steady stream of reports were being received by telephone from the radar, but it was difficult to differentiate the reports and to decide whether they were all the same aircraft or several different ones.

The next day I arranged to have a mooring board on the bridge with a number of coloured pins with which different aircraft could be plotted. I gave this duty to Lieutenant Commander Reece, who soon became very good at producing a clear picture of what was happening. I remember that during a subsequent night raid on Alexandria after we had been closed up for well over an hour and had opened fire half a dozen times ourselves, I asked him how the attack was developing. He replied that he thought there were 12 enemy aircraft, and that so far 11 had attacked. He was quite right, there was one more burst of firing when the last enemy attacked, and then we got the all clear.

Early the next morning we received orders to prepare for sea, followed shortly after by the orders for the operation. Once again, we were to escort the same Glen ship to Crete with stores for the army, but in place of the two frigates on this occasion the anti-submarine screen consisted of three Australian destroyers including the flotilla leader *Stuart* commanded by Captain Walker. As Captain Walker was the senior officer, he was in command of the whole force.

We were due to leave harbour at 6pm. I was already in my seagoing clothes waiting in my day cabin for the First Lieutenant to report 'ready for sea' and listening to the 6pm BBC news (owing to the use of double summertime in England, British summertime corresponded to the Eastern Mediterranean time we were using). I was horrified to hear an announcement from the Admiralty that the *Hood* had been sunk during the previous day. This news seemed to be a very bad omen just as we were setting out on what must prove to be a pretty hazardous enterprise. I suddenly remembered that the day was my 43rd birthday. These two facts, the bad news coming on my birthday, cast a gloom over me; but I realised that it was important that I did not give any indication of my inward feelings. In the privacy of my cabin, I pulled myself together so that when a few minutes later the First Lieutenant reported that we were all ready for sea, I was able to walk up to the bridge without, I hope, giving any indication of my inward thoughts.

Our passage that night was uneventful and at dawn it appeared that we should arrive with our convoy at Sfakia where she was to discharge her cargo soon after dark. But air activity developed in the day; the radar was constantly reporting echoes. *Coventry* was the only ship in the force with radar so that we were constantly passing reports to the *Stuart* to keep the senior officer up-to-date with the situation.

While most of the reports referred to hostile aircraft attacking other forces – it was the day that the *Formidable* was bombed – two attacks developed on our force during daylight hours. Neither of these caused any damage, though one bomb fell unpleasantly close to the *Coventry* with that increasing whistling noise which is so unnerving.

Towards dusk a more serious attack developed by a number of aircraft which continued for a considerable time in the rapidly failing light, firstly by bombers and then by at least one torpedo plane. *Coventry* was steaming close astern of the Glen ship to cover her as far as possible with our AA armament while the destroyers were on a comparatively close antisubmarine screen. As each aircraft came into attack, we passed radar bearings and ranges to the destroyers who endeavoured to back up our barrage with their AA guns. Then when the hostile aircraft got really close, the destroyers fired a barrage of shrapnel from their 4.7-inch guns to burst over the convoy.

The Australian destroyers were magnificent, switching their barrages to follow *Coventry* so that each opponent as he came into attack was met by a considerable barrage which, if not very accurate, must have been very frightening.

It was the rapid and continuous fire which we developed to which I put down the fact that the force escaped almost, though not quite, immune. Early on, the Glen ship was hit well aft and a large quantity of cased petrol stored on deck over her aft holds was set on fire. This blazed up making an excellent aiming mark in the dusk for the enemy.

The petrol was in four-gallon tins, almost a dozen tins to a case, stored conveniently to pass it rapidly over the side when we arrived at our destination. Somehow the crew of the Glen ship managed to shove each burning case over the side. At intervals of two or three minutes another flaming case would fall into the sea, to make a pool of burning petrol which silhouetted the *Coventry* as we steamed past. Every moment I thought the

Glen was bound to burst into flames and become a total wreck. But somehow, they contained the fire to the petrol and eventually got rid of the last case.

I can't remember how long this attack lasted, but at the time it seemed to be interminable, made all the more dramatic by the failing light which enhanced the glare from the flaming petrol, the gun flashes and the flashes in the sky from the bursting shells. It was towards the end of the attack, when the last of the cased petrol was being pushed over the side, that the radar picked up an echo very low down and unpleasantly close. We got off a salvo or two at it but almost at once, the plane, whatever it was, turned away and was lost off the screen. I originally thought it was a torpedo plane coming in to make its attack, but it did not appear to come sufficiently close to deliver a torpedo. I came to the conclusion it was an aircraft that had delivered its load of bombs and was circling around, endeavouring to see the results of its attack. I dismissed the idea of a torpedo attack as there seemed to be more important things to think about. However, a few minutes later the ship was considerably shaken by an underwater explosion and looking aft we saw an upsurge in the wake, very similar to that caused by a depth charge. At that moment there were no aircraft overhead, so it could not have been caused by a bomb. Further, the disturbance was quite different to that caused by a bomb. I had little doubt but that the explosion was caused by some form of torpedo which had been dropped by the low-flying aircraft. There had been various very vague intelligence reports of the enemy developing a torpedo which turned into the wake of the target and followed it up. Could this explosion be something on that line which had fired prematurely? Anyway, that was something for my successor as Fleet Torpedo Officer to worry about; all I had to do was to make a note of the known facts and report them which, in due course, I did.

As darkness closed down and the radar reported that the screen was at last clear, I was wondering what our next move should be. Besides losing all her cased petrol, was the Glen ship seriously damaged? Was it worthwhile going on to land such stores as remained? I was glad I was not senior officer and had not to make a decision on this question. But I need not have worried. Shortly after, we received a signal recalling us to Alexandria. Apparently, the policy had been changed, instead of continuing the battle for Crete, it had been decided to withdraw all forces.

I cannot remember whether we were actually attacked during the next day as we made our way back across the Mediterranean, but I remember that the air was full of aircraft which we were reporting all day long to the *Stuart*. Every radar report was passed out by 10-inch light, and from time to time I sent *Stuart* a situation report as I had appreciated the situation from my mooring board. I think these reports were useful and appreciated as the last signal *Stuart* made to me as we went into Alexandria harbour was one to congratulate me on the efficiency of what he called my 'aerial ping men'. I think we deserved that little pat on the back. Our radar had given us early warning of every attack and, during the dusk attack, had enabled us to put up an effective barrage as each attack developed and so allowed us to escape with little damage.

Once we arrived in Alexandria that evening, we went to our usual berth on the breakwater and fuelled and early the next morning, ammunition lighters came alongside to replace the rounds we had fired. Each projectile had to be fused before it was stored away after which we could have done with a little rest but that was not to be thought of. Long before we had finished ammunitioning, we received orders to raise steam and to be ready to leave harbour that evening.

During the afternoon, I was summoned onboard the *Phoebe* in which ship Admiral King, who was to command the next operation, had hoisted his flag. As *Calcutta* was also to form part of the force Captain Lees and I went together.

Admiral King explained that the object of the operation was to evacuate as many men as possible from Sfakia. What remained of the army in Crete were retreating towards Sfakia and it was anticipated that by tomorrow night there would be several thousand men ready for embarkation. In order that our approach to the coast and retreat from it should be carried out as far as possible under the cover of darkness, he intended to arrive off Sfakia at 1am. Any men not embarked by then were to be left behind.

The force consisted of two cruisers, the *Phoebe* and the Australian cruiser *Perth*, two anti-aircraft cruisers *Calcutta* and *Coventry*, another Glen ship called the *Glengyle* fitted with a number of landing craft and an anti-submarine screen of destroyers whose names I cannot remember. On arrival off Sfakia, the *Glengyle* was to anchor as close in as possible and without further orders, lower her landing craft and start ferrying men off to the *Glengyle*, *Phoebe* and *Perth* who would anchor close alongside. Destroyers were to assist as far as their boats would allow, but it was intended that the main lift should be by the *Glengyle* whose landing craft were much more suitable than ships' boats.

During the operation of embarking the soldiers *Calcutta* and *Coventry* were to patrol close off the anchorage as a defence against attack by aircraft. Admiral King thought that the enemy would anticipate an operation to embark troops from Sfakia. After he had explained his intentions, Admiral King asked us if we had any questions or suggestions. Nobody had much to say, we were all weary ourselves and were only too well aware that our ships' companies were exhausted and badly in need of a decent rest. The Admiral had explained that the position of the army in Crete was desperate; if we could not get them away, they would have to surrender. So obviously we had to go and make as good a show as possible, but nobody looked forward to the operation one little bit.

The captain of the *Phoebe*, Captain 'Granny' Grantham, tried to put a more cheerful look on the conference by giving us each a whisky and soda. I was sitting near the outboard bulkhead under a scuttle which was fitted with a scuttle shoot through which came a pleasant cool breeze. *Phoebe* was preparing for sea and in furling the quarterdeck awning someone caught a rope in the shoot and tipped it inboard. As the shoot fell it hit my right arm, causing me to upset most of my whisky and soda over my nice clean white uniform that I had put on to call on the Admiral. Captain Grantham was most distressed and apologetic and wanted to lend me one of his own white uniforms. But I refused to accept his offer, thinking that if nothing worse than a scuttle should fall on me during the next two days, I shouldn't do too badly.

On our arrival in harbour I had been informed that my experienced navigating officer was to be relieved, and as I returned from the *Phoebe* the new navigating officer came to report to me. I was distressed at losing my experienced navigator, who had been a great help to me, but I need not have worried. His relief, Lieutenant Kerruish RAN, proved to be a skillful navigator and to have the cheerful courage which one had learnt to expect from the Australian naval officers serving in the Mediterranean[19].

---

[19] Robert H.E. Kerruish survived the war. He retired in 1956 and died in Australia in 1967.

We sailed at dusk that evening, and by the next morning we were well on our way to Crete. As far as I remember we were attacked twice that day and I have little doubt but that we were reported. Admiral King steered a course as though we were making for the Western Med', and then, as darkness fell, altered course directly for Sfakia. The defence we put up during the day was successful and the force approached Crete undamaged.

The night was very dark, under cover of which some 7000 men were embarked in the *Glengyle, Phoebe* and *Perth. Calcutta* and *Coventry* patrolled along a line ten miles long close off the coast, but there was no interference by the enemy. The force left Sfakia at 4.00 am and proceeded at *Glengyle's* best speed which was about 18 ½ knots. *Calcutta* and *Coventry* followed up astern and rejoined the convoy at daylight, the AA cruisers taking station on either bow of the *Glengyle*, while the *Phoebe* and *Perth* were on either quarter.

HMS Glengyle

We were reported soon after daylight, and the attack arrived early in the forenoon watch. The enemy consisted of ten or twelve planes and came in from astern. *Glengyle* zig-zagged madly, I told Kerruish to keep close to her port bow, which he did to such good measure that once we must have been within half a cable of her. *Calcutta* was in a similar position on her starboard bow so that, as each plane attacked from astern, we put up a very affective barrage which few of the enemy penetrated. They preferred to drop their bombs on the cruisers.

We made full use of our multiple pom-pom which, with several pom-poms on the *Glengyle* and *Calcutta's* close-range weapons, put up a formidable barrage. As the enemy came in, they were engaged first by *Phoebe* and *Perth* and then by the 4-inch guns of *Coventry* and *Calcutta*. Few pressed their attacks but preferred to diverge either to port or starboard and release their bombs over the cruisers or destroyers. *Perth*, during one zig-zag, allowed herself to become detached from the rest of the force and immediately became the target of two or three of the enemy, one of which succeeded in putting a bomb into her forward boiler room. Although her full speed was considerably reduced, she was still able to keep up with the force and our retreat to Alexandria was not therefore delayed.

Once again it was shown that if a number of ships kept well together, had a good warning of an attack and the visibility to see the target and fired hard and fast, only the most determined enemy would press his attack sufficiently close to have a good chance of obtaining a hit. Unfortunately, it was not always possible to ensure early warning and good visibility, on which a rapid volume of fire was dependent. Our next trip to Crete showed only too clearly that if these conditions were not present, then a determined and skillful enemy could cause us great loss.

The remainder of our voyage back to Alexandria was without incident, and we again secured at the detached breakwater astern of the *Calcutta* in the small hours of the next morning. Early in the day, a fueler came along side followed by a lighter full of ammunition from which we replaced the rounds which had been fired. The speed with which the stores were placed alongside was a good indication that we should be required for service again very shortly.

Soon after breakfast, Captain Lees walked along the breakwater and suggested we should both visit the Commander-in-Chief's office to, as he expressed it, 'find out the form'. During the almost continuous series of operations during the previous month, all ship's boats had suffered considerably and there had been no opportunity for repair and maintenance. *Calcutta* had not got a power boat that was reasonably reliable and *Coventry's* motorboat was under repair, but the First Lieutenant had lowered the motor cutter which appeared to be running satisfactorily, so we both went in that boat.

Once we had arrived at the office, we were immediately shown into see the Commander-in-Chief, who wanted an account of our last operation, expressed himself very disappointed that we could not report having seen any of the enemy fall into the sea, and told us that we must fire harder and faster and a damned sight straighter. What was the good of an AA cruiser if she could not shoot down every hostile aircraft that came in range? Then he went on to talk a little about the whole series of operations, of how the army were up against impossible odds, and that we must do our best to get as many of them out of Crete as possible.

Lees said that we had lost 60,000 men during the first day of the Battle of the Somme, was it worthwhile to lose the whole of the Mediterranean fleet for the 30,000 men in Crete? Admiral Cunningham turned on him at once and repeated that remark which he made on more than one occasion during those tense and trying days, namely, that it takes three years to build a ship but 300 years to build a tradition. The Navy always stands by the army and we were not going to break a tradition now.

Then he went on to say that there would be a few more men to be collected from Sfakia that night, and that he had sent his only available destroyers to pick them up. He wanted *Calcutta* and *Coventry* to go to sea at 1.00 am and meet the destroyers roughly halfway to Crete and come back with them to give additional AA support. Further, he had arranged with the RAF that we should have fighter cover. Two fighters with long range tanks would cover us during our return to Alexandria. After which, he said with one of his more cheerful laughs, we might be allowed a day or so in the harbour to refurbish ourselves.

So, we made our way back to our ships, neither of us feeling very cheerful to find that the operational signal had arrived. I desperately wanted to rest, but a lot of paperwork had arrived; some of which my secretary was very insistent that I should deal with before we sailed. The First Lieutenant wanted me to see requisitions and various officers wanted to talk to me and, indeed, I wanted to talk to them. So far, I had had very little chance of getting to know any of my officers but come what may, I was determined to go to bed early and get a little sleep before we sailed at 1am. Vain hope. I had hardly got to sleep before I was awakened to be told that a preliminary air raid warning signal had been received.

Scrambling into my clothes, I hurried up to the bridge only to be faced with a long wait. The actual raid did not develop until after 11pm. We opened fire on several occasions. The enemy attacked with one plane at a time with considerable gaps between each attack. It was nearly 1am before we received the all clear, and we were just singling up our wires preparatory to slipping when RAL closed the port.

During the raid, splashes had been seen in Great Pass which might have been magnetic mines. No ships were therefore allowed out through the boom until the splashes had been investigated. It was after 4am before we were given permission to sail, and it was not until 5.30 am that we were clear of the swept channel and steady on a course for Crete. Then it was time for dawn action stations after which it was too late to think of sleep, so I shaved and dressed and had an early breakfast.

The sun had come up into a clear cloudless sky and there was every promise of a hot Eastern Mediterranean summer day. In fact, by 9am it was already very hot when the radar first picked up an echo fine on our port quarter roughly in the direction of Alexandria. My first reaction was that the RAF fighters had not heard that we had sailed three hours late from Alex, and had therefore come out too early. As soon as we received the report of the echo on the bridge, we repeated it by 10-inch light to *Calcutta*, who was not fitted with radar.

We were doing a No 10 zig-zag, which meant that at 9.10am we both altered twenty degrees to starboard together, which brought *Coventry* fine on *Calcutta's* starboard quarter and, more importantly, brought the echo of the approaching aircraft dead astern in the funnel haze and straight up sun.

The echo continued to come straight towards us and at a range of about 10 miles was observed to be two aircraft, obviously the two fighters from Alexandria.

The sun was a flaming orb in a sky of burnished brass as we stared through the dancing funnel haze to catch a glimpse of the approaching aircraft who came steadily on straight for us. I cannot remember at which moment I became suspicious. In any event, not nearly soon enough, as I was too tired for my brain to work quickly. Of course, being RAF planes, they would not have IFF[20] but surely they would indicate their friendly character before coming too close; either by firing a recognition signal or making a circuit around us outside gun range so that we could identify them? All our guns were trained in the direction of the approaching aircraft, but the director could see nothing.

The radar had the echo absolutely firm; reports were coming up to the bridge every 15-20 seconds and were being passed on to the *Calcutta* as fast as the 10-inch light could transmit them. I could see that *Calcutta* had all her guns trained on the bearing of the approaching aircraft, but she did not open fire or make any alteration of course signal. I had every lookout on the bridge, signalman, officer of the watch and navigator searching the sky astern of us. Nobody saw anything until the chief yeoman, Slausen, who I had already learnt had the eyes of a hawk and was a most reliable man, was searching the sky through his signalman's telescope and shouted, 'It's a JU'. Immediately, I gave the order 'starboard 25'. (When steaming 22 kn as we were on this occasion, we found that for all practical purposes the ship answered her helm as quickly on 25 degrees of rudder as on 35 degrees and did not lose so much way). Stepping to the starboard side of the compass platform I shouted up the voicepipe to the foretop to 'open fire', and then ran to the after end of the wing of the bridge to try and get a view clear of the funnel haze.

Immediately I saw the leading enemy aircraft coming straight towards us, now well into her dive and looking terribly menacing. Almost at once she let drive with her machine guns. The first rounds hit the sea just clear of the port quarter. The splashes from the following rounds moved up the port side, just missing the ship. Watching them, they seemed to move quite slowly, though I don't suppose there was much more than a second between the first and last splash.

I had been passed over for promotion the preceding December by another officer on the Commander-in-Chief's staff. On promotion he had been appointed to command an AA cruiser and had been killed a month

---

[20] "Identification, friend or foe" (IFF) was a radar based system to avoid the problems of friendly fire.

or so previously by a machine gun bullet when his ship was shot up by a diving aircraft. Had I not been passed over for promotion I would certainly have been in his place. I had been congratulating myself that, if I had had to wait for my promotion, at least I was still alive. Now, as I watched death approaching me across the water, it passed through my mind that after all I was to suffer the same fate.

But I had just got the wheel over in time and the *Coventry*, witch that she was then and always, was swinging fast, too fast for the enemy to adjust his aim. His machine gun bullets just missed us and a second or so later, when the bombs arrived, they were also just clear of the port side, but the centre one of three was sufficiently close to drench the first waist with spray. An officer who was in the port waist subsequently told me that the bomb fell 17 feet from the ship's side. How he measured the distance so accurately I cannot imagine, but at least his estimate indicates that the bomb was much too close. The force of its explosion gave that jerk to the ship which gives the impression that the whole ship is being lifted.

The aircraft passed close overhead, I shouted myself hoarse for someone to open fire with something, but our close-range weapons were as ponderous as the four-inch guns and had no hope of catching up with the diving aircraft at that short range. If only we had had Oerlikan or single-barrelled Bofors we might have done something, but an eight barreled pom-pom was still lumbering around from right astern to right ahead when the enemy was nearly over the horizon.

In the meantime, the second aircraft was attacking *Calcutta*. Lees had seen *Coventry* start to swing and had immediately put his own wheel over to conform, but the slight delay had not given *Calcutta* time to alter course appreciably and she was hit by two bombs straight up the centreline.

It was at once obvious that *Calcutta* was seriously damaged. My first reaction was that the attack must be reported; it looked as though *Calcutta*'s wireless might be out of action and therefore it was up to me to make the necessary signal. I shouted to Slausen to make the signal 'I'm being bombed'. In those days there was a signal group for the signal, I think it was OEAB – it was a group we used to see frequently in those days. I think I said to Slausen, 'OEAB *Calcutta* hit' and followed it up by telling Kerruish to give our position. He had foreseen the requirement and was already taking it off the chart.

I hurriedly took the wheel off and brought *Coventry* back close to *Calcutta* who, it was at once clear, was slowing and was down by the bows. All this time the radar was reporting aircraft. Actually, I think the two aircraft that attacked us separated and circled around to see the effects of their attack. The radar kept picking them up on different bearings which gave me the impression there were more aircraft waiting to attack.

Soon it was clear that the Calcuttas were preparing to abandon the ship. They started to lower boats but there was no time, the fo'c'sle was nearly underwater. Her stern came up so that one of her four propellers could be seen. Then men started jumping over the side; I saw one who seemed to fall into the propeller. Then suddenly she was gone, and there was nothing to see but a large pool of oil fuel in which were one or two carby rafts and flotta nets that they had succeeded in launching, and a large number of heads bobbing in the oily water.

I told Kerruish to circle round the survivors and reduce speed; we were still doing 22 knots. Obviously, we would have to stop and pick up survivors, but were we going to be attacked again? I tried to get a picture from the radar of what aircraft were in the vicinity at the same time sending for the First Lieutenant, and directing him to prepare to pick up survivors, but he must do it with the repair parties. With the menace of air attack at any moment, I refused to fall out any guns' crew or control parties. At the same time, I made another signal to the Commander-in-Chief reporting that *Calcutta* had sunk. Just 4½ minutes elapsed between the moment *Calcutta* was hit and she sank.

There was not even a breath of wind, the sea was flat calm, a perfect summer day in the Eastern Med. On the surface of the sea was a circle of black oil now nearly half a mile in diameter. How to approach to pick up survivors? I had vivid memories of being told of a destroyer in the First War who, anxious to get among a crowd of survivors as quickly as possible, went in too fast and had to go violently astern on her engines to avoid overshooting. The result was that she chewed up a lot of men in her propellers. I was determined not to make the same mistake. In the event I was too cautious. We turned through almost 360 degrees and approached on roughly our original course and stopped the ship with her fo'c'sle just in the circle of oil. The survivors swam towards us many giving a cheer and shouting, 'good old Coventry' as they came. *Calcutta* was our chummy ship and every man had one or two friends in her.

As we arrived alongside, they were exhausted with their swim in the oil, and could not climb the flotta nets to the height of the fo'c'sle. Many got halfway up and hung exhausted. Further, the flare of the fo'c'sle added to their difficulties. I had to move the ship ahead. Impossible to make men who were already grasping the flotta nets and ropes under the fo'c'sle to let go. I had to tow them with us, giving just a touch ahead on the screws and immediately stopping again so that the ship just moved ahead.

All the time the radar was reporting aircraft; I was terrified we were going to be attacked while we were stopped with the upper deck littered with survivors, many in not too good shape, gasping out oil fuel and water.

In the water all the heads looked exactly alike, smeared as they were with oil fuel. From the upper deck came shouts of pleasure as individuals were recognised as they were hauled in over the berthing rails. I kept trying to pick out Bunny Lees and, leaning over the bridge, I shouted to an officer on the fo'c'sle to look out for him and bring him up to me. Nothing happened. I kept shouting for Captain Lees. Then a quiet voice behind me said, 'It's alright William, I'm here'. Turning around I saw a bedraggled figure sitting on the step up from the bridge to the compass platform. Without his cap and much smeared with oil fuel, no one had recognised him. I ran to him asking silly questions 'Was he alright, was he hurt'. He was very calm, sad and resigned. I asked him to go down to my cabin and ask my steward to give him some clean clothes. But he said 'No, no, don't worry about me, you are doing a magnificent job, get on with it'[21]. Realising that I could best comfort him by rescuing as many as possible of his ship's company, I turned back to considering the next move.

Before the *Calcutta* sank, she had managed to launch two or three flotta nets, on which they had placed some of their more seriously injured men. These were being swum towards us by some of the stronger swimmers. We endeavoured to ease the ship towards them, and prepared with heaving lines to haul them the last few yards alongside the waist where we could best hoist

---

[21] Captain Dennis M. Lees DSO ("Bunny") survived the war and was promoted to Rear Admiral in 1949. He retired in 1953 and died in 1973.

inboard the injured men. At the same time, we realised there were some men on the far side of the pool of oil who were going to take a long time to reach us, if they ever got to us at all. I called away a whaler; she had to be manned by a scratch crew, as all the seaman ratings were closed up at the guns. I sent away in her a sub-lieutenant whose name I cannot remember. He had only joined us a few days days before, had not yet been properly worked into the organisation, and was therefore more or less a spare number.

As the boat was being lowered, I hailed him and told him that if I was attacked, I should immediately get underway. He was to remain in the same area and I would come back and pick him up after dark. I didn't add 'If I am still afloat', although that thought was very much at the back of my mind. But in fact, he picked up the half dozen survivors who were making heavy weather of their swim to the ship, had a look around for any others, and came back just as we hoisted the last survivor inboard.

We hooked on the boat full speed and I directed every man on the upper deck to man the falls, ships company and any survivors who could stand, and as the boat left the water, I put both telegraphs to full speed ahead.

Coventry seemed to almost leap out of the water as she got going; I think she was as nervous as I was to get away. We had been stopped exactly twenty-five minutes, the longest twenty-five minutes through which I have ever lived.

With our patched lines our speed had been limited to 22 knots. But the sea was a flat calm, I felt that if our bow was safe at 22 knots zig-zagging in a bit of a seaway, it was safe to go a little faster in such calm conditions. So, we whacked her up to revs for 29 knots, which was about all her ancient engines would do. I felt that the spot where such great disaster had come upon us was a place of ill omens, and the sooner we got away the better. And the *Coventry* thought so too, she went like a bird.

Then it was time to sum up the situation. We found that we had onboard 255 of the Calcuttas which included 32 more or less seriously injured men. I think it shows what a high standard of discipline there must have been in the *Calcutta* that in the 4 $\frac{1}{2}$ minutes from the time that she was first hit, to the moment when she finally disappeared, that they had got 32 injured men onto rolled up flotta nets and organised gangs of swimmers to swim the nets to the *Coventry*. But it meant that about a hundred men were missing. I can't remember now whether we were exactly a 100 short and one or two more subsequently died in hospital, or whether the deaths in hospital brought the number up to a hundred.

We were back in Alexandria in the early afternoon with orders to go alongside in the dockyard and land our survivors. We had to go the far side of the main jetty into a space between the *Resource* and a convoy of trawlers and drifters. Kerruish sketched out the track we must follow on the large-scale chart, pointing out to me that having made our big swing around the end of the jetty, we must then immediately reverse the swing on the ship to get into the only small space vacant and then quickly take the swing off the ship again before we hit the wall broadside on. Easy to explain on a chart what was required, but when I saw the small space into which I had to fit the *Coventry*, it looked almost impossible that I could get her in.

But it was no use hesitating; the sooner I got these injured men into hospital the better. I had asked for the assistance of a tug but had been told that none would be available for at least an hour. It was early afternoon so the sea breeze had hardly started to blow which helped. Kerruish encouraged me to use plenty of power on the engines and the *Coventry*, always a perfect lady, did exactly as I told her so that as I finally reversed engines and rudder we arrived in our berth alongside the wall, and I don't think we should have cracked an egg had anyone been fool enough to hang one over the edge.

The Captain of the Fleet and one or two officers from the Commander-in-Chief's office were on the wall to welcome us, together with several ambulances and a mobile canteen run by Alexandrian ladies. Several people congratulated me on the way I had bought the *Coventry* alongside, but I felt such a load of gloom on my shoulders that I could not appreciate their remarks.

My cabin was of course a first aid station and full of injured men, so I walked out on the jetty where everyone I met told me of disasters to the Med Fleet, and it was clear that poor old *Coventry* with her damaged bow was one of the few units which was still a going concern.

We got the injured men away in the ambulances as soon as possible, then divided the survivors up into groups while they were fed on tea and buns by the ladies, ready to be put into transport as soon as it arrived to take them to temporary accommodation. Then I collected Captain Lees and persuaded him to accept the loan of one of my suitcases filled with a few clothes.

He was loathe to take them, but I knew it would take him several days to collect together an outfit from the much-depleted shops of Alexandria. So eventually he took the suitcase, extracting a promise from my steward that he could come and collect it from the place Captain Lees was going to be accommodated.

Then the officer who was carrying out the duty of harbour master came and asked me to take the *Coventry* back to her usual berth on the detached breakwater, as he wanted our berth alongside again immediately. He apologised for not having a tug available to help, but remarked that after the way he had seen me bring the ship alongside, he didn't think I should have any difficulty.

I took the *Coventry* back to the detached breakwater and so ended my first ten days in the ship. It can be given to few officers to take their first command into action quite as often in their first ten days of command. On the other hand, there can be few officers who have had the good fortune to take over such an experienced set of officers and ship's company who, to such a remarkable degree, combined the major virtues of loyalty, efficiency and courage, combined with the minor virtue, if indeed it is a minor virtue, of cheerfulness. From their pirate of a First Lieutenant to the junior rating they were the most cheerful ship's company I have ever known, and I suppose that is what stood us in such good stead, not only in the Ten Days of Crete but also in the months to follow.

This account was first published in 'HMS Coventry *anti-aircraft cruiser', a narrative by George Sims, 1972. Chapter 16 was titled 'Ten Days – from the Recollections of Captain Carne RN'*

Rescue of the Hospital Ship Aba by the Coventry, painting by Charles Peers

This engagement took place immediately preceding A/Captain Carne's appointment. Petty Officer Alfred Sephton was awarded a posthumous VC for his "great courage and endurance" while HMS *Coventry* was attacked on 17th May 1941. Captain Carne recommended Sephton to the Commander-in-Chief for an award when he heard of his heroism on joining the *Coventry*.

HMS *Coventry* was sunk on the 14th September 1942. She had been taking part in a largely unsuccessful attack on Tobruk and was going to the aid of HMS *Zulu* when she was hit by four bombs from JU87 dive bombers. 63 crew were killed, with the remainder being rescued by HMS *Beaufort*, which came alongside, and HMS *Dulverton* that rescued men from the water. HMS *Zulu* was sunk an hour later after being attacked by nineteen JU87 dive bombers.

3/6/41

Darling,

We had a complete day in harbour yesterday, the first since I have been in command of this ship. I have taken her to sea four times, and on each occasion there has been almost continuous air action. On three occasions ships have been hit, we got in the first two but on Sunday I and my consort Calcutta were proceeding to a rendezvous when we were attacked straight out of the sun by two JU 88's. By the Grace of God one of my chaps saw one for an instant just out of the sun and I put my wheel hard over a starboard. Thirty seconds later his stick pf bombs fell in my wake and up my port side as he came over machine gunning us. My alteration of course had saved the ship. The second followed about twenty seconds later and hit the Calcutta with two bombs and she sank in four and a half minutes. The sea was covered in men. I turned and stopped and in just over half an hour we got every man still alive, 255 altogether. I cant think how we did it as 32 were seriously injured and quite helpless. If I live to be a thousand I hope I shall not pass through such a half hour of anxiety again, the ship was helpless while we were picking up the men and I expected more aircraft at any instant but I couldn't leave the chaps in the water. The only bright moment of the day was when I got back to harbour I made an almost perfect alongside into a very difficult berth with most of the C⁻in⁻C's staff, who had come down to receive the survivors, looking on. In the meantime I am having a few other troubles, one man gone off his head and jumped overboard, one attempted suicide, one breaking out of the ship just before we sailed because he was frightened, one leading sailor I shall have to court martial for failing to do his duty in the face of the enemy. Every time we have gone to sea, we have done so in pitch darkness and from difficult berths which would turn my hair grey if it weren't white already. I am afraid that the casualties have been very heavy over the last ten days. Beck was killed on Orion and Rawlings was wounded. Hampton who had the other AA cruiser was killed by machine gun bullets.

I am well looked after in this ship, the food is good and my petty officer steward excellent.

All my love,
William

Text of original messages retained by William Carne relating to the evacuation from Crete 1941:

General   C in C Med.

Following received begins. To C-in-C Med. From ADMIRALTY

For many weeks the Mediterranean Fleet has been engaged in a series of operations which have been carried out in a most successful manner but which have followed one another with such rapidity that there has been little, and in some cases no time for proper maintenance of ships or rest for their crews. That the Fleet has continued to fight and operate with maximum efficiency under these conditions is a remarkable tribute to your fighting spirit and determination of Officers and men under your command. The Battle of the Mediterranean is not yet won, and owing to casualties to some of your ships, an additional strain will be thrown on those now operating. Their Lordships have no doubt the Mediterranean Fleet will run true to form and that this strain will be borne in the same unflinching manner until the Battle is won. Thus will be added further laurels to the reputation of the Officers and men of the Mediterranean Fleet which already stands so high.

To Mediterranean Fleet   C-in-C

I wish all Officers and men in the Fleet to know that I fully realise the strain and fatigue they have been under during the last fortnight as well as the courage that has been displayed, and I appreciate to the full what has been done. I hear from all sides of the unselfishness of ships' companies in disregarding all question of their own comfort in their endeavour to make things easier for those being evacuated in conditions of great over-crowding. These things are a credit to the Mediterranean Fleet, and are the reasons that it's prestige stands so high at Home and in the Dominions.

   We are not out of the woods yet, and I will not disguise from you that we have some rough times ahead to weather. Any man who allows his resolution to falter is playing the enemy's game. We can face the difficult times just as they have at home, and we can stand up to it, I'm quite sure.

General   C in C Med.

Following received. To C-in-C Med. From MIDEAST

Personal for Admiral Cunningham from General Wavell.
   I send you and all under your Command the deepest admiration and gratitude of the Army in the Middle East for the magnificent work of the Royal Navy in bringing back the troops from Crete.
   The skill and self sacrifice with which this difficult and dangerous operation was carried out will never be forgotten and will form another strong link between our two services. Our thanks to you all and our sympathy for your losses.

Following reply has been made. C in C ME to C in C Med

Many thanks for your kind signal which has been promulgated to all concerned. I am sorry I was not able to do more.

Following received from C in C Med. From H.Q., RAF, ME

Personal for C in C Med from TEDDER.
May I express on behalf of myself and the the RAF Middle East our deep admiration of the way in which the Royal Navy has once again succeeded in doing what seemed almost impossible.

The following reply has been made AO C in C Med from C in C Med
Personal. Thank you so much for your signal. Both our Services seemed to be faced with the problem of doing the impossible but I think that our present close co-operation will go far to allow us to do so.

Following received from the Acting Prime Minister of New Zealand. Admiral Cunningham Commander-in-Chief Mediterranean Fleet., Alexandria. We have read, and our Prime Minister has told us of the wonderful work of yourself and the men under your command in sustaining, succouring and relieving our men in Crete. Your efforts have inspired the people of New Zealand to continue to give all that they have to free the World from the menace of Nazi domination. Will you please accept yourself and convey to your officers and men the heartfelt thanks of the Government and people of New Zealand for your magnificent enterprise and courage during the past twelve days. Walter Nash, Acting Prime Minister.

CHAPTER 18
POST-1941 YEARS

The notes and letters written by William Carne end with the account of the first ten days of HMS *Coventry*. The following chapter records some of the events in the rest of his Naval career until his retirement in 1956.

In late 1941 *Coventry* was sent to Bombay for a refit, and he left her and brought the cruiser *Colombo* through the Indian Ocean and South Atlantic back to England in 1942. He was then sent as part of the British Admiralty delegation to Washington, the Americans having now joined the war, and spent about a year there, primarily on purchasing American stores and torpedoes for the Royal Navy.

He returned to the UK in about April 1943 and was appointed Captain of the escort aircraft-carrier HMS *Striker* which, at that stage, was operating with the Home Fleet out of Scapa Flow. She escorted numerous convoys in the Atlantic and around the north cape to Russia and was also involved in attacking German shipping using the Norwegian coastal routes, hunting and attacking U-boats and attacking installations in Norwegian harbours.

HMS Striker

As one example, On March 10th 1944, *Striker* was detached with the Frigate *Baynton* and Corvette *Clover* to conduct air attacks on U575 which had torpedoed and sunk the Corvette *Asphodel* west-northwest of Cape Finisterre. This was not the *Asphodel* that William Carne had sailed in in the First World War; this Corvette had been launched in 1940. Only five survivors out of *Asphodel's* crew of 97 were picked up by *Clover*. After the attack the U-boat was hunted for 18 hours but managed to escape. U575 was, however, sunk just two days later on the 13th March in the North Atlantic by depth charges. Thirty-seven men survived of the crew of fifty-five.

In April 1944 *Striker* was involved in Operations Planet, Ridge Able and Hoops which involved planned strikes against the German battleship *Tirpitz* and merchant shipping. Bad weather impacted the effectiveness of these operations, although a number of ships were successfully sunk.

Wt.22313/97997. 12-42. 2,000M. E.N.M. & S. :

NAVAL MESSAGE.

S. 1320a.
(Established—May, 1930.)
(Revised—December, 1931.)

To:

CARRIERS (R) R.A.E.C.

FROM:

V.A.2.

WELL DONE. PRELIMINARY REPORTS SHOW THAT IN SPITE OF BAD WEATHER, FOUR SHIPS AND ONE ESCORT WERE HIT. I MUCH REGRET YOUR LOSSES OF ONE BARRACUDA AND FOUR FIGHTERS

(1000/26/4/44)

HOME FLEET AT SCAPA.   FROM.   C IN C H.F.

AIRCRAFT FROM HOME FLEET CARRIERS HAVE CAUSED IMPORTANT DAMAGE TO ENEMY SHIPPING OFF THE NORWEGIAN COAST.
     SOUTH OF BODO AT LEAST FOUR MERCHANT SHIPS IN CONVOY AND ONE ESCORT VESSEL WERE SO HEAVILY DAMAGED BY BOMBS THAT TOTAL LOSS IS ASSUMED.
     HITS WERE OBTAINED ON A MERCHANT SHIP ALREADY BEACHED AND SHIPPING INSIDE BODO HARBOUR.
     FURTHER NORTH A TANKER WAS SHOT UP AND POSSIBLY SET ON FIRE.

(2) FIVE AIRCRAFT WERE LOST.

(3) CARRIERS AND SURFACE FORCES SUPPORTING THEM WERE UNDER THE COMMAND OF THE V.A.2ND IN COMMAND HOME FLEET.

(291230B/APRIL)

(OPERATION RIDGE ABLE)

HMS Striker – *Photo by William Power Carne*

On 11th May 1944 His Majesty King George VI visited the fleet at Scapa Flow and came aboard HMS Striker. *Captain W.P. Carne is standing to the right of the King.*

4/9/44

Darling,

I have not been able to write to you for some three weeks as we have been busy. Nor have I had any letters from you but we should be back in harbour in the next forty-eight hours when I shall hope to get a good budget from you. We have been for a fortnight in the Arctic Circle, we were lucky with the weather and it was astonishingly salubrious but I don't know that it is an area which I should recommend for a holiday. We had another unfortunate accident soon after starting, a wildcat went into the barrier and killed a rating and injured four others. The poor devil who was killed had only joined the ship two days before and I don't think he was sufficiently alive to the necessity to dodge when these things go haywire. None of the injured men were at all serious and were all back to duty in a few days. It has been a very busy period, two of our wildcats shot down a BV137 after a most exciting hunt in the clouds which lasted nearly an hour. We have also had considerable fun with the U-boats.

One interesting experience was lunch onboard a Russian flagship as guest of the Admiral. We all sat down around a large table covered with enormous piles of caviar, smoked salmon, slices of ham and tongue and various pickled vegetables and drank vast quantities of vodka. One's glass was kept continuously topped up and there were innumerable toasts to be drunk. Conversation was a bit limited as the longest phrase any of the Russians knew in English was, "I love you, my darling" and none of the Englishmen were even as good as that in Russian. However there was not much necessity to talk as we were entertained by a very good concert party from the Moscow Conservatoire. They each came in turn and played or sang behind the Admiral's chair and were each rewarded in turn by a ferocious scowl from him. When I finally left the flagship, as I had taken part in an operation with the Russian Admiral, I was given a present of a bottle of vodka. After all the rude things I have said to my sailors about getting drunk on shore I felt slightly ashamed of myself arriving back on board my ship rather flushed, not quite steady and clutching a bottle. The same evening the same concert party gave a performance onboard the Striker in the hanger and to my surprise, were very well received by the sailors. All their stuff was pretty high brow classical stuff, not the sort of thing you would expect the sailors to like, but they listened in absolute dead silence and then their applause nearly lifted the flight deck. The Russians were obviously very pleased. Afterwards I had the whole party in my cabin and fed them on tea and coffee and cakes. Luckily I had a little chocolate which went down very well. Apparently it is almost unknown in Russia now. Again conversation was a bit limited but one or two of my officers did some good eye work with some of the young women, who were quite good to look at.

I meant Richard to be with me for this operation. It would have been a good experience for him. But the letter from the College to the Admiralty saying in which ship it was intended cadets should do their training was not sent off until the 9th August. I got my copy on the 13th, too late to do anything about it.

All my love

William

At the end of October 1944, *Striker* was sent to the Far East to join the war against the Japanese. In March 1945 William Carne was appointed Commodore in charge of the 30th Aircraft squadron and *Striker* became the Squadron's flagship. The primary job of the escort carriers was to provide logistic and aircraft supplies to the main fleet carriers who were operating with the United States Fleet against the Japanese in the Pacific, north and east of the Philippine Islands. So, *Striker* was, in fact, trying to support a fleet which was operating several thousand miles away from its base in Sydney, Australia.

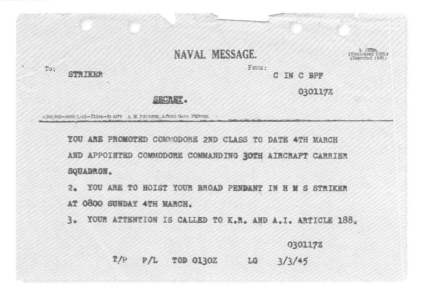

NAVAL MESSAGE.

To: STRIKER

FROM: C IN C BPF

030117Z

SECRET.

YOU ARE PROMOTED COMMODORE 2ND CLASS TO DATE 4TH MARCH AND APPOINTED COMMODORE COMMANDING 30TH AIRCRAFT CARRIER SQUADRON.

2. YOU ARE TO HOIST YOUR BROAD PENDANT IN H M S STRIKER AT 0800 SUNDAY 4TH MARCH.

3. YOUR ATTENTION IS CALLED TO K.R. AND A.I. ARTICLE 188.

030117Z

T/P   P/L   TOD 0130Z   LG   3/3/45

By July 1945 *Striker* was off the coast of Japan continuing the replenishment duties. At the time of the Japanese surrender she was actually at anchor in Seeadler Harbour, Manus Islands, Papua New Guinea.

Immediately after the surrender *Striker* was employed on humanitarian relief work, repatriating refugees and POWs. All aircraft and related equipment was off loaded and large quantities of food and medical supplies were embarked for delivery to Hong Kong along with folding beds and spare clothing, for the men, women and children they were to embark as passengers for the return leg. Even in these difficult times, weddings took place and Commodore Carne was the guest of honour at one.

NAVAL MESSAGE.

S. 1320A
(Established—Mar, 1930.)
(Revised—January, 1933.)

To: FROM:

A.C.30.   CTF 111.

St 5021

I have watched the work of the Escort Carriers in their many
and varied tasks during the last few months. I know how much
the Fleet has appreciated your help and there are now many men
who will always be grateful to your squadron for the work they
have done in evacuation.
My best wishes to yourself and your ships.

                                       050813.

W/T   P/L.   TOR 1335/6/10.   SRW

Striker came home to England at the end of 1945 and was then returned
to the United States.

William Carne was then appointed Captain of *Defiance*, the torpedo
school at Devonport, which was in the process of converting into a torpedo
and anti-submarine school. He was then appointed Captain of the cruiser
Nigeria, the flagship of the Royal Navy's squadron in the South Atlantic,
based at Simonstown. He held this job for eighteen months and it was his last
sea job in the Navy. On his return he was chairman of a committee which
reviewed the training of torpedo electrical and anti-submarine ratings.

He retired in June 1950, but shortly afterwards was offered a job at
the Admiralty in Bath on the torpedo and anti-submarine materials side.
He probably didn't enjoy that much, and it didn't last very long, but soon
afterwards he was offered a job as Captain Superintendent of Contract Built
Ships, responsible for the Admiralty liaison with all ship builders building
Royal Naval warships in private yards and this job was upgraded to a
Commodore soon afterwards.

He was thus a Commodore twice, in 1944 and again in 1954. He had
about two or three years as Commodore Superintendent and then finally
retired from the Navy in 1956. He was appointed a Commander of the
British Empire (CBE) in 1955.

Captain William Carne, Valentine Carne, Admiral of the Fleet Andrew Browne Cunningham, 1st Viscount Cunningham of Hyndhope, KT, GCB, OM, DSO and Lady Cunningham. Probably taken at a memorial event in the 1960's

Commodore Carne CBE with his four sons, from left to right, Oliver, Rodney, Gyles and Richard. Taken at Rodney's wedding to Jill Trench Fox in 1955.

EPILOGUE

This book tells of an extraordinary life, led through the harshest of times. A career spanning the two World Wars. These times seem unimaginable to us today; appalling losses were accepted as a fact of life. And the letters give an insight into the uncertain and frightening world that the extraordinarily brave and resourceful loved ones had to endure.

In their retirement in Cornwall, William and Valentine had many grandchildren, and there were years of idyllic summer holidays spent playing in the beautiful woodland garden at Tresahor, the family home they lived in, and where my father still lives today. William created treasure hunts for us children and erected an old shed deep in the woods which was the official meeting house for SPOG – the Society for the Protection of Old Grandfathers. We had a blissful childhood. We were far too young to know anything about war and the sacrifices that had been made by his generation. And when I became old enough to become curious, in my teenage years, he was at the end of his life, somewhat silent and removed, and regrettably, we never had the conversations that I now wish we could have had.

On one occasion, I must have been about sixteen, I thought I would be helpful and cut the grass down in the wood. There was a fearsome machine called a cultivator that had huge teeth along the front. It was unwieldy and very heavy. I didn't really know how to control it, and at one point it careered off the path and embedded itself in the roots of a rhododendron. I looked up, and to my absolute horror, saw my grandfather on the path above, in breeches and stockings with tweed jacket, looking sternly down at me. I was, frankly, terrified at the telling off I expected. But his leadership experience had obviously taught him that nothing he could say would make me feel any better, or any more humiliated than I already felt. So, without a word, he walked down the hill and helped me drag the cultivator back onto the path.

Now that I know him much better, having spent so long compiling this book, I think I know what he must have been thinking as he looked down at the nervous, callow youth in front of him. I couldn't control a lawnmower, while at the same age, he had been taking part in one of the greatest sea battles – Jutland. Quite a thought.

William Carne, painted by Frank Jameson

INDEX

Page numbers in *italic* indicate figures.

1st Battle Cruiser Squadron, Battle of Jutland 68, 84
2nd Battle Cruiser Squadron 52, 65, *67*, 84
2nd Light Cruiser Squadron 41, 97
3rd Battle Cruiser Squadron 52, 84, 87, 234
3rd Light Cruiser Squadron 97
4-inch guns 312
4.7-inch guns 17
5th Battle Squadron 66; Battle of Jutland 71, 72, 79–80, 82–83, 86; Rosyth repairs 95
6-inch guns 17
12-inch guns 42, 52
13th Destroyer Flotilla 52, 79
13.5-inch guns 42, 52
14th Flotilla 201, 205, 206, 207, 208
30th Aircraft Squadron, Commodore Carne 331, *331*

A
Aba (hospital ship), rescue by *Coventry* *322*
academic education, naval cadets 208, 209
accident 158–175; bandages 159, 162–163; Board of Enquiry 166, 169–170; Captain *(Asphodel)* visit 167; certificate of wounds and hurts *175*; complete daze 162; conversance 173–174; deafness 160, 169; details of 167–168; discharged fit for duty 174; first aid 158–159; gun defect 166–167; gun modification 169; lacerated ear and scalp 162; letter home *165*, 169; other sailors injured/killed 166, 167–168; pain (nothing for) 162; senior doctor 159, 167; visit to *Asphodel* 172 *See also* Royal Naval Hospital Bighi
Aegean convoys 243–244, 266
Alexandria: air raid 305–306; breakwater berth 309, 312, 321; floating dock 230, 266; Great Pass 242; land and sea breezes 123; minesweeping 236–238, 239; ratings shortage 119–120; travel to 111 *See also* Mediterranean posting (First World War)
Alexandria Harbour, Great Pass 123
Alexandrian ladies 320
'Alteration and Addition' (A&A) 126–127
Army and Navy Stores 103–104
Arthur Cavanagh 285
Artigliere (sinking) 274, 275
Asphodel 100, 114–154; armament exercise (Carne) 124–126; armament maintenance 120–121;

based in Malta 139; Base Engineer Officer 128–129; blackboard (gun control) 136–137, 158; Cameron (engineer officer) 117, 134, 141, 142, 153, 178; Captain 116–117, 127; Captain (relieved) 118, 134, 148–149; Carne's predecessor 123–124; Carroll (Petty Officer) 120, 121, 124, 158, 168; coal (trim from deck to bunkers) 141–142; convoy escort duty 139–151, 155–157, 176–186; convoy (last) 181–182; convoy policy arguments 130–131; convoy ship torpedoed 144–150; deck cargo of coal 140–141, 142, 143; depth charge pistols 151–152; depth charges 121, 137, 149, 151; dog (Vic) 147–148, 152; easy conditions (sun and warmth) 122–123, 127; first days 118–126; fo'c'sle gun 121; foreign service leave 181–182; full power trial 128–129, 133; Galbraith (mother's letter) 153–154; Gale (torpedoman) 125–126, 132, 149, 151–152; gun defect 166–167; guns (control from bridge) 126–127, 135–137, 158; guns (electric firing) 125–126, 131–132; guns (firing practice) 158, 168–169; guns (modification) 132–133, 169; guns (percussion firing) 132–133; main engine bearers 117, 128–129, 133–134, 139; major repairs 129, 133–134, 139; Malta dockyard 117; Mediterranean anti-submarine policy 123; minesweeper 118–119; 'Modified Sweep' 122; officer reliefs 134; officers return from leave 138; Port Said to Gibraltar convoy escort 141–151; Port Said to Malta convoys 129–132; QF gun 124–125; ship's complement 119; signals (improvised) 129–130; sinking 327; sister ship (*Wisteria*) *115*; Skerki Channel 144; special duty orders 140–141; Staples (Chief Petty Officer) 120, 142; sub-lieutenant duties 115–116; submarine spotted on surface 178–179; team spirit 115–116; tow torpedoed ship 176–177; troop ship escort 123; voicepipes 126–127, 135–136; zig-zag alterations of course 140 *See also* accident

Aurora 41

Australia 52; zig-zag alterations accident 63–64, 65

axis war 230

B

Baker, Philip (midshipman) *58*, 81

Bartolomeo Colleoni 265

Barton, D.H.: based in Alexandria 179–180; Battle of Jutland 86; cigarettes 82, 88; Mediterranean posting 100–101, 104–105; *New Zealand* 54–55, *67*, 70–71, 73, 75, 79; Royal Naval Hospital Bighi 109–110

Battenberg, Prince George 53

Battle Cruiser Force 52, 93

battle damage: cordite fire 46–47;
   Jutland 46–47

Battle Fleet, Scapa Flow 93

Battle of Calabria 244–257; AA fire
   255–256; *Bartolomeo Colleoni* 265;
   causalities 263; 'Conti de Cavour'
   252; Cunningham 245, 255, 257,
   261; enemy air attack 255; enemy
   cruiser under tow 256–257; enemy
   turned away 254–255; enemy vessel
   identification 253; fleet formation
   249, 250–252, *251*; Gulf of Messina
   256–257; knocked over by blast
   (Carne) 253, 257, 260; letter to
   Valentine *262*; 'loose formation'
   256; luck (British) 264; nervous
   tension 252–253; 'pattern bombing'
   255–256, 261, 263; return to Malta
   257, 258; smoke 254; splinter holes
   263

Battle of Dogger Bank 41–49; *Blücher*
   sinking 46, 47–49, *47*; coal fired
   ships 42, 43; enemy Battle Cruiser
   Squadron 41; enemy Light Cruiser
   Squadron 41; fleet movement *42*;
   letter Feb 5th *46*; 'Salvoes' 43;
   Transmitting Station (TS) 42, 43

Battle of Heligoland 20

Battle of Jutland 65–93, 334; 1st Battle
   Cruiser Squadron 68, 84; 2nd
   Battle Cruiser Squadron 68, 84;
   3rd Battle Cruiser Squadron 84,
   87; 5th Battle Squadron 66, 71, 72,
   79–80, 82–83, 86; 13th Destroyer

Flotilla 79; Admiral Beatty 76, 87,
   93; Admiral Jellicoe 84, 93; battle
   cruiser action May 31st *69*; Beatty's
   battle cruisers gunnery standard
   79–80; big gun action 70, 82; British
   Grand Fleet 82; communication
   in battle 102; controversy 68–69,
   79, 92–93, 102; cordite fire 47;
   defective materials 93; *Defence* 85;
   direct firing 70; German battle
   cruisers 68; German High Sea
   Fleet 81–82, 83, 84, 85, 89, 102;
   German light cruisers 84; German
   Peltravic system 70; German rate of
   fire 71–72; Grand Fleet 83, 84, 86,
   89; *Indefatigable* 72–73, *74*, 81, 102;
   Indomitable 87; *Inflexible* 87; *Invincible*
   84, *85*; lack of enemy reports 87,
   88; *Lion* 79, 86, 88, 93; lives lost
   102; lull 79, 81; main engagement
   80; movements 30-31 May (1916)
   67, *69*; newspaper reports 91, *92*;
   New Zealand hit 76–78, *78*, 80–81;
   noise 71; peril 69; *Queen Mary* 76,
   77, 81; range finding 71–72; 'Rapid
   Salvoes' 72; retrospective view 102;
   Rosyth (repairs/casualties) 90; 'Run
   to the South' 79–84; ships lost 102;
   smoke 70, 71, 86–87; *Southampton* 81;
   statistics 80–81; strict censorship 91;
   van of the battle fleet 86–87; *Warrior*
   84–85; *Warspite* 85; 'Windy Corner'
   85–86

Battle of Matapan 276, 278–281, *282*

Battle of Scapa Flow 23–24

Battle of Taranto 276, 277–278, *279*

Baynton 327

Beatty, Admiral 27, 52, 95, 99; Battle of Jutland 70, 76, 87, 93

Beaufort 322

Benghazi, Carne's hope to press on to 293

Bighi Hospital *See* Royal Naval Hospital Bighi

Birch, Assistant Paymaster *54*

Bizerta 152, 182

Blücher 43, 44; Prize Bounty *62*; sinking 46, 47–49, *47*

Boulogne 107

Bowlby, Cuthbert (midshipman) *58*

Boyd 283–284

British Eastern Mediterranean Fleet 233, 242

British Grand Fleet, Battle of Jutland 82

British submarines, losses in Mediterranean 267–268

British Supply Mission 326; Bullard Company 276–282

Buckingham Place, crowds eve of First World War 11–12

C

cabin baths 16, 25

Caius College (Cambridge) 208

Calcutta 272, 273, 305, 309–310, 311, 312; 4-inch guns 312; air attack 316; 'Bunny' Lees (Captain) 305, 309, 312, 318, 320, 321; flotta nets 318–319; missing men 319–320; No 10 zig-zag 314; signals from *Coventry* 314–315; sinking 316–317; survivors pick up *Coventry* 317–319, *323*

Caledon 234

Callaghan, Admiral 14

Calypso 234

Canadian troop convey, October (1914) 24

Capetown 225

Cape Wrath 200

Captains Courageous (Kipling) 50

Captain Superintendent of Contract Built Ships 332

Carne, Annie (mother) *51*

Carne, Mark (grandson) 7, 214–216, 334

Carne, Valentine (wife) 214, *215*, 216, *333*

Carne, William: Captain *329*; Commander *231*; home with family (1916) *66*; Lieutenant *215*; marriage 214, *215*; memorial event (1960s) *333*; Midshipman 27, *51*, *54*, *56*, *66*; naval cadet *6*; parents' home *103*; political thoughts 216; post-1941 years 326–334; professional instruction 32, 33, 52, 97–98; retirement 332, 334; sons 214, *330*, *333*; Sub-Lieutenant *106*, *135*

Chatfield, Lord (Admiral of the Fleet) 99

Christmas card (1940) *281*

Christmas (onboard *New Zealand*) 38–39

cigarettes 82, 88

Cingalese Prince (first merchant ship Tobruk) 289

clothes: *Asphodel* 164, 166; London shopping 187–188, 189; wardrobe overhaul 104

Clover 327

coal fired ships: Battle of Dogger Bank 42; smoke at full power 43; stoking/trimming coal 56–60

coaling: *New Zealand* 29, 31–32, 46, 51, 90; *Sappho* 14–15; speed 32

Colombo, Carne sailed back to England 326

convoy escort duty: *Asphodel* 123, 139–140, 141–151, 155–157, 176–186; Port Said to Gibraltar 143, 144–146; *Striker* 326–327, *329–330*

cordite fire 46–47

Cotton (Chief Petty Officer, Sappho) 17, 18, 21, 22, 28

Coventry 272, 273, 300–325, *302*; 4-inch guns 312; AA fire 307, 313; *Aba* (hospital ship) *322*; air attack 314, 315–316; aircraft reported 302–303, 314–315; air raid 305–306; Alexandria breakwater berth 309, 312, 321; Alexandria docking 320; *Calcutta* survivors pick up 317–319, *323*; Captain Carne 300–325; Crete (enemy activity) 302–303; evacuate men from Sfakia (Crete) 309–312, 313–317; evacuation of Crete (original messages to Carne) *324–325*; Gilmore, David *300*, 301; Glen ship fire 307–308; Glen ships to Crete escort 301–304, 306–308; high-priority signal 303, 304;

Kerruish, Robert H.E. (Lieutenant RAN) 310, 311, 316–317, 320; movement 28th May- 1st June (1941) 303; navigating officer 305, 310; pom-pom 312, 316; radar 302, 306, 307, 308, 309; RAF bomber (lost/ditched) 304–305; Reece (Lieutenant Commander) 306; refit (1941) 326; report back attack/Calcutta damaged/sunk 316–317; return to Alexandria 304–305, 308, 319–320; Sephton, Alfred (Petty Officer) 322; sinking 322

Crete: enemy activity 302–303; evacuate men from Sfakia (Crete) 309–312, 313–317; evacuation of Crete (original messages to Carne) *324–325*; Kasso Strait 244; Sfakia 307, 309–312; Suda Bay 243

Cromarty Firth 31

Cunningham, Admiral 230, 232, 235, 238, 239, *333*; Battle of Calabria 245, 255, 257, 261; Carne's minesweeping duties 294; high-priority signal 304; Navy always stands by the army 313; Tobruk (capture 1941) 290–291

Cunningham, Lady *333*

D

Dainty 265

Danae 214, 217, 226

Dardanelles 60

Dartmouth, naval cadets 11–13

dawn action stations 35

Defence 85

Defiance 214

depth charge: *Asphodel* (failure) 149,
151; 'D' type 121, 137; mine
clearing 294; *Tactician* 195–196, 207

depth charge pistols 151–152

Derna 291; minesweeping (Carne)
292–293; Navy Office 292

Devonport, torpedo school 214, 332

dghaisa 110

dhows 123

direct firing 43, 49, 60–61, 70

Dorsetshire 222

Dulverto 322

Dunkirk 233

E

Eagle 244, 249; air striking force
254, 255, 258; Battle of Calabria
252, 254; Captain 266; Gladiator
aircraft 264–265; reconnaissance
aircraft 248, 254, 256, 258–259;
Swordfish aircraft 240–241, 244,
264, 267; Tobruk attack 265–266,
284; torpedo bombers 248; torpedo
supplies 260

Eastern Mediterranean (1917) *108*

Eastern Mediterranean (1940) *243*

East Indies Squadron 267

Edinburgh 13, 37, 65

Engine Room training, ex-Dartmouth
cadets 55–56

England, rationing system (WW1) 187

Express of Asia 217

F

Falmouth 97

Ferryville 152

Fiona 285, 286, 287, 290; Griffiths 285,
286; return to Malta 293

First Light Cruiser Squadron 52

First World War: anti-climax 203–204;
armistice 203–204, 207; certificate
of recognition *212*; crowds at
Buckingham Place 11–12; German
fleet surrender 205–206; great naval
battle to end 202; little idea of the end
coming 189; rationing system 187

Fisher, Admiral 118

Fleet Torpedo Officer (FTO), Carne
231, 294, 301

Force 'H' from Gibraltar 272, 273

Formidable 307

Fort Capuzzo (bombardment) 269–270

Free French 235

French armistice 235

French soldiers 183

G

Galatea 52, 65–66

Galbraith *(Asphodel* letter and gift)
153–154

George VI, King (visit to Scapa Flow)
329

German High Sea Fleet 95–97; Battle
of Jutland 81–82, 83, 84, 85, 89, 102

German light cruisers, Battle of Jutland
84

German submarines: armistice
surrender 205; lack of weapons to

attack 41; *Sappho* hunt for 20–22; threat 23, 63; zig-zag alterations of course 63

Gibraltar 152; Straights of Gibraltar 242 *See also* Port Said to Gibraltar convoy escort

Gieves (naval tailors) 23, 26–27

Gilmore, David *300*, 301

Gladiator aircraft, *Eagle* 264

Glengyle 309–310, 311, *311*

Glen ships to Crete escort 301–304, 306–308

Gloucester 234, 244, 247, 249, 252, 260, 263

Godfroy, Vice-Admiral 233, 235, 236, 239–240

Goodenough, Commodore 25–27, 52

Gough-Calthorpe, Admiral 134

Grace, Captain 194, 196–197

Graham navyphone 73, 75

Grand Fleet: additional destroyers 202; Battle of Jutland 83, 84, 86, 89; hopes of return to 180, 181; Jellicoe 233; Loch Ewe 24; memos 198; *New Zealand* 65–66; Rosyth 201; Scapa Flow 38, 200–201; threat from German submarines 23

Graziani 268

'Green Mice' squadron 246–247

Greenock, Tail of the Bank 194

Greyhound 280

Griffiths, Arthur 285, 286

gunroom argument 91

guns: *Asphodel* modification 132–133; blackboard (gun control) 136–137,

158; direct firing 43, 49, 60–61, 70; electric firing 125–126, 131–132; German Peltravic system 70; percussion firing 132–133; unloading (*New Zealand*) 45–46

H

Haka 34

Hands Across The Sea (Operation HATS) 272–275; *Artigliere (sinking) 274, 275*; letters to Valentine *273–274*

Hannibal 118, 128

Havoc 265

Hawkins 194, 196–197

Heligoland 20, 38, 44

Hickling, *Captain* (SNOIS) 284, 285, 290, 291, 293

Home Fleet, Kronstadt 34

Homeward Eastern Number One (HE1) 141

Hood, sinking BBC radio news 306

Hood, Admiral 52, 84

Huntley 291–292

I

IFF (Identification, Friend or Foe) 315

Illustrious 272, 273, 277

Indefatigable 52, 72–73, *74*, 81, 102

Indomitable 42, 43, 44, 45, 46, 52, 87

Inflexible 52, 87

Invincible 52, 84, *85*

Iron Duke 23, 24, 96

Isonzo 109

Italian convoys, Italy to Albania 277

J

Jellicoe, Admiral 14, 84, 93, 233
Jervis 266
Junior Officers' Club (JOC), South
    Queensferry 99

K

Keighly-Peach, Charles (Commander)
    264–265
Kent 269
Kerruish, Robert H.E. (Lieutenant
    RAN) 310, 311, 316–317, 320
King, Admiral 309, 310, 311
King's Cross 11
Kipling, R.: *Captains Courageous* 50; 'The
    Scholars' 209–210, *211*
Kronstadt 34

L

Land Girls 188
leave: Christmas (1918) 207–208;
    Edinburgh 37; foreign service leave
    181–182; London hotel 49–50; long
    train journeys 49–50; Mediterranean
    May (1941) *300*; Mediterranean
    posting 103–105; *New Zealand* (May
    1915) 49–50; *New Zealand* (November
    1915) 61; *New Zealand* (repairs 1916)
    65; Portsmouth torpedo school 187
Lechanché battery 17, 125–126
Lees, 'Bunny' (Captain) 305, 309, 312,
    318, 320, 321
letters: accident *165*; armistice (not
    expecting 6/11/18) *204*; Battle of
    Calabria *262*; Battle of Dogger Bank

46; Battle of Jutland (to Mona) 96;
    Battle of Matapan *282*, 297–299;
    Battle of Taranto *279*; *Calcutta*
    survivors pick up *323*; Carne home
    bombed *295–296*; censor 154;
    Fort Capuzzo (bombardment) *271*;
    Hands Across The Sea (Operation
    HATS) *273–274*; hopes of return
    from Mediterranean WWII *297*,
    299; *Striker* convoy escort duty
    329–330; Tobruk (capture 1941)
    283, *295*
Lewis, Signal Boatswain *54*
Liguria 286
Lion 31, 43, 44, 49, 52, 53, 96; 13.5-
    inch guns 42; Admiral Beatty 95;
    Battle of Jutland 68, 70, 79, 86, 88,
    93; damage 46–47; evening shows
    99; 'Flag, Lion' 94; limping home
    45, 46
Liverpool 234, 244, 263
London: clothes shopping 187–188,
    189; return from Mediterranean
    posting 186
Lorraine (French battleship) 233, 234
Lovatt, Richard (midshipman) 81
Lyster, Lumley (Admiral) 283–284

M

machine guns exercise 305
magazine doors 93
magnetic mines 'cucumbers' 283–284,
    285, 286, 287
mails: irregular 152–153; *Sappho* 24;
    South Queensferry 40–41

Malaya 232, 244, 249, 252, 254

Maleme airfield 305

Malta: Admiral's Office 110; air attack 314; Baracca lift 173; Comino channel 177; convoy runs to 242, 258; Customs House 110; ferry to 109; Grand Fleet 314; Grand Harbour 109, 110, 171, 177; Great Pass 301; journey to 107–108; Marsa Scirocco 177; Osborne (hotel) 110; Sliema Harbour 110; Tigné 134; Union Club 134, 173–174; Valletta *109*, 110, 134 *See also* Royal Naval Hospital Bighi

Marder, A.J. 100

Maund, Loben E.H. (Captain) 226

Mediterranean fleet formation (WWII) 230–241; air attack 244–247, 270; British submarine losses 267–268; Carne's hope of relief from *297, 299*; Commander-in-Chief, Mediterranean 272; contraband patrols 231, 237; Cunningham 232, 235, 238, 239, 245; enemy aircraft (making 'longs') 245, 259; Fleet Gunnery Officer (FGO) 250, 253; French armistice 235, 242, 244; French battleships 232; French libertymen plan to ambush 238–239; French ships surrender 235–236, 238–240; fuel base (between Alexandria and Malta) 243; Godfroy 233, 235, 236, 239–240; Gulf of Bardia 269; Gulf of Bomba 267; gun crews 245–246;

Italian minefields 234, 236–238; Italian submarine commanders 234; Italy remaining neutral 230–231, 237; lack of small craft 232–233, 312–313; luck (British) *273*; Malta 231, 257–258; minesweeping (Carne's plan) 236–238, 239; patrol of fighters overhead (British) 265, 269; 'pattern bombing' 245, 246–247, *247*, 261, 270; 'Pooh trap' 268–270; RAF aerodromes 240–241; refueling 243; reinforcements 272, 277; Suda Bay (Crete) 243; Tobruk (torpedo attack) 240–241, 265–266 *See also* Battle of Calabria; Battle of Matapan; Battle of Taranto; *Coventry*; Tobruk (capture 1941)

Mediterranean posting (First World War) 100–101; appointment of reliefs 181; Christmas (1917) 155; leave before 103–105; looking forward to return to Grand Fleet 180, 181; *Revenge* 214; travel back to England 182–186; travel to 104–109; wardrobe overhaul 104 *See also Asphodel*

Milford Countess 285

minesweeping: Alexandria 236–238, 239; depth charge clearing 294; Derna 292–293 *See also* Tobruk (capture 1941)

Ministry of Shipping 104

'Modified Sweep,' submarine detection 122

Moore, Admiral 44

mosquitoes 134–135

Moy 285, 291

N

Naval Assistant to the Second Sea Lord (NA2SL) 188

naval cadets: academic education 208, 209; deaths autumn (1914) 23; Engine Room training (ex-Dartmouth) 55–56; travel from Dartmouth 11–13

Neptune 244

Nereide 111–114; Captain 112, 114; First Lieutenant 113–114; passage to Alexandria 114

New Zealand 29–62, *30*; 4-inch control officer 55; 4-inch gun crews 79, 81, 82, 86, 87; 12-inch guns 42; Admiral Moore's flag 44; Admiral Packenham's flag 65; auxiliary oil fire 56; Battle of Dogger Bank 41–49; Battle of Jutland hit 76–78, *78*, 80–81; bunting ensigns 68, 88; 'Cable Officers' 30, 34; Chief Stoker (Lake) 57–58, 59–60, 86; Christmas 38–39; coal bunkers 56, 57; coaling 29, 31–32, 46, 51, 90; communication in battle 72, 73–74, 75, 78; Conning Tower 73, 79; Devonport dockyard 61; direct firing (fitting) 60–61; Engine Room training (Carne) 55–56; First Lieutenant 32, 39; fo'c'sle deck 29; full power 42, 60; gunroom 29; gunroom rugger team 98; guns (unloading) 45–46; Haka 34; leave (due to ship repairs) 65; leave (May 1915) 49–50; leave (November 1915) 61; lower deck rumours 60; Maori Chief's prophesy 33–34, 91; midshipman 'A' turret (Carne) 52–53; midshipmen (new batch) 52, 99; Mr. Battenberg 53; newspaper reports *92*; picket boat duty 39–41, 89–90, 91, 94, 95; professional instruction 32, 33; 'P' turret 30; 'Q' Marines turret 30, 45; 'rabbit hutch' 71, 75, *77*, 79, 82, 86; Rosyth 36–37, 46, 61, 64–65, 89; Scapa Flow 31, 95; secondary torpedo control officer (Carne) 53; secondary torpedo control position 53, 55, *67*; shell rooms 90; ship's company (lack of information) 36; South Queensferry mail incident 40–41; stokers (feeding after battle) 87–88; stokers (number and watches) 60; stoking/trimming coal 56–60; torpedo net booms 34–35, 64; torpedo officer 53–54; torpedo range finder 33; tour of the ship 29–31; traditions and customs 33; Transmitting Station (TS) 32–33, 35–36, 42, 43, 44, 52; 'A' turret 30, 33, 90; voicepipe men 71, 75; Wardroom flat 30; west country ship 35; 'X' turret 29–30, 33–34, 53, 75, 77–78, 81; zig-zag alterations of course accident 63–64 *See also* Battle of Jutland

New Zealanders 171

Nigella 100, 179

Nigeria 332

night fighting equipment 93–94

North Roma Island 20–22

Notices to Mariners 193, 194, 200

Nottingham 97

O

Officer of the Watch 63, 100

Orion 244

Orkney Islands 19–20 *See also* Scapa Flow

Osborne 11, 107, 188, 237

Outer Hebrides 20

P

Pakenham, Admiral 52, 65, 68

Paris 184–186

Pelorus Jack *54*

Pennington, L.G. (midshipman) *54*

Perth 309–310, 311, 312

Phoebe 309–310, 311, 312

photography (Carne) 73

'Pooh trap' 268–270

Port Edgar 207

Port Said to Gibraltar convoy escort 141–151; dog left onboard ship 147–148; order to return to Malta 150; periscope sighted 149; torpedoed ship 143, 144–150

Portsmouth 12–13; torpedo school 187

Princess Royal 42, 43, 49, 52

pyjamas 26–27

Q

Queen Alexandra's Royal Naval

Nursing Service Reserve 171

Queen Mary 49, 52, 76, *77*, 81

Quintinshill rail disaster 49

R

RAF aerodromes, Western desert 240–241, 266, 267, 269

Railway Transport Officers (RTOs) 11

Resolution 55

Resource 320

Revenge 214

Rifleman 111–114

RNR lieutenants 18–19, 26

Rodi 293

Rosyth: Grand Fleet 201; Kirkliston route march 37–38; new dockyard 94–95; *New Zealand* 36–37, 46; picket boat duty 94; repairs/casualties (Battle of Jutland) 90; submarine defences 39, 64–65; *Tactician* 201

Royal Naval Hospital Bighi 109–110, 160–174, *161*, 180; Chief Sick Berth Petty Officer 161; chocolate and lizards 171–172; clothes 164, 166; 'Officers Surgical' 160–161, 165; sick berth attendants 164; Sister 164–166, 170–171, 172–174; visitors 167, 169

Royal Sovereign 232, 244, 249, 257–258

rum 38

S

sailor's flannel 26–27

sand flies 135

San Grigio 285, 286, *287*

Sappho 14–28, *16*; 4.7-inch guns 17; 6-inch guns 17; Battle of Scapa Flow 23–24; cabin baths 16, 25; cabin flat 16, 25; coal dust 15; coaling 14–15; Cotton (Chief Petty Officer) 17, 18, 21, 22, 28; deck scrubbing 15; First Lieutenant 18, 21; fresh mutton 21–22; fresh provisions 20, 25; guard ship for Holm Sound 18; mail for the fleet 24; midshipmen promotion 23; Muckle Flugga patrol 24–25; Navigating Officer 21; North Roma Island 20–22; Orkney Islands 19–20, *19*; reservists 18–19, 26; Scapa Flow 14, 18, 25–26; search for German submarines 20–22; as yacht for CNC 17; yardarm groups 15

Scapa Flow: battle cruisers 27–28; Battle Fleet 93; Battle of Scapa Flow 23–24; George VI *329*; German destroyers escorted to 206; Grand Fleet 38, 200–201; Hoxa Sound 23; Long Hope 200–201; *New Zealand* 31, 95; Ronaldshay 210; rough waters 25–26; *Sappho* 14, 18; *Striker* 326

Scarborough, bombarded 36–37

seaboot stockings 153

sea chests 11, 101, 107, 111, 183–184

seasickness 19, 22, 25, 109, 114, 155

sea warfare professionals 22–23

Second Light Cruiser Squadron 52

Second World War *See* Mediterranean fleet formation (WWII)

Senior British Naval Officer Canal Area (SBNOC) 291

Sephton, Alfred (Petty Officer) 322

Seydlitz 47

Sfaki evacuation 309–312, 313–317

Shanghai evacuation (1937) 217–227; *Capetown* 225; Chinese snipers (Pooting point) 224; *Dorsetshire* 222; fires 220; food shortages 223; Japanese aeroplanes Nantao bombing 222; letters to Valentine *218*, *220*, 222–226; map of war zone *221*; photo from *The Times 219*, 225; Pooting bombing 222, 224, 225; Shanghai Club 220; signal from the Admiralty *227 See also Danae*

Shetland Islands, Muckle Flugga 24–25

Sims, George 321

Sinclair, Alexander (Commodore) 52

sloop maintenance party 157–158

Southampton 25–26, 36, 41, 52, 81, 289

South Queensferry 13; Junior Officers' Club (JOC) 99

Spanish 'Flu 188; *Tactician* 189, 191, 195–197

Straights of Gibraltar 242

Striker 326, 328; 30th Aircraft Squadron 331; Captain Carne 326–332; convoy escort duty 326–327, *329–330*; humanitarian relief work 331, *332*; Japanese surrender 331; Operations April (1944) 327; return England (1945) 332; sent to Far East (October 1944) 331

Stuart 306, 309

sub-lieutenant exam 97–98, 99–100

submarine defences: barrage (mouth

of Adriatic) 176; picket boat patrol 39–41; Rosyth 39–41, 64–65; zig-zag alterations of course 63

submarine detection, 'Modified Sweep' 122

submarines: British boats lost 267–268; German armistice surrender 205; German lack of weapons against 41; German *Sappho* hunt for 20–22; German threat 23, 63; Italian commanders 234

Sunderland, intended bombardment 95–96, 97

Swordfish aircraft: *Eagle* 244, 264, 267; Tobruk 240–241; *Warspite* 250, 256; Western desert 267

Sydney 244, 265

T

Tactical School 248–249

Tactician 188–208, *190*; acceptance trial 192, 193, 194–195; armistice 203–204, 207; Beardmore's Yard 188, 189; cable officer duties 194–195; Captain 190, 191, 194, 195–196, 207; Captain (relief) 197, 198–199, 202; Captain (return from illness) 204; Captain (second relief) 202; Captain (Spanish 'Flu) 195–197; chart house 192–193, 194; Christmas leave (1918) 207–208; 'comforts' parcel 201; confidential books 197–198; correspondence (commanding officer) 197–198; coxswain 190, 192, 200; depth charge throwers 195–196, 207; Engineer Captain 189–190; escort German destroyers to Scapa 206; escort 'K' class submarine (Scapa) 199–200; First Lieutenant 191, 207; First Lieutenant (missing due to illness) 189, 191, 195; First Lieutenant (relief) 197, 202; German fleet surrender 205–206; Grand Fleet memos 198; Gunner (T) 189–190, 195–196, 197, 198, 203, 206, 207; Notices to Mariners 193, 200; Rosyth 201; 'Rounds' 193–194, 199; Spanish 'Flu 189, 191, 195–197; sub-lieutenant duties 192–193; temporary engineer officer 191–192, 198, 202; wardroom atmosphere 202; wardroom wines and spirits 206; watch bill 199; whaler 192; working up period 201, 205

Taranto 108

Terror 284, 290

'The Scholars' (Kipling) 209–210, *211*

Tiger 42, 43, 52

Tobruk, torpedo attack (British on) 240–241, 265–266

Tobruk (capture 1941) 283–299; 'Admiralty House' 288; alarm of aircraft 291–292; Australian soldiers 293; *Australian soldiers* 287–288; Benghazi (hope to press on to) 293; booby-traps 288–289, *289*; boom buoys 286, 288; *Cingalese Prince* (first merchant ship) 289; Clearance Officer Tobruk (COT) 285;

Cunningham, Admiral 290–291; Derna as next harbour to open 291–293; *Eagle* (torpedo attach on) 284; 'Enter Tobruk Harbour (ETH) 285; *Fiona* 285, 286, 287, 290, 293; Fyson 288, 289, 290; harbour's sandy bottom 286; letter *295*; *Liguria* 286; magnetic mines 'cucumbers' 283–284, 285, 286, 287; Maltby 285, 286; minesweeping (Carne's plan) 284; *Moy* 285, 291, 292; oil fuel tanks (burning) 286, 287; prisoner transport 289–290; *San Grigio* 285, 286, *287*; Smith, Captain 287, 289, 290, 291; swept channel 285–286; William volunteers *283*, 284

torpedo manufacture, Bullard Company 276–282

torpedo officer 214

torpedo range finder 33

Tovey, Admiral 237, 238, 239, 244

trains, forces transport 12, 49

Transmitting Station (TS): *New Zealand* 32–33, 35–36, 42, 43, 44, 52; range finding 71

troop convoys, Palestine to France 180

troop ship escort 111–114, 123

Turkey, surrender 202

U

Union Club Malta 134, 173–174

Usborne Willis, Sir Algernon (Admiral of the Fleet) 284, 291

V

Valiant 272, 273

Venus 52

Vernon 187, 214

Veronica 119

Very Light 143

Very pistol 145

Vice-Admiral, Malta (VAM) 258

Victoria Station 11

voicepipes 126–127, 135–136

Voyager 234, 292–293

W

Walker, Captain 306

Warrior 117

Warspite 236, 244, 261; Admiral's bridge 246, 260, 270; air attack 259–260, 261, 270; Battle of Calabria 246–262, *247*; Battle of Jutland 85; Battle of Matapan 280; Carne knocked over by blast 253, 257, 260; Cunningham, Admiral 232, 237; Fort Capuzzo (bombardment) 269–270; Italian air attack tactics 260; maximum speed 249, 259; plot 256; staff dispersal (air attacks) 260; Swordfish aircraft 250, 256, 266; tin hat wearing 260–261

Waterloo station 104

Watson (relief for Carne Mediterranean WWII) *297*, *299*, *300*

west country ship 35

Wilson, Henry (Field Marshal) 292–293

Wireless Teletype (W/T) 157, 177

Wisteria 115

X

Xerces 214

Z

zig-zag alterations of course: *Asphodel*
140; *Calcutta/Coventry* 314; *New
Zealand* accident 63–64
Zulu 322

The staff of the Mediterranean Fleet on the deck of HMS Warspite while docked in Malta, circa 1940. Commander Carne, Fleet Torpedo Officer, seated front row, second from the end on the right.